A MENORAH

FOR ATHENA

A

MENORAH

F O R

A T H E N A

CHARLES

REZNIKOFF

AND THE

JEWISH

DILEMMAS OF

OBJECTIVIST

POETRY

S T E P H E N
F R E D M A N

THE UNIVERSITY OF
CHICAGO PRESS
CHICAGO AND LONDON

STEPHEN FREDMAN is professor of English and the Joseph Morahan Director
of the Arts and Letters Core Course at the University of Notre Dame. He is the
author of two books of criticism, *Poet's Prose: The Crisis in American Verse* and
The Grounding of American Poetry: Charles Olson and the Emersonian Tradition,
three books of translation, and a book of poetry.

The University of Chicago Press, Chicago 60637
The University of Chicago Press, Ltd., London
© 2001 by The University of Chicago
All rights reserved. Published 2001
Printed in the United States of America
10 09 08 07 06 05 04 03 02 01   1 2 3 4 5

ISBN: 0-226-26138-7 (cloth)
ISBN: 0-226-26139-5 (paper)

The University of Chicago Press gratefully acknowledges the support of the Institute
for Scholarship in the Liberal Arts of the College of Arts and Letters of the University
of Notre Dame in the publication of this book.

Library of Congress Cataloging-in-Publication Data

Fredman, Stephen, 1948–
    A menorah for Athena : Charles Reznikoff and the Jewish dilemmas of objectivist
poetry / Stephen Fredman.
        p. cm.
    Includes bibliographical references and index.
    ISBN 0-226-26138-7 (cloth : alk. paper) — ISBN 0-226-26139-5 (pbk. : alk.
paper)
    1. Reznikoff, Charles, 1894–1976—Criticism and interpretation. 2. Judaism and
literature—United States—History—20th century. 3. Reznikoff, Charles, 1894–
1976—Religion. 4. Modernism (Literature)—United States. 5. Jewish poetry—
History and criticism. 6. Objectivity in literature. 7. Judaism in literature. 8. Jews in
literature. I. Title.
PS3535.E98 Z64 2001
811'.52—dc21   00-055953

CONTENTS

This book had its inception in research I conducted in 1993 among the papers of Charles Reznikoff, in preparation for a talk at the conference "The First Postmodernists: American Poets of the 1930s Generation," organized by the National Poetry Foundation at the University of Maine. As I studied Reznikoff's papers, housed in the Archive for New Poetry, Mandeville Special Collections Library of the University of California at San Diego, I was captivated to witness the struggle he waged to create a Jewish-American poetic identity. Then, digesting what I had read, I realized that investigating the issues involved in this struggle would provide significant new ways to read Reznikoff's poetry and that of the other Jewish Objectivists, for they all faced serious dilemmas in trying to articulate a poetic position that takes cognizance both of Jewish issues and of the latest trends in modern poetry.

At the time I began to reflect on Reznikoff's Jewish dilemmas, no one seemed particularly interested in studying the influence of Jewish issues upon modern poetry; nor were the Objectivist poets exciting much comment except by other poets. Concurrent with my working on this book, a welcome explosion has occurred in the field of Jewish studies, and modern poetry has begun to come in for its share of attention. The Objectivists, too, are achieving much greater visibility in anthologies and critical works. Much of the credit for this increased presence goes to the National Poetry Foundation, which not only sponsored the groundbreaking conference mentioned above, but also has published invaluable critical/biographical/ bibliographical volumes on Charles Reznikoff, Louis Zukofsky, George Oppen, Carl Rakosi, Basil Bunting, and Lorine Niedecker, and has devoted much space, including special issues, to essays on these poets in the journal *Sagetrieb*. The person primarily responsible for all this activity by the foundation is Burton Hatlen; readers of the Objectivists owe him a great debt of gratitude. Although the present study is the first single-author treatment of Reznikoff, a number of books on Zukofsky have been published, and substantial works of criticism now include excellent chapters devoted to all of the Objectivists. As this study reaches completion a new volume has appeared: *The Objectivist Nexus: Essays in Cultural Poetics,* edited by Rachel Blau DuPlessis and Peter Quartermain, which makes a convincing case for the importance of the Objectivist contribution to twentieth-century poetry and culture.

For readers unfamiliar with the Objectivist movement, a few words of introduction might be helpful. In a strict sense, the movement consists of the poets listed in the preceding paragraph. Zukofsky initially called the group into existence by editing an issue of *Poetry* in 1931 and *An "Objectivists" Anthology* in 1932; both publications featured these poets (except for Niedecker) alongside a number of others and included manifestos about Objectivism by Zukofsky. Because the other poets did not ratify Zukofsky's essays, and the essays themselves are not particularly transparent, the term *Objectivist* is not easily definable. DuPlessis gives a good encapsulation of its various facets: "the term *objectivist* usefully designates a general aesthetic position in modern and contemporary poetry encompassing work based, generally, on 'the real,' on history not myth, on empiricism not projection, on the discrete not the unified, on vernacular prosodies and not traditional poetic rhetoric, on 'imagism,' not 'symbolism' or 'surrealism,' and on particulars with a dynamic relation to universals" (Oppen, *Selected Letters* ix). As this definition implies, the term *objectivist* has been employed in literary history not only to designate a particular poetic movement that came to prominence in the thirties, disappeared in the forties and fifties, and was seemingly reborn and newly influential in the sixties and seventies, but also to give a name to a poetics that is empirical, socially engaged, and linguistically compressed—a poetics that has played a major role in twentieth-century American poetry.

By stressing the Jewish dilemmas faced by Reznikoff and his cohort, I aim to open up new ways of understanding a poetry that can be seen fruitfully from many other vantage points. In the case of Reznikoff, for instance, Charles Bernstein has published a superb essay, "Reznikoff's Nearness," that places more emphasis upon formal innovation in Objectivist poetry than does the present study. Rather than offering "the last word" on these poets, I hope to provoke further thinking about the function of ethnic and religious issues in their work and that of other modern writers.

It is hard to summarize in a few words my enjoyment of working on this book. Aside from the writer's twin joys of discovery and expression, most of the pleasure has come from the enthusiastic and penetrating responses of the people with whom I have discussed the project. More than anything else, the lively discussions I've had make it clear to me that Reznikoff and the issues constellating around him make a compelling

story for people interested in modern poetry and in Jewish identity. I want
to thank all of the interlocutors I have had—readers, listeners at con-
ferences, students, and others with whom I have shared ideas. The following includes, to the best of my memory, the people whose wisdom has
been made available to me: David Antin, Nancy Arnson, Charles Bern-
stein, Kathleen Biddick, Barbara Black, Jonathan Boyarin, Gerald Bruns,
Geneviève Cohen-Cheminet, Robert Creeley, Rachel Blau DuPlessis,
Norman Finkelstein, Robert Franciosi, Herbert Fredman, Alexander
Gelley, Albert Gelpi, Alan Golding, Sandra Gustafson, Heidi Hartwig,
Burton Hatlen, Michael Heller, Kathryn Hellerstein, Glenn Hendler,
Milton Hindus, Susan Howe, Romana Huk, Swami Ishwarananda,
Grant Jenkins, Cyraina Johnson-Roullier, Feng Lan, Edward Levy,
Shirley Lim, John Matthias, Milton Meltzer, David O'Connor, Ranen
Omer-Sherman, Alicia Ostriker, Marjorie Perloff, Jerome Rothenberg,
Anthony Rudolf, Armand Schwerner, Mark Scroggins, Percy Seitlin,
Vincent Sherry, Maeera Shreiber, Hazel Smith, Piotr Sommer, John
Taggart, Kremena Todorova, Chris VandenBossche, Henry Weinfield,
Tim Woods, Ewa Ziarek, Paul Zukofsky, and two anonymous readers
for the University of Chicago Press. At the Press, I have had the benefit
of careful editorial attention from Alan Thomas, Randolph Petilos, and
Sandra Hazel. My immediate family has provided the fertile ground in
which this work could flourish.

Quotations from unpublished materials by Charles Reznikoff residing
in the Mandeville Special Collections Library, University of California,
San Diego, are used with the permission of the library and of David
Bodansky. Quotations from unpublished materials by Louis Zukofsky
residing in the Mandeville Special Collections Library, University of
California, San Diego, are used with the permission of the library and of
Paul Zukofsky. Reprint permission for an earlier version of chapter 1 is
granted by *Sagetrieb* 13.1–2 (1994). Reprint permission is granted by the
University of Notre Dame, *Religion & Literature* 30.3 (Autumn 1998), for
the afterword.

A MENORAH FOR ATHENA

In the first half of the twentieth century, there was no expectation that American Jews would begin to write influential poetry in English. With the single exception of Emma Lazarus in the nineteenth century, no recognizably Jewish voice made itself heard in the elite world of English-language poetry until the advent of Allen Ginsberg in the mid-fifties. To be sure, there were major poets writing in Yiddish in the United States during this period, but their works were not translated in little magazines or intellectual quarterlies, and so they remained virtually unknown to mainstream readers of poetry. There was, however, one group of Jewish poets writing in English, known as the Objectivists, who did make a significant impact prior to Ginsberg—during the thirties. Because they entered the literary world under the guidance of Ezra Pound, the Objectivists have been subsumed by critics into the avant-garde wing of poetry that was launched in the teens by Imagism and Vorticism, movements in which Pound took a leading role. Viewing the Objectivists from this perspective has almost completely obscured the Jewish content appearing in their work as well as the fascinating Jewish dilemmas lurking behind it. Yet if examined from the vantage point I am proposing, the Objectivists represent a major and surprisingly neglected opportunity for investigating Jewish issues that have made a difference in twentieth-century American poetry.

In the standard narrative of modern American poetry, Charles Reznikoff (1894–1976) and the other Jewish Objectivist poets—Louis Zukofsky (1904–78), George Oppen (1908–84), and Carl Rakosi (b. 1903)—have occupied a rather peculiar spot. Perhaps Hugh Kenner best articulates the prevailing opinion: "The quality of their very youthful work is that of men who have inherited a formed tradition: the tradition over the cradle of which, less than twenty years previously, Ezra Pound had hoped to have Henry James, O.M., speak a few sponsoring words." In other words, the Objectivists, according to Kenner, must be placed in the realist tradition of American literature that runs from Henry James into the Imagism of Ezra Pound. Because they so thoroughly imbibed that tradition, "The Objectivists seem to have been born mature, not to say middle-aged" (Kenner 169). Kenner contrives a story in which the birth of Objectivism in 1931 reprises, in a minor key, the birth of Imagism in 1912: "sponsored" by Ezra Pound, it thus emerges into a dynasty already in full swing. To compare Imagists to Objectivists, then, would be something like comparing embattled revolutionaries to the heirs of a comfortable legacy.[1] Ironically, given the ethnic marginality and Marxist sympathies of the Objectivists and the cultural centrality and right-wing, oftentimes anti-Semitic, views of many of the poets around Imagism, it would be easy to switch the valences in this account, designating the Objectivists as revolutionaries and poets like Ezra Pound (1885–1972), T. S. Eliot (1888–1965), and H.D. (1886–1961) as inheritors of "a formed tradition." But regardless of the extent to which formal or political considerations have prevailed in a particular account of American modernist poetry, the basic narrative with respect to Objectivism has remained thus far firmly in place: Ezra Pound and William Carlos Williams (1883–1963) are seen as dominant fathers, with the Objectivists as their dutiful sons.[2]

To be sure, there is ample evidence for such a narrative, and I will provide a sketch of that evidence below. A narrative of Objectivism told from the vantage point of Imagism, however, risks ignoring much of what is distinctive about these poets, for without an account of the compelling Jewish dilemmas they faced, a major portion of the story remains untold. In addition to their adept pursuit of the Imagist goals of verbal concision, formal density and suppleness, and eschewal of subjective effusions, these poets make a strong claim for our attention based on their inventive negotiations between literary modernism and a Jewish heritage. Charles Reznikoff, in particular, undertook such negotiations throughout his career; the depth and persistence of his efforts make him suitable as the representative Objectivist in the story I wish to tell. Like many of the most influential Jewish writers of the twentieth century, such as Sigmund Freud, Franz Kafka, Martin Buber, Walter Benjamin, and Hannah Arendt, the Objectivists used their liminal position between cultures as a basis for groundbreaking work—in their case, the invention of a poetics capable of registering the tensions of the multiethnic urban world. Rather than simply regarding Objectivism as the consolidation of formal experiments inaugurated by predecessors, we can gain much by observing how the poets turn a precarious situation—that of immigrant Jews in American culture prior to World War II—to remarkable advantage. Both stylistically and thematically, the Objectivists create a poetry of ethical interaction, based upon a new relationship of equality among poet, language, and society. Arising out of a welter of modern Jewish dilemmas, this poetics has borne ample fruit for a surprising number of succeeding poets, both Jewish and Gentile: the influence of Objectivism ranges across a broad spectrum of American poetry, from poets of the succeeding generation like Charles Olson, Robert Duncan, Robert Creeley, Cid Corman, David Ignatow, and Allen Ginsberg, to a range of contemporary Jewish poets like Jerome Rothenberg, David Antin, Armand Schwerner, Michael Heller, and Paul Auster, to the many poets grouped under the rubric of Language poetry. If there is one story already in place that portrays the Objectivists as the inheritors of a formed tradition, there is another story awaiting narration in which the Objectivists contribute mightily to the development of an entire strain of American poetry—and this latter story cannot be told properly without accounting for the element of Jewishness.[3]

Before moving on to consider how Jewish dilemmas have participated in the development of Objectivist poetry, I will employ the figure of Pound to indicate some of the ways in which the Objectivists take their bearings from the earlier modernists. Among the Objectivists, Louis Zukofsky, who gave the group its name, maintained the closest contact with Pound. Their surviving correspondence includes more than four hundred items, covering the years between 1927 and 1963 (Ahearn, *Pound/Zukofsky* vii). As a young poet, Zukofsky modeled himself in many ways on Pound, claiming in the dedication to *An "Objectivists" Anthology* that Pound is "for the poets of our time / the / most important" (27). A zealous disciple, Zukofsky goes so far as to refer to himself as "sonny" and to Pound as "papa" in some of his early letters—a mode of address that Pound adopts as well (Ahearn, *Pound/Zukofsky* xix). But most important, the elder poet returned the younger's regard by publishing Zukofsky's first major effort, "Poem beginning 'The,'" in his magazine *The Exile* and by procuring the February 1931 issue of *Poetry* for Zukofsky to edit. By virtue of opening this editorial space to Zukofsky and advising him closely on how to go about filling it, Pound became, along with Williams (with whom Zukofsky also had close contact), a primary advocate for the Objectivist movement.

Beyond the timely support he offered in the early phases of Zukof-sky's career, Pound continued to inspire him in a number of significant ways. For example, the formal hygiene prescribed by Pound for rid-ding modern poetry of what he perceived as the stylistic excrescences inherited from the nineteenth century became the basis for the even stricter hygiene adhered to by Zukofsky—not only in his own carefully wrought poetry, but also in his criticism and in his anthology of exem-plary texts, *A Test of Poetry* (1948). Zukofsky's often gnomic, highly pre-cise poetics bears an unmistakable Poundian cast, as when he compresses Pound's pseudo-Greek terms for describing the poetic function—*phano-poeia, melopoeia,* and *logopoeia*—into a single sentence: "The test of po-etry is the range of pleasure it affords as sight, sound, and intellection" (*Test* vii). Moreover, Zukofsky acquired from Pound the conviction that the highest poetic ambition must bear fruit in an epic poem running to many hundreds of pages and encompassing both the poet's life and his attempts to make sense of history. In the contest to write an epic that defined the modern era, Zukofsky entered his epic *"A"* (1928–74) as the rightful (superior?) companion to Pound's definitive entry, *The Cantos* (1919–70).

In the cases of Rakosi, Oppen, and Reznikoff, the relationship with Pound did not take on the intensity of an oedipal struggle; nonetheless, Pound's ideas, example, and sponsorship contributed in varying degrees to the careers of all three poets. Some of Rakosi's first significant publications came in Pound's *Exile,* where they caught Zukofsky's attention and caused him to invite Rakosi to contribute to the "Objectivists" issue of *Poetry* and to *An "Objectivists" Anthology* (1932). Like the other Objectiv-ists, Rakosi sat at the feet of Pound when it came to matters of style. He expressed particular gratitude to Pound for shunting aside the "very flabby stuff" that represented poetry at the beginning of the twentieth century. Reinforcing part of the story told by Kenner, Rakosi states: "Now, the Objectivists who followed, of course, had Pound's work already done. We were free, for the first time, to be absolutely honest, absolutely sincere, and to write in exactly the form that we wanted to write in. That's a big thing!" (Cohn 47). It is important to note that "Pound's work," as Rakosi sees it, did not consist of forming and passing along a tradition (as Kenner would have it), but rather of rendering certain formal and thematic con-straints outmoded and urging other poets to seek new ways to express new realities. As in the case of Rakosi, Pound also played a marked personal and formal role in the work of George Oppen. As Rachel Blau DuPlessis points out, Pound's criticism makes explicit a crucial equation between form and ethics, an equation whose import Oppen's own writing and thinking greatly amplifies. In an apothegm from Pound's "Credo," "I believe in technique as the test of a man's sincerity" (Pound, *Literary Essays* 9), DuPlessis locates the origin of the Objectivist concern with "sincerity," which will occupy our attention in chapter 4: "The Pound on whom Zukofsky and Oppen drew was indeed the Pound of sincerity and ethical-social awareness: 'technique as the test of a man's sincerity' does not separate craft from the whole social and moral being of the person" ("Objectivist Poets" 127). Although Oppen's ethical and political views diverged widely from those of Pound, the elder poet provided a crucial example of a modernist social poetics.

Much closer in age to Pound than were the other Objectivists, Reznikoff, too, found Pound's Imagist style liberatory.[4] "When I was twenty-one," he recalls, "I was particularly impressed by the new kind of poetry being written by Ezra Pound, H.D., and others. . . . It seemed to me just right, not cut to patterns, however cleverly, nor poured into ready molds . . . but words and phrases flowing as the thought" (*MP* 98). In an interview, Reznikoff directs attention to the achievements of Pound's he most valued: "I think the first two Cantos have a magnificence, and his translations especially. But all the people I knew who were interested in writing were very much moved by his prose articles in *Poetry*" (130–31). Reznikoff explicitly ties Pound's critical thinking to the origins of Objectivism in an unpublished "Note on the Objectivist Press": "We called our firm The Objectivist Press, not because—as far as I was concerned—we had any new doctrine to offer: the name was suggested by Pound's stress on 'objectivity' in his correspondence as printed in *Poetry* and we—at least Zukofsky and I—heartily agreed with his do's and don't's" (UCSD 9.19.3). The qualities that Reznikoff most appreciated in Pound—his supple verse technique, his elevation of the "image" to a place of self-sufficiency in poetry, and his "objectivity"—can also be seen as components of Reznikoff's "painstaking verbal craftsmanship" (Hindus, *Reznikoff* 13). Like Pound, H.D., and Eliot, all of whom he admired, Reznikoff sought classical (particularly Greek) models for this sort of artistry. Milton Hindus praises Reznikoff for being capable, like the Imagists, "of creating little artifacts out of words of jewel-like perfection not unworthy of comparison with the inscriptions and epigrams conserved in the Classic anthologies" (13).

In delivering this just praise, Hindus does not mention the fact that, in marked distinction to his Imagist predecessors, Reznikoff had to purchase classicism at a high price and was never assured of retaining its possession. In a striking poem on this theme, Reznikoff meditates upon the costs and the risks of employing this style:

Hellenist

As I, barbarian, at last, although slowly, could read Greek,
at "blue-eyed Athena"
I greeted her picture that had long been on the wall:
the head slightly bent forward under the heavy helmet,
as if to listen; the beautiful lips slightly scornful.
(*CP* 1.107)

This poem identifies Reznikoff as an outsider ("barbarian") to the entire
Greek tradition, a tradition drawn upon extensively by Imagist poets such
as Pound and H.D. The long, slow-moving, incessantly qualified first
line renders palpable the painstaking, stumbling effort he makes to learn
"Greek"—in which the language stands for the entire body of non-Jewish
thinking that contributes to Western culture. Having achieved some
halting success in this arduous acquisition of learning, the poet takes
delight in his new ability to salute the goddess of wisdom (to "greet"
the "Greek")—only to find himself mutely regarded with scorn. The
provisionality of his command of Greek is underlined by the repeti-
tion of "slightly"—as if the slightest imbalance in the Jewish poet's ac-
cord with the Greek goddess would be enough to end their colloquy
abruptly.

In poems such as this, Reznikoff's Jewish "difference" from the Imagist
poets begins to emerge. His work renders this difference explicit in a variety of ways, disclosing memorably just how much is at stake in an encounter between Judaism and modernism. The story I would like to tell about
the Jewish dilemmas of Objectivism begins with and depends in crucial
ways upon the poetry of Charles Reznikoff. In the present context it is
important to consider how, for a Jewish poet of eastern European background such as Reznikoff, becoming a "Hellenist" means something entirely different than it does for Pound or H.D. For one thing, as a Jewish
participant in the high culture of the West, Reznikoff cannot conceive of
Hellenism without also calling upon the counterterm, *Hebraism*. In the
poems surrounding "Hellenist" in *Jerusalem the Golden* (1934), for example, Reznikoff specifically invokes things "Hebrew": the preceding
poem in the book apostrophizes "The Hebrew of your poets, Zion,"
and the succeeding poem acknowledges the erotic temptation of the
moon for "the Hebrews" (*CP* 1.107). In the latter poem, "throw[ing]
kisses at the moon" represents a succumbing to the pagan quality of
Hellenism. Evoking such desires and their associated dangers, the guilty
poet asks, "What then must happen, you Jeremiahs, / to me who look at
moon and stars and trees?" (107). Placing himself in a symbolic position of
betweenness—between Hebraism and Hellenism, between Judaism and

modernism, and, in this poem, between religion and nature—Reznikoff joins not only the other Objectivist poets but also an entire generation of American Jewish intellectuals. Sensing an opportunity to overcome a two-thousand-year history of marginalization, these Jews are hungry to enter the mainstream of American culture. The most ready route that presents itself involves refiguring the authoritative dichotomy between Hebraism and Hellenism in such a way that it supports rather than impedes their entry.

This dichotomy, evoked in Reznikoff's "Hellenist" and ubiquitous in the intellectual discourse of early twentieth-century American Jews, will form a major theme of this book. The dichotomy has both historical and transhistorical aspects, which are summarized by David Stern, editor of a recent collection of essays on Hellenism and Hebraism. At the transhistorical level, "The two terms have been yoked together to represent virtually every important type of opposition that has figured in Western cultural and intellectual tradition: paganism/monotheism, 'right-thinking'/ 'right-doing,' philosophy/revelation, spatial/temporal thinking, static/ dynamic being, and so on. Indeed, the very idea that these two terms represent an essential opposition is itself a virtual founding myth of Western tradition" (1). In the eyes of modern historians, however, who look at the period of direct contact between Judaism and Hellenistic culture (from 330 B.C.E. to the fifth century C.E.), no such fundamental opposition can be found. In this postbiblical period, the religion of Judaism "was itself the product of the fusion of native Israelite culture with the world of Hellenism. . . . [E]arly Judaism, far from being a rejection of Hellenism, was the embodiment of a *successful* encounter with it" (3, 6). If historians have proven that no actual dichotomy between "Hellenism" and "Hebraism" existed, they have not succeeded in erasing the influence of this "founding myth" on subsequent eras—particularly the last two hundred years. In Stern's judgment,

> *Hellenism* and *Hebraism* have continuously been reformulated and differently applied by individual thinkers, who attributed new values to the terms as though they were the great original tabulae rasae of Western culture. Perhaps the only thing that can consistently be said about these terms is that . . . they have been used to refer to inner cultural meanings or values that bear little relation to the actual cultures alluded to. Hellenism and Hebraism . . . are by now virtually pure abstractions that have no connection to anything concretely or historically Hebraic or Greek.
> (11)

The degree to which this dichotomy has slipped free of historical grounding may well be directly proportional to the degree of its ideologi-

cal usefulness to modern thinkers. For nineteenth-century writers such as
Heinrich Heine (who first explicitly formulated the opposition), Friedrich
Nietzsche, Herman Melville, and Matthew Arnold, the dichotomy allowed tremendous leverage for affirming or stigmatizing particular values
and the people who presumably held the values. In Arnold's rhetoric, for
example, "Hebraism" corresponds to the puritanical strain in English culture, whose moralistic influence he hopes to leaven by counterposing the
more esthetic values he associates with "Hellenism." Because Arnold's
cultural pronouncements still carried a great deal of weight in America at
the beginning of the twentieth century, Jewish intellectuals sensed that
grappling with his formulation of the dichotomy might allow them both
to undo attitudes prejudicial to Jewish intellectual aspirations and to assert
a new valuation for Jewish thought and experience. This initial generation
of American Jewish intellectuals consisted mainly of eastern European immigrants and their children, who had arrived in the United States during
the major period of immigration from 1881 through 1925. Often coming from the intensely scholastic world of talmudic study, these young
people also comprised the first Jews to enter American universities in significant numbers. The leap from the enclosed, in many ways medieval,
world of eastern European Jewry to the genteel Protestant world of early
twentieth-century American intellectual culture was immense; it required
as a bridge a set of extremely malleable and vast abstractions such as the
Hebraism/Hellenism dichotomy.

The bridging was accomplished, to a remarkable extent, in a particular
American Jewish cultural movement that spawned a highly influential periodical, the *Menorah Journal* (1915–62); the collegiate Menorah movement from which it sprang made crucial contributions to the negotiations
between Judaism and the emergent cultural modernism.[5] Especially during the period between 1906, when the first Menorah Society at Harvard
was formed, and 1931, when the Great Depression began to assert its own
imperatives, this nonsectarian attempt to make the study of Jewish culture
both academically viable and a force in the construction of a pluralistic
American society gained recognition as a major presence on the cultural
scene. There are a number of ways to gauge its impact. For instance, it is
noteworthy that the first major Jewish literary critic to teach in an Ivy
League school, Lionel Trilling, cut his teeth on the *Menorah Journal,* publishing all of his early fiction and reviews there. In addition, Horace Kallen, the social thinker who coined the phrase "cultural pluralism" and
helped launch the New School for Social Research, was a founder of the
Harvard Menorah Society and played an important role in the journal.
Rabbi Mordecai Kaplan used the pages of the journal to popularize Re-

constructionism, a new American form of Judaism that continues as an active denomination today. In cultural terms, the most significant fact about the *Menorah Journal* would be that the premier American Jewish thinkers of the period, the New York Intellectuals, coalesced around it and its most creative editor, Elliot Cohen, who went on to found a successor journal, *Commentary,* after World War II. Because the journal placed Jewish issues in the context of national and international concerns that often exercised American intellectuals in general, it attracted prominent non-Jewish social thinkers such as Randolph Bourne, John Dewey, and Lewis Mumford.[6] In the international context, it also paid close attention to events in Palestine and was critical of Zionist attempts to shunt aside Arab Palestinians. Finally, the journal introduced a number of European Jewish intellectuals and artists to an American audience through translation and photo-reproduction.

Bringing into view the *Menorah Journal* and the meditations it provoked on the Hebraism/Hellenism dichotomy helps to flesh out the Jewish context in which Charles Reznikoff and the other Objectivists wrote. Reznikoff himself was keenly aware of the journal's intellectual agenda, and he participated in it by publishing more of his writing there than in any other venue. During the twenty-five-year stretch from 1924 through 1949, the full range of his work—poetry (including an entire book, *In Memoriam: 1933*), plays, fiction, anecdotes, commentaries, and historical sketches—appeared in twenty-eight issues of the journal; two of his books received reviews there; and he was a contributing editor from 1940 to 1962.[7] The *Menorah Journal* also played an important part in his social world in New York City, where he attended dinners hosted by its publisher, Henry Hurwitz, along with other Jewish intellectuals. Because of Reznikoff's participation in the *Menorah Journal,* Louis Zukofsky planned for his essay on the poet to be published there in the late twenties—along with other work of his for which he was seeking acceptance for publication. Rejected by the journal, the essay, "Sincerity and Objectification: With Special Reference to the Work of Charles Reznikoff," was featured by Zukofsky as the central theoretical statement in the issue of *Poetry* that inaugurated the Objectivist movement.

The major question agitating Reznikoff and the *Menorah* writers—a question that reverberates in a variety of ways throughout the work of the other Objectivists—is how to climb aboard the invigorating enterprise of modernism while securing vital ties to the Jewish past. This is by no means an easy task, as Harold Bloom points out in his pessimistic essay, "The Sorrows of American Jewish Poetry." Bloom believes that the cultivation of a prophetic style and of certain Jewish attitudes ("the relative naturalism and humanism of Jewish tradition") are the essential prerequisites for effective Jewish poetry, and he finds these prerequisites largely missing in American Jewish works. Turning to the "impressive testament" of Reznikoff's volume of selected poems, *By the Waters of Manhattan* (1962), Bloom affirms that Reznikoff "should have been the American-Jewish poet in whom younger writers could find a precursor of real strength" (251), but he denies Reznikoff that stature because of the poet's own choice of precursors. Lamenting this choice, Bloom complains that "prolonged reading in him depresses me with the sense of unnecessary loss. Why attempt to translate Yehudah Halevy into the idiom of Pound and William Carlos Williams?" (251–52). By contrast, Bloom praises Reznikoff's contemporary, the English poet Isaac Rosenberg, for his "quasi-biblical fragments" (248) that achieve a Blakean prophetic style in which "moral insights fuse into a powerful Hebraic pattern" (249). In other words, by adopting an Imagist style rather than an English prophetic style, Reznikoff eschews the offering of explicit "moral insights" and thus forfeits the prerogative of creating "a powerful Hebraic pattern." By using a reified notion of "Hebraism" in his discussion of American Jewish poetry, Bloom seems intent on pushing the Hebraism/Hellenism dichotomy toward an absolute antinomy: for an American Jewish poetry to be authentic, it must abandon the "Hellenic" completely.

Where Kenner sees Reznikoff and the other Objectivists as minor modernists in the wake of Pound the master, Bloom sees Reznikoff as a minor Jewish poet because he abjures the prophetic style favored by Romanticism.[8] Setting aside these complementary judgments for the moment, it is instructive to note that at the time Reznikoff began writing, his decision to follow the "Hellenist" example of the Imagists was anything but inevitable. When he published his first slim volume, *Rhythms* (1918), the dominant figures in American poetry were neither Pound nor Stevens but Midwesterners including Edgar Lee Masters, Vachel Lindsay, and Carl Sandburg; Chicago, headquarters of *Poetry,* was the hub of a new, Whitmanian strain in American letters. Ironically, the biblical cadences and prophetic voice of Walt Whitman would have provided a "Hebraic" model such as Bloom might recommend for an American Jewish poet (although, admittedly, Bloom does not rank highly any of the "Whitmanian" poets mentioned above). Indeed, a number of Jewish poets—particularly the committed leftists—chose such a model. Following a similar poetic route would, no doubt, have been easier for Reznikoff; instead, he embarked on the more exacting and, I believe, the more rewarding search for a hybrid position, combining the Jewish and the modernist by interweaving the Hebraic and the Hellenic.

Believing in their own seductive but relatively foreshortened narratives of modern poetry, Kenner and Bloom cannot properly appreciate the merits of Objectivist poetry. Their damaging assessments have unfortunately contributed to the relative obscurity of the writing of the Objectivists in general and Reznikoff in particular. In 1974, at a reading given by Reznikoff in San Francisco to a large and devoted audience of poets and students, George Oppen complained in his introduction about "the length of time it has taken to notice Charles Reznikoff" ("On Reznikoff" 39). Like the purloined letter in Poe's famous tale, Reznikoff's poetry may have been extremely difficult for critics like Kenner and Bloom to see because it resides in plain sight, inviting neither reference-hunting nor interpretation as a psychodynamic struggle. In opposition to the modes of twentieth-century poetry that have managed to gain critical acclaim, Reznikoff devoted himself to banishing obscurities from his poetry, presenting instead a bare pattern of events in the brightest possible light. His scrupulous attention to detail—in the individual word, in the poetic line, in the person or object before him—had by the late twenties already come to stand as a shining example of sincerity for both Oppen and Zukofsky.

In his seminal essay, "Reznikoff's Nearness," contemporary poet Charles Bernstein points out the paradox that occurs through Reznikoff's concision and his heightened attention to detail: "Reznikoff's very extreme attitude toward elision and condensation has the supplemental effect of producing density in exact proportion to its desire for clarity" (219). In other words, what lies in plain sight still may not be wholly transparent. Under the heading of "nearness," Bernstein explores a number of the qualities in Reznikoff's writing that bring him "near" to the concerns of Language poetry: his treatment of subjects that are common and near at hand (214), the intimacy of his address to his subjects and his readers (215), his moral outlook in which "others exist prior to oneself" (217), and a formal cohesion that operates by "adjacency" rather than by subordinating parts to the whole (205).[9]

To an attentive reader willing to shed the blinders of critical orthodoxies, the dense clarity in the unemphatic music and plain language of Reznikoff's poetry can unfold as provocatively as a tightly furled flower bud. In his introduction to Reznikoff's reading, Oppen testifies, "I don't know of any poems more pure, or more purely spoken, or more revelatory." The "purity" of the poetry is at once stylistic and ethical, with each dimension reflecting back upon the other. The ethical impact arises from clear-eyed attitudes of humility and self-abnegation, balanced by inexhaustible respect for and obligation to others—particularly for those not used to drawing attention to themselves—and this impact occurs because of the "purity" of an extremely concise, vernacular style. For many poets, Reznikoff's purity has become an unforgettable touchstone. Speaking for Zukofsky and others, Oppen explains, "I think the young of my generation were luckier than the youngest in this audience, in that we had to go searching for our own tradition and our own poets. What we found was Reznikoff . . . and I cannot say how important he has been to us" ("On Reznikoff" 40).

This book seeks to "find" Reznikoff through a series of interlinked arguments. First, I contend that to fathom the origins of the Objectivist movement—particularly in its negotiations between Judaism and modernism—it is necessary to understand the Jewish dilemmas of Charles Reznikoff, the first and in many ways the model Objectivist. My second contention is that for a nuanced reading of Reznikoff, it is essential to explore the contextual influence of the Menorah movement and its journal. The Menorah context is especially crucial for Reznikoff in his investigations of Jewish history: in the *Menorah Journal* he participated alongside distinguished Jewish historians such as Salo Baron and Cecil Roth in a modern redefinition of Jewish culture based upon historical research. Third, I argue that to grasp fully the Jewish dilemmas of writers such as the Objectivists and the *Menorah* intellectuals, we need to lay out a genealogy of the modern Jewish condition of betweenness, a genealogy that runs back through the Hebraism/Hellenism dichotomy of Arnold and Heine to the Marrano *(converso)* background of the first Jewish thinker of modernity, Baruch Spinoza. With the larger Jewish context for Objectivism in view, it becomes possible to make some telling distinctions between the Objectivists and other early twentieth-century American Jewish poets and also among the Objectivists themselves. In particular, I contrast a central tension between English and Hebrew in Reznikoff's poetry with a different but equally significant tension between English and Yiddish in Zukofsky's poetry. Although the issue of a "Jewish language" does not arise in Oppen's poetry, his work, too, evinces key dilemmas faced by the Jewish poet in America, and his responses to these dilemmas have had a striking influence upon other poets—many of whom are not Jewish. Finally, I contend that regarding the Objectivists as modern *Jewish* poets makes apparent not only their distinctiveness as modernist poets but also some of the reasons for their profound impact upon poets of later generations.

ONE

CALL HIM CHARLES

"NO MIDDLE NAME"

I have no middle name. My Hebrew name is just like the prophet Ezekiel's but when my mother asked her doctor for equivalent in English
so that she could name me after her father, the doctor answered, "Call
him Charles," and I have been called Charles officially all my life, except
on those rare occasions when I have been called up to the Torah in
synagogue.
(UCSD 9.2.21)

One way to get to the heart of the Jewish dilemmas in Charles Reznikoff's writing is to look at the symbolic role the Hebrew language assumes
and at the complex interplay between Hebrew and English to be found in
both his life and his work. Reznikoff associates Jewishness with the Hebrew language. This is by no means idiosyncratic: for two thousand years
of diaspora Jewish men have learned Hebrew as an initiatory language,
alongside whatever other language or languages they require for daily
commerce or intellectual activity. As with most national languages, the
term *Hebrew* denominates both the language and the people who speak it.
Given the cultural weight of the Hebrew language, one can readily imagine the dilemma an immigrant family of 1894 might face in Brownsville,
the Jewish ghetto of Brooklyn, when bestowing a name on their firstborn.
They want to give the child a Jewish identity by using a Hebrew name,
and yet the name must translate easily into English in order to make him
fit for American life. In the passage that started this chapter (taken from
one of Reznikoff's letters), the tension between Hebrew and English

makes itself felt not only in the swerve from Ezekiel to Charles, but also
in the complementary, though negative, form of a gap: the baby receives
"no middle name." The lack of a middle name signals an instability, which
appears as a fissure between what we call the "Christian" name and the
(Jewish) surname. In place of a culturally reassuring mediator such as the
mother's maiden name or another family name, there is just the baffling
incongruity of "Charles" + "Reznikoff." In America middle names carry
considerable weight: they signify solidity, a sturdy triangular base upon
which to erect fame and fortune. Ralph Waldo Emerson, John Greenleaf
Whittier, Henry Wadsworth Longfellow: how could one hope to become
an author and enter public life without a disyllabic middle name as bridge?

As if to compensate for the missing middle name, many American
Jewish men have borrowed a bit of gentility by adopting as their first
name a disyllabic English surname—particularly that of a famous English
author—such as Morris, Sydney, Milton, Burton, or Herbert. In Reznikoff's case, rather than receiving his grandfather's name, Ezekiel (in
Hebrew, *Yehezqiel*), he was given the common though also regal English
name of Charles—not by his immigrant mother but by the doctor who
said—callously? offhandedly? obligingly? imperiously? reassuringly? pa-
ternalistically?—"Call him Charles." "Call him Charles" says both that
his name is not really Charles and that he must be known as Charles. By
naming someone else's child, the doctor becomes, in effect, a demiurge,
creating an entire world for the child to live in—a duplicitous world. At
the moment of naming, the baby is called by an invented name, a fictitious
name, an "official" English name that hides a Hebrew name behind it. As
American citizen, as poet, as husband—in every official capacity—he is
known as Charles. In the ancestral Jewish world he is Ezekiel, for one
cannot be "called up to the Torah in synagogue" except by a Hebrew
name. In accordance with Jewish law, one becomes a man, a Bar Mitzvah,
by answering the (Hebrew) call and coming up to read the Torah (in Hebrew). Ezekiel is called up, but Charles is merely called.

Reconciling his American and Jewish names becomes a central dilemma
for Reznikoff's writing. Surprisingly, though, critics have given this issue
little mention, tending to regard Reznikoff as either a Charles—an American modernist poet, whose short poems and *Testimony* reveal a close ob-
server of the urban world and of the social costs it exacts—or as an Ezekiel—an American Jewish man of letters, whose autobiographical poetry
and fiction and extensive renderings of biblical, talmudic, and other historical Jewish sources address in multiple ways the question of Jewish
identity in America.[1] The contemporary American novelist and poet Paul
Auster gives an insightful description of the uncanny position Reznikoff
occupies as both Objectivist and Jew:

It is a precarious position, to say the least. Neither fully assimilated nor fully unassimilated, Reznikoff occupies the unstable middle ground between two worlds and is never able to claim either one as his own. Nevertheless, and no doubt precisely because of this ambiguity, it is an extremely fertile ground—leading some to consider him primarily as a Jewish poet (whatever that term might mean) and others to look on him as a quintessentially American poet (whatever *that* term might mean). . . . Reznikoff's poems are what Reznikoff is: the poems of an American Jew, or, if you will, of a hyphenated American, a Jewish-American, with the two terms combining to form a third and wholly different term: the condition of being in two places at the same time, or, quite simply, the condition of being nowhere.
(*MP* 156–57)

In a short poem that records his effort to overcome this uncanny "condition of being nowhere," Reznikoff endeavors to stretch Jewish tradition wide enough to encompass both his English and his Hebrew names. He does this by pointing out that the meanings of both names can be construed as referring to his position as the first-born child, who traditionally belongs to God:

> Because, the first-born, I was not redeemed,
> I belong to my Lord, not to myself or you:
> by my name, in English, I am one of His house,
> one of the carles—a Charles, a churl;
> and by my name in Hebrew which is Ezekiel
> (whom God strengthened)
> my strength, such as it is, is His.
> (*CP* 2.80–81)

This is an elegant attempt at synthesis, evincing a subtle midrashic interpretive ability; but the attractive braiding of cultures unravels when one notices the incommensurability of the social worlds of feudal England and traditional Judaism—an incommensurability Reznikoff himself depicts so decisively in *The Lionhearted,* his novel about medieval England. As ersatz artifact, this poem has a rhythmical and exegetical elegance that makes it similar to a genealogy skillfully patched together for a Jewish financier who has just acquired a coat of arms. In other words, this is an instance of a creative attempt to overcome the fissure at the heart of Reznikoff's name. Another appealing but unconvincing attempt at bridging can be found in Milton Hindus's ex post facto speculation that a Yiddish "middle" name effects the transfer from "Ezekiel" to "Charles": *Chatzkl,* he points out, is the Yiddish nickname for *Yehezqiel,* and it sounds a bit like "Charles" (*Reznikoff* 20–22).

In an interview with Reinhold Schiffer, Reznikoff tenders a much fuller explanation of the derivation of his English name than any we have examined thus far. At one point, Schiffer comments on the way Reznikoff, in the aforementioned poem, inflects "Charles" to place himself squarely in Jewish tradition; then Schiffer wonders whether that gesture of incorporation is consistent with a statement, "I have a very poor Jewish background" (*MP* 116), which the poet had just made. As though to probe behind Reznikoff's evasive humility—which the poet wields deftly as a shield for parrying both praise and requests for self-revelation—Schiffer asks, "Do you really think that?" Reznikoff answers:

> CR: Well, the "Charles" might explain it. Now, let me tell you why I'm called "Charles." My parents came here as immigrants, and shortly after they were married, and of course afterwards I was born, the oldest of the family. My mother's English was very limited. Her doctor, who attended her at my birth, a Jew, but an anarchist, had no use for Jewish affairs, as anarchists wouldn't. Later, at every great fast day, he gave a feast (laughs) . . . [ellipses in original]
>
> RS: Just to spite them?
>
> CR: Yes. He was an excellent doctor and had a great reputation in that community. My mother told him the following: you see, her father, for whom she had an enormous amount of affection, was named Ezekiel, in English, and *Yehezqel,* in the Hebrew. She wanted to name me, her child, her firstborn, and her son, after her father, who had been dead then for about twenty years or so . . . and he said, "Well, what's your father's name?" She said, "Yehezqel," which in English is Ezekiel, the prophet. So he said, "Well," he said, "call him Charlie. He'll be grateful to you." (Laughs) So all that is on my birth certificate and everywhere is Charles. Reznikoff, the last name, is Slavic. *Reznik* is a Slavic word which stands for a Hebrew word. The emperor of Austria at one time, insisted that all Jews take German names, and I suppose the Russians followed to some extent. The Jews when called up in the synagogue to read from prayer or from Torah, would be called, "so and so, son of so and so," as the Bible has it all the time. But they had to change their names, so they changed it to Reznik or in Russian, Reznikoff. Now, to change that name in English, when you came here, as many Jews do, is regarded with contempt: not because they're hiding their Jewishness but they're hiding themselves, as it were. So my father never changed his name.
> (*MP* 117–18)[2]

After following Reznikoff through such a detailed account of the derivation of his names, it may be hard to recall that he offers this in support of his contention, "I have a very poor Jewish background." At base, he seems to make the extraordinary claim that his English name, and the manner of its bestowal, has compromised his Jewish identity. What an odd way to make the point! Why not blame the sense of estrangement from his Jewish background on his secular education in a public school, for instance? The explanation he fashions operates on a completely different level, for it revolves around "Charles"—as though his own name bespeaks a fundamental self-division, an uneasiness about being Jewish in America that won't go away.[3] The naming scene itself provides a number of clues about the origin of Reznikoff's self-division. This scene, which the poet cannot actually remember, of course, has become a part of his personal mythology, as related to him most likely by his mother. She must have felt not only some anger and dismay at having her wishes thwarted, but also a measure of guilt at betraying her own father—which may explain why the justifying detail about the doctor's skill and reputation survives in the story. The fact that this doctor was a Jew is also very telling. One might have inferred from the version of the story quoted at the head of this chapter that Reznikoff was the unwitting victim of anti-Semitism. In one sense, this is true, since his doctor knows that bearing the name of Charles in America will be infinitely easier than living with the name of Ezekiel. But beneath the pragmatic value of the name lies a more disturbing issue, which has been called "Jewish self-hatred"—that is, discomfort with a public display of Jewishness. In its fullest sense, Jewish self-hatred refers to a range of responses to the virulent stigmatization of anti-Semitism. In Reznikoff's case, it lends a characteristic coloring to the family story about the naming of the first son.

Analyzing the origins of Jewish self-hatred, Sander Gilman argues that this baffling phenomenon, which is at the core of modern Jewish self-division, does not originate within Judaism itself but is a direct aftermath of anti-Semitism. In social-psychological terms, Gilman delineates how the members of any oppressed group subconsciously accept the stigma imputed to them and then, in a classic response to a double bind, attempt to escape from it by passing it on with unabated virulence to other members of their group, whom they designate as the true possessors of the stigmatized qualities. For example, German Jews often professed shock and disdain at the language, dress, and behavior of "Eastern" Jews, to whom they applied all of the stigmas that German society directed toward themselves (Gilman, *Jewish Self-Hatred* 1–21). In this way the stigmas applied by European society, created to marginalize the Jews, have been continuously recycled within Jewish culture. In fact, stigmas that socially dominant groups use to establish insider/outsider relations are some of the most powerful fictions that human beings invent: once the stigma is in place it takes on a life of its own, and it bores to the psychological core of "insiders" and "outsiders" alike. For the social insiders, the artifact of the stigma establishes the conditions for legitimating discrimination, coercion, and physical brutality against those they consider to be outsiders. Outsiders not only bear the brunt of social and political exclusionary practices and bodily attack; they also find the fiction of the stigma coiled around their own self-image: "Self-hatred results from outsiders' acceptance of the mirage of themselves generated by their reference group—that group in society which they see as defining them—as a reality" (2).

Reznikoff received his name Charles from an anarchist Jewish doctor, whose embarrassment at Jewish Otherness emerges in his reaction to religious festivals and the bestowal of names. At first glance, there appears to be a contradiction between the doctor's transgression of cultural codes and his ministration to the Jewish community of Brooklyn. Such paradoxes, however, are legion in Jewish history. As Gilman argues, the pervasiveness of Jewish self-hatred is such that it enters every layer of social and individual life; historically, it has run like a black thread through an entire range of self-divisive reactions to normative Judaism—from the Sabbatian messianism and apostasy of the seventeenth and eighteenth centuries to Freud's psychoanalysis. In Schiffer's 1974 interview, the emotional scars Reznikoff bears that correspond to his doctor's self-division become apparent when the poet laughs embarrassedly at each profound moment of Jewish self-transgression in the story about his naming. He laughs first after noting that the doctor gave a feast during the days of fasting, the holiest days of the Jewish calendar; he laughs again after reporting the outcome of the naming scene as "Call him Charlie. He'll be grateful to you." Moreover, in that one statement, "He'll be grateful to you," many voices can be heard: the doctor's canny assessment of Reznikoff's life opportunities in anti-Semitic America and, beneath that, the doctor's own self-division and reactions against normative Judaism; the mother's attempt to assuage her guilt (or calm her outrage?) by reassuring her son that he will "fit in" as an American and thus be less susceptible to the anti-Semitic attacks that had punctuated her life in Russia; and the rueful irony of the poet, for whom the conflict between his English and Hebrew names mirrors a self-division that anti-Semitism exacerbates.

Anti-Semitism was a prominent feature of the social landscape that Reznikoff navigated from the moment of his birth in Brownsville to his last book of poetry, *Holocaust* (1975). In an early poem he depicts a youthful encounter with this landscape:

It had long been dark, though still an hour before supper-time.
The boy stood at the window behind the curtain.
The street under the black sky was bluish white with snow.
Across the street, where the lot sloped to the pavement,
boys and girls were going down on sleds.
The boys were after him because he was a Jew.

At last his father and mother slept. He got up and dressed.
In the hall he took his sled and went out on tiptoe.
No one was in the street. The slide was worn smooth and slippery—
    just right.
He laid himself on the sled and shot away. He went down only twice.
He stood knee-deep in snow:
no one was in the street, the windows were darkened;
those near the street-lamps were ashine, but the rooms inside were
    dark;
on the street were long shadows of clods of snow.
He took his sled and went back into the house.
(*CP* 1.45–46)

This marvelous poem is one of twenty-seven published under the heading
"Jews" in *Uriel Acosta: A Play and a Fourth Group of Verse* (1921). Although
it is composed almost exclusively of simple, declarative sentences, the
poem manages to convey, through the skillful use of understatement and
narrative jumping, a range of compelling emotions: loneliness, furtive-
ness, fear, desire, and exhilaration. In the social landscape portrayed by
the poem, "It had long been dark, though still an hour before supper-
time," for the wintry darkness of social exclusion has stained the entire
day. At the end of the poem there is a moment of paralysis, which represents the double bind provoked by anti-Semitism. After two runs with his
sled, the boy stops still, "knee-deep in snow." He becomes aware of the
social world, in which he is an outsider. Noticing the lack of human witness to his pleasure, he looks into the windows of the houses that harbor
his tormentors. The windows are dark. They reflect the light of the street
lamps, but they reveal nothing of the beings who peer malevolently out
of them during the day. For the Jewish boy, the mentality of anti-Semitism
is opaque; he cannot penetrate the consciousness that sees him as Other.
Neither can the street lamps, which Reznikoff celebrates in a number of
poems as diminutive equivalents to the moon (as though the moon were
"humanized"), illuminate this implacable darkness. In fact, the warm, reasonable light from the street lamps is converted into the projector of "long

shadows of clods of snow." "Clod" is the perfect word, for it denotes both a "dull, ignorant, or stupid person" and "a lump or chunk, especially of earth or clay" *(American Heritage Dictionary)*. These clods are the souls of the boys, his tormentors, earth-bound, ready to bury him, arrayed against the humanistic light, casting long shadows on his inner world.

On another level, we can read the central activity of sledding as a metaphor for writing poetry. In the landscape Reznikoff inhabited, "The boys were after him because he was a Jew," so he wrote poetry in the shadows, appearing mainly in Jewish magazines and printing nearly all of his books of verse at his own expense. Tellingly, the poet Michael Palmer once recalled in conversation with me that when he was editing *Joglars* with Clark Coolidge in the mid-sixties, he asked Louis Zukofsky how to approach Reznikoff for a submission to the magazine. Zukofsky told him, "Oh, Charles only publishes in Jewish magazines." When Palmer later met Reznikoff, he asked whether this was true. "No," he was told, "they're the only ones that accept my work." The sledding poem seems to speak about the costs and rewards of Reznikoff's social position as a writer, depicting both the lonely courage necessary to pursue a long career with almost no external encouragement and the victory in struggling through an opaque urban world to glimpses of uncanny purity. Through the imagery associated with sledding, the act of writing poetry is figured as an exhilarating, even vertiginous, spiritual release. At the same time in this fairy-tale setting, "He went down only twice" instead of completing an anticipated three runs and achieving full satisfaction, for the "long shadows of clods of snow" enforce a painful forbearance, which translates in Reznikoff's poetry into the disciplined incompleteness of his style.

Anti-Semitism, as L. S. Dembo notes, "seems to be always on the poet's mind—or in the back of it." Dembo underscores its presence in many facets of Reznikoff's life and works: "Indeed, his life as a loner and wanderer, no less than much of his irony and wit, has its source in the fears and anxieties elicited by Jew-baiting youths" *(MP* 191). Like the shy humility that marked his social behavior, the seemingly simple, bland surface of Reznikoff's poetry represents a highly studied attempt both to escape notice by appearing inconspicuous and to control powerful emotions such as rage, desire, and fear. The suppressed emotions, in particular, create a tensely muffled undertone that accounts for much of the striking fascination of this stark poetry, comprising mainly portraits of resistance, long-suffering, and sheer survival. His wife, Marie Syrkin, could not help but be aware of the sway these emotions held over the poet. In "Charles: A Memoir," she points out, "He was not as indifferent as he pretended. In one of his rare ventures into self-analysis he wrote after a discussion with

Al [Lewin—an old friend and movie producer, who brought him to Hollywood]: 'I sat wondering if we had not both uncovered the emotional springs of our being, what makes us tick; vanity perhaps in his case; fear perhaps in mine' " (50).

In Jewish history, Reznikoff found many examples of successful responses to the emotions generated by persecution. During a life devoted in good part to writing Jewish history, he was moved most by the qualities of stubborn tenacity and healing compassion that he encountered. "The Jews typify," he claims, "perhaps more than any other people, constant and often victorious struggle against a hostile environment and hostile elements within itself, a struggle which has constantly evolved Jews that are symbols of the admirable" (Sharp, "Reznikoff's *Nine Plays*" 272–73). Through his identification as a Jew, Reznikoff's ability to thematize the anxiety evoked by anti-Semitism makes him a valuable poet not only for an understanding of American Jewish experience, but also for an illumination of similar anxieties experienced by everyone in the modern world. In this sense, the terrible burden of anti-Semitism may be transformed into a wise tutor, for, as Gilman notes:

> The internalization of such stereotypes can lead to self-destructive behavior ("self-hatred"), but it can also lead to productive and successful means of resistance. Poets, scientists, critics, philosophers, physicians can take the doubts which are embodied in racial concepts and transform them into constructive actions for the individual, if not for the group. For these projected concerns mirror doubts which all human beings have about their own authenticity: the sense of our own lack of control over destiny, the rigidity which we demand from the world so that we can control our own anxieties, the need to locate where danger lies— these factors are shared by all human beings.
> (*Jew's Body* 240–41)

The vulnerability and paranoia that result from racial stereotyping may be converted into productive virtues, such as an alert sensitivity to exclusionary practices, a rigorous commitment to self-analysis, and a subtle demythologizing bent. Jewish exercise of these virtues has led both to battles against a variety of corrosive human delusions and to an active compassion for the victims of such delusions: everyone.

Many of Reznikoff's poems present a carefully observed person or group whose existence is precarious and whose struggles are habitually ignored by others. In one poem, for instance, Reznikoff speaks of a long-suffering elevator operator, who "must greet each passenger / pleasantly." The elevator man is a kind of sentinel, required to open himself to each person he meets, although the subject of their encounter can be seldom more than "dull and trivial." Commenting upon the elevator man's fate with a perfectly modulated tone, Reznikoff proclaims, "to be so heroic / he wears a uniform" (*CP* 2.30–31). The tone manages to convey a beautiful conjunction of irony and praise: of course, the uniform worn by the elevator man grants him no authority but marks him as a servant; and yet the poem expresses genuine admiration for the man's ability to proffer a humane greeting to strangers from his subservient position. Another poem about underdogs portrays a casual moment during the Great Depression, in which a destitute man discovers an innate generosity lying beneath the cynicism he wears to shield himself from inimical economic conditions:

> The young fellow walks about
> with nothing to do: he has lost his job.
> "If I ever get another, I'll be hard!
> You've got to be hard
> to get on. I'll be hard, all right,"
> he says bitterly. Takes out his cigarettes.
> Only four or five left.
> Looks at me out of the corner of his eye—
> a stranger he has just met; hesitates;
> and offers me a cigarette.
> (33)

In both of these poems, Reznikoff observes how a heroic yet commonplace virtue like openness to strangers allows a subject at the mercy of implacable social forces to win a crucial measure of self-respect. In Reznikoff's own case, his confrontations with anti-Semitism gave rise not only to fear and self-divisiveness, but also to an adamant self-respect and a stance of compassionate advocacy. Basing his pleas for respecting the dignity of outsiders upon his own experience of the shadows, Reznikoff writes a poetry that shows us "where danger lies" and how an awareness of it can cut through self-delusion and open us to humane encounters beyond the bounds of the social group with which we identify.[4] Defending the truth revealed by his unflinching gaze into "the long shadows" cast by "clods," Reznikoff says, "A reviewer wrote that when he read *Testimony* a second time he saw a world of horror and violence. I didn't invent the world, but I felt it" (*MP* 107). Making a commitment to viewing the world without illusions results for Reznikoff not in bitterness or disillusionment, but in "feeling"—that is, in pathos and compassion. Eliot Weinberger, too, notes how Reznikoff's reflections upon the human condition partake of a rueful wisdom: "It was a world of injustice without ultimate justice, of disembodied outbursts of violent passion, of suffering without the illusion of a political redemption. If Reznikoff's life is ever known, I suspect that what we saw as an untiring humility will be far more tragic" (78). Weinberger goes too far, perhaps, in calling Reznikoff's life itself tragic, but he is right to consider the wisdom of Reznikoff's work as the product of an unyielding gaze directed at an unredeemed world—a compassionate gaze that has the power to wither delusion.[5] Surely, it is the power of this gaze that has attracted the artist Ann Hamilton to cover gallery walls of the 1999 Venice Biennale with passages from Reznikoff's *Testimony,* which gives a history of the United States from 1885 to 1915, drawn from the courtroom testimony of victims of social forces such as slavery, industrialization, and class strife. Speaking of her installation, Hamilton says, "I'm thinking that I am the American representative, and it's the eve of the millennium. . . . I want to bring to the surface the questions we should be asking" (Dobrzynski 1, 30).

"THE HEBREW OF YOUR POETS, ZION / IS LIKE OIL UPON A BURN"

I would like to return to the issue of Reznikoff's "poor Jewish background" by looking at how the strife between his American and Jewish names represents for him a larger tension between two languages, English and Hebrew, each with its own powerful associations. In normal conversation, when someone confesses to a "poor Jewish background," he or she is often referring to an inability to read or speak Hebrew, especially biblical or talmudic Hebrew. Having learned at his mother's insistence to speak only English at home, Reznikoff did not read Hebrew, the language of his Jewish heritage, until he was an adult. Of the other languages in Reznikoff's cultural background, Yiddish was the language of the eastern European Jewish community, still spoken by many Jews when they came to America; Russian was the national language of the country in which Reznikoff's parents had been born. It would have been possible for either of these, especially Yiddish (the *mame loshn,* or "mother tongue"), to function as a "middle" language for Reznikoff, mediating between the ancient religious and the modern cosmopolitan tongues. But as the poet explains to Reinhold Schiffer,

> Now, I don't know any Russian, except a word or two, nothing whatever, my folks never spoke it. At least my father, my mother was against that, mother's discipline was we should learn English. And she emphasized that constantly, because when my grandparents came to this country, it [Russian] was the only speech they understood. Well of course,

my grandfather knew Hebrew, but they never used it in their daily
speech, that was just the religious speech. We spoke Yiddish to them;
my Yiddish is very bad. People who really know Yiddish run out of the
room when I try to talk. But I think I understand most of it, and in
Hebrew I know very little, but what I can I read with great pleasure.
And as I say, maybe it's the ethnic background, but really ethnic, because
I was never taught any Hebrew as a child.
(*MP* 123–24)

Hebrew and English had no common ground in the world in which
Reznikoff grew up. His paternal grandfather, who emigrated when
Charles was a boy, had been a Hebrew teacher in Russia, but Charles
remained ignorant of the sacred language. And he takes a dismissive attitude toward Yiddish: when discussing the conflict between speaking English and Russian in his household, he claims that Russian was "the only
speech" his grandparents understood, completely ignoring the fact that
"we spoke Yiddish to them"; his own Yiddish, learned at an early age, he
brushes aside as "very bad." In fact, he seems embarrassed about Yiddish,
both in his use of it (which he claims forces native speakers to turn aside
in pain), and in his banishing the language itself from his "ethnic background"—which he purifies to include only Hebrew. Hebrew is the pres-
tige language, which he idealizes and sets in opposition to the low, vernacular dialect of Yiddish that he repudiates. Despite the thriving Yiddish
culture in New York City, most of the immigrant Jews there felt that
becoming American meant mastering English and suppressing Yiddish.
In reality, Reznikoff seems to have feigned his lack of competence in Yiddish, as George Oppen reveals in the following anecdote: "[A]s Reznikoff
knows, my Yiddish is completely fake. It's nowhere that I know in my
ancestry. Reznikoff will not permit me to say anything on the subject. I
remember signing books with him when our first New Directions books
came out and, in a moment when there was no one around, I signed one
and handed it to him and said, 'Read it in health.' Charles said, 'No: read
it in *good* health.' The Yiddish was wrong" ("An Interview" 194).

Reznikoff's schooling reinforced the separation of Hebrew and English
(and the suppression of Yiddish and Russian), for in Brooklyn one could
attend either a New York public school or a Jewish religious school. In
later life, he still recalls the contrast between the two in stark terms:

I remember my mother took me into what they call a *cheder,* where they
teach children Hebrew. I had been going to public school at the time.
Well, public school, you sat in their beautiful building, comparatively.
If you went to a *cheder* in those days (now they're better built), it was in
the cellar, or a basement, and they were teaching it according to the

standard that every pupil was working on a different passage and was shouting it aloud. There was terrific turmoil and in comparison to the ordinary public school, it was atrocious! And in addition, the man who was teaching was armed with a strap; a child who wasn't paying any attention was spanked. So all this, coming from an American public school, was very unpleasant to the child and even the mother. But a religious person wouldn't have minded it.

(*MP* 124)

In his memory, the public school was aboveground, well lit, orderly, quiet, English speaking, and replete with up-to-date knowledge that allowed immigrant children to assimilate quickly; the *cheder* was underground, dark, chaotic, noisy, physically threatening, Hebrew-speaking, and inculcated a knowledge of Jewish law that reinforced religious orthodoxy.[6] Distancing himself from what he implies are the irrational beliefs and acceptable sufferings of a "religious person," Reznikoff maintains that nothing but an overriding religious motive would have made one choose the *cheder* of those days over the public school.

In contrast, the child and his family opted for assimilation rather than religious orthodoxy, English rather than Hebrew (or Yiddish), but the poet remained haunted throughout his life by a longing for Hebrew, as though he had lost the divine language along with his Hebrew name— and with the language lost his proof of belonging to the Jewish people and to the Hebrew God:

How difficult for me is Hebrew:
even the Hebrew for *mother,* for *bread,* for *sun*
is foreign. How far have I been exiled, Zion.
(*CP* 1.72)

Reznikoff equates the loss of Hebrew directly with the constantly displaced life of exile, in which the simplest words and the most intimate features of the world appear as if at a distance. Like racial stereotyping, the condition of exile also has an internal replication as self-exile, in which Ezekiel seems to dwell beyond the reach of Charles. And within Ezekiel reside the emotionally laden Hebrew words for *mother, bread,* and *sun,* as though the primary forms of nurture and the sources of growth and knowledge were not native to this Jewish Charles. In Reznikoff's private lexicon, "bread" stands for the gift of sustenance, over which one offers a (Hebrew) prayer; "sun" represents the universal (nonparochial) supplier of illumination and warmth; and "mother" symbolizes the fundament, with which the poet (having repudiated the *mame loshn*) must maintain contact at all costs.

In his arresting poem, "Kaddish," written after his mother's death, Reznikoff posits "mother" as a primary locus of value; in doing so, he places the ritual "prayers and words and lights" of bereavement beneath her. It's as if he could bridge the gap between Charles and Ezekiel by returning not to the womb but to maternal mourning. Although the Kaddish, the Jewish prayer of mourning, is normally recited on the anniversary of a death and is intended to comfort the mourner by its affirmation of faith in God's goodness, Reznikoff's poem for his mother is in many ways a counter-Kaddish, consisting of an unsentimental description of her in her last days and in the period after her death. In the penultimate stanza, the poet portrays his family as comfortless during the ritual mourning period following her demise, as though they were left speechless by the loss of the mother:

> We looked at the light burning slowly before your picture
> and looked away;
> we thought of you as we talked but could not bring ourselves to
>   speak—
> to strangers who do not care, yes,
> but not among ourselves.

Speaking of her to friends offering condolence was easy, a formality, but from within this family caught between Jewish and American cultures, the loss of mother was equivalent to the loss of language. "Among ourselves" speech breaks down in grief, for now neither the mother nor the mother tongue nor the solace of belief makes communication possible. The extremely powerful resonances of the traditional Kaddish as a locus for grief and as a source of solace remain inaudible, as though Hebrew (or, in this case, Aramaic) were being muffled by English.

In the final stanza, in the present tense, Reznikoff addresses his mother directly. Paradoxically, though, he fashions speechlessness and the absence of Jewish ritual into signs of intimacy:

> I know you do not mind
> (if you mind at all)
> that I do not pray for you
> or burn a light
> on the day of your death:
> we do not need these trifles
> between us—
> prayers and words and lights.
> (CP 2.56)

One of the remarkable qualities of Reznikoff's poetry is the combination of a scrupulous commitment to ordinary diction with an intense pressure applied to each word. In this stanza I would like to single out the word *between,* which receives an unexpected rhythmic and syntactic stress. This normally unobtrusive preposition bears the traces of all of Reznikoff's concerns about mediation—about language, about ritual, about kinship—concerns that endlessly haunt a poet with "no middle name."[7] The word *between* signals simultaneously distance and connection; like any medium, it brings things together and holds them apart. On the one hand, the poem figures mediation (such as language or ritual) as a "trifle" that intervenes between two communing souls; on the other hand, the separate phrase "between us," like the earlier "among ourselves," speaks of a plural identity, an *inside,* that resists mediation from outside. We could say that the term *between* carries the entire freight of Reznikoff's double-bind condition, for if he is trying to eliminate the medium and reach an "immediate" rapport with his mother, then he will be forced to ignore not only his mediatory role as poet (for whom language is essential), but also the very space of betweenness, of American Jewishness, in which, as Charles/Ezekiel, he exists. As Reznikoff well knows, "prayers and words and lights" are anything but "trifles," and yet from the perspective of his multiple losses—of mother, of Hebrew, and of religious belief—he wishes they were so.

In addition to the nurturing matriarchal resonances of Hebrew ("for *mother,* for *bread,* for *sun*"), the language also has for Reznikoff a powerful patriarchal ring, in which, by contrast, prayers occupy a place of central importance. In his sequence "Early History of a Writer" (1969), he includes a poem that expresses in patriarchal terms the religious and cultural discontinuity he felt in not learning Hebrew. In Russia, his grandfather had taught Hebrew to boys; in America, the sixteen-year-old grandson cannot even understand the benediction pronounced over him:

I went to my grandfather's to say good-bye:
I was going away to a school out West.
As I came in,
my grandfather turned from the window at which he sat
(sick, skin yellow, eyes bleary—
but his hair still dark,
for my grandfather had hardly any grey hair in his beard or on his
    head—
he would sit at the window, reading a Hebrew book).
He rose with difficulty—

he had been expecting me, it seemed—
stretched out his hands and blessed me in a loud voice:
in Hebrew, of course,
and I did not know what he was saying.
When he had blessed me,
my grandfather turned aside and burst into tears.
"It is only for a little while, Grandpa," I said
in my broken Yiddish. "I'll be back in June."
(By June my grandfather was dead.)
He did not answer.
Perhaps my grandfather was in tears for other reasons:
perhaps, because, in spite of all the learning I had acquired in high
    school,
I knew not a word of the sacred text of the Torah
and was going out into the world
with none of the accumulated wisdom of my people to guide me,
with no prayers with which to talk to the God of my people,
a soul—
for it is not easy to be a Jew or, perhaps, a man—
doomed by his ignorance to stumble and blunder.
(*CP* 2.167)

If the ungraying hair on the grandfather's head stands for the ageless wisdom of the Jews, expressed through Hebrew books and prayers, then the Hebrew-less child feels himself barred from this wisdom and from the solace stored in the Jews' collective experience. By imbibing the religious laws and sayings, the practicing Jew prepares to meet life under the protection of righteousness; observing the commandments, he or she gains not only collective support but also a ritually sanctioned status of "purity." Eschewing religious purity, Reznikoff achieves a compensatory purity by poetic means: through scrupulous technique, simple diction, and the investment of emotion in the choice of subject matter rather than in "self-expression." His relentless pursuit of this type of purity made him an exemplary poet, as Oppen testified. Still, the efficacy of poetry extends only so far: without Hebrew at his command, the poet ruptures the continuity of the millennia during which generations of Jewish lips have uttered the same prayers countless times; so that the loss of his grandfather, like that of his mother, transposes into the loss of Hebrew. Not knowing the language—and therefore the prayers—of his people, he would be, in his grandfather's eyes, like so many deracinated immigrants, "doomed . . . to stumble and blunder" in the New World, adrift in a secular milieu that cannot be redeemed through sacred language.

During World War II, when the "old world" of European Jewry was effectively demolished, Reznikoff pursued his investigation of the relations between the new language, English, and the old language, Hebrew, by using England as the setting for his novel *The Lionhearted: A Story about the Jews in Medieval England* (1944). Drawing on Sir Walter Scott's *Ivanhoe* and the Romance tradition, Reznikoff inverts the point of view of his story of twelfth-century England from the English to the Jewish and shifts the ascription of lionheartedness from the English (the persecutors) to the Jews (the persecuted). In the novel, the English language functions first as a sign of cosmopolitanism and assimilation, of the ability of Jews to make their way into any corner of the world and find a means to survive—often by playing the intermediary among diverse groups of people. This intermediate position is that of the translator; in this sense, Walter Benjamin's classic treatise, "The Task of the Translator"—with its messianic notion of a pure, unpronounceable language, of which translation offers us glimpses—can be seen as a covert essay in Jewish historiography, in which Hebrew would be the unmentioned "pure language." But in a more sinister sense, the cosmopolitan language has often operated historically to occlude Hebrew through a dark veil of anti-Semitism, and so a correspondingly urgent desire arises among certain Jewish writers—such as Benjamin's friend Gershom Scholem—to break free of the dominant language and return to Hebrew.[8]

Reznikoff thematizes the conflict between "cosmopolitan" English (itself an international language composed of Old English, Norman French, Latin, Greek, etc.) and "pure" Hebrew in two passages of the novel. In the first, a young Norman (ostensibly French-speaking) knight is lecturing his friend, a Jewish physician, who is also a poet:

> You Jews, even if none of you could ever hope to write a chanson like that about Roland, or songs as good as those of Guilhem of Poitiers, have a knack for words, the least and worst of you. Now I know only French. That is enough for me. Let the priest speak Latin and my serf Saxon. When they want me to understand they must speak French. But you, or your father, or your cousins, must know the churl's Saxon if he is to fee you for your medicine; must understand my French if I am to buy your furs and spice; why, you must understand Latin to dispute my priest and Greek and Arabic to read your books of medicine. And, of course, Hebrew to talk among yourselves or to your God. If you are driven out of France, as Philip Augustus has just driven you out of Paris, or you are banished from Germany, say, to the land of the Polacks— you must set about learning Polish to earn a living. But I do not even need French. My language is the sword's, which every man understands. Yes, both the French and English have understood it.
>
> (*Lionhearted* 5–6)

In this passage, Reznikoff shows how the Jewish poet becomes cosmopolitan by necessity, speaking all the world's languages. This poet, however, will always be in some sense a translator, whose songs can never be "native" to the language in which he composes and thus never "as good as those of Guilhem of Poitiers." Instead, the Jewish writer will create a polyglot's literature, in which linguistic purity can become a pressing issue—as in the uncannily "pure" German of Franz Kafka, the violently corroded and annealed German of Paul Celan, and the crisp, compressed English of Reznikoff, which strives to replicate the grammatical compactness of Hebrew.

The hallmarks of Hebrew—biblical Hebrew, in particular—are condensation and terseness, qualities that Reznikoff values highly and dedicates himself to achieving. Coincidentally, these qualities were also promoted by the Imagists, especially Ezra Pound, so that Reznikoff implicitly finds the Hebraic reinforcing the Hellenic at the level of style. In his own way, though, Reznikoff focuses so intently upon the single word—as we have seen, for instance, with the word *between* in the poem "Kaddish"—that he asks it to bear a weight not frequently expected of English words. In this he mimics, instead, a defining feature of Hebrew poetry, for "[t]he condensed, laconic nature of biblical Hebrew also contributes to the prominence of each word within the line" (Hrushovski 1201). In order to achieve such prominence, Reznikoff labors unceasingly at revision; for all their ordinary diction, his poems constitute anything but spontaneous remarks. In a note to himself found among his papers, Reznikoff lays out the regimen of condensation to be followed in his practice of revision:

The Method of Revision
1. Write all seemingly good lines
2. Examine every word to remove all possible latinisms and unnecessary words
3. Examine the meaning of the sentences in their order
4. Examine the rhythm of the lines
5. Examine the rhythm of the whole
6. Then revision by contemplation
(UCSD 9.19.2)

This note begins to illuminate the extensive, multilayered method Reznikoff followed to "purify" his poetry. As can be seen by consulting the extensive textual variants in his *Poems 1918–1975,* this method mainly involved cutting away words, phrases, and even entire sentences, so that by a kind of alchemical process of reduction the remaining words would glow with the strongest possible light. Although the poems are written in idiomatic English, their language appears to be bulging at the seams with an unaccustomed weight, as though there were Hebrew words confined within. Reznikoff makes this quality explicit in the poem "Joshua at Shechem": "and God looked and saw the Hebrews / citizens of the great cities, / talking Hebrew in every language under the sun" (*CP* 1.126).

Like Walter Benjamin, Reznikoff believes that a pure language hides behind the constant translations performed by the cosmopolitan Jew. In the Diaspora, "talking Hebrew in every language under the sun" may be a necessary subterfuge, through which, on the one hand, a "Hebrew" identity survives and, on the other hand, a Jewish mark is imparted to the cosmopolitan language—as, for example, in the impact of Kafka and Celan upon German literature or that of Yiddish phrases upon American English. Having translated into English many portions of the Hebrew Bible himself, Reznikoff might even go so far as to agree with Benjamin when he speaks of "the Scriptures" as "unconditionally translatable"— that is, as requiring continual translation. In the case of the Scriptures, which are "supposed to be 'the true language' . . . , translations are called for only because of the plurality of languages" (Benjamin 82). Although Benjamin speaks ecumenically of "the Scriptures," one could argue that from his quasi-kabbalistic perspective Hebrew forms the model and substratum of all languages. Because it is closest to the "pure language— which no longer means or expresses anything but is, as expressionless and creative Word, that which is meant in all languages" (80), Hebrew is *always* being spoken "in every language under the sun."[9]

The notion of infinite translatability also revisits the question of mediation. In the passage quoted from *The Lionhearted,* Reznikoff proposes another, more sinister, "immediate" language—not the wordless communion of the poet with his mother, as in "Kaddish," but the fleshly speech of the sword wielded by the Norman knight. In this novel that Reznikoff completed during World War II, more rides on the question of mediation than a linguistic analysis. In 1942 *Jewish Frontier,* a Labor Zionist monthly coedited by his wife, Marie Syrkin, published the first news account in the United States of the Holocaust. When the State Department received word from the World Jewish Congress that Hitler had embarked upon a systematic attempt to annihilate European Jewry, Syrkin learned of the atrocity at a small meeting for Jewish journalists. In spite of all they knew about the campaign Hitler had waged against the Jews since he came to power in 1933, the journalists found it impossible to accept what they were being told. Syrkin later explained that because she and the rest of the *Jewish Frontier* staff were uncertain how to proceed, "we hit on what in retrospect appears a disgraceful compromise: we buried the fearful re-

port in the back page of the September issue in small type, thus indicating
that we could not vouch for its accuracy. But by the next issue the small
staff of the magazine had uncovered enough material so that the truth had
to be acknowledged" (Kessner 60–61). For that November issue, published with black borders, Syrkin wrote the editorial statement: "In the
occupied countries of Europe, a policy is now being put into effect whose
avowed object is the extermination of a whole people. It is a policy of
systematic murder of innocent civilians which in its ferocity, its dimensions and its organization is unique in the history of mankind."[10]

Reznikoff was by no means immune to the collective reaction of anger, impotence, nightmarish fear, and guilt that swept through American Jewry on the heels of that announcement. If his invocation of "the
churl's Saxon" reminds us of his English "Christian" name, Charles, then
does this novel represent a site where the guilt of the American Jewish
poet, brought to a crisis by the Holocaust, breaks out? English/Hebrew,
secular/sacred, American/European, son/father, doctor/mother: all of
these oppositions engage the anxious narrative of this novel about a cosmopolitan Jewish poet in a time of persecution. As the action of the novel
proceeds, the language of the sword speaks loudly to the Jews and severs
the "Hebrew" from "every language under the sun," rendering the cosmopolitan tongue a dead weight in the poet's mouth. Or, to use Reznikoff's own paradoxical image, the cosmopolitan idiom becomes "blood-
less—and tasting of blood." At such a time, Reznikoff has his Jewish poet
seek the "purity" of Hebrew with redoubled passion. As he attends to the
mounting physical impact of the persecution of the Jews, the increasingly
harrowed physician/poet looks for solace in "the speech of his fathers":

> The sweet rhymes and, for that matter, even the speech of the Gentiles
> in which David had been writing now seemed to him bloodless—and
> tasting of blood. He thirsted for Hebrew as the wounded do for water.
> Even when he had been working in the language of the country, he had
> tried for full sounds and tight sentences; in the speech of his fathers he
> found all this ready at hand. He knew now that he must read and still read
> all that had been hallowed by the lips of his father and the generations of
> Israel, not only as a pious Jew but, as a poet, for pleasure in meaning and
> sounds. And he could make music out of the legalistic, the driest, of this
> reading, he thought, as a savage can out of sticks and a hide.
> (*Lionhearted* 172)

In this passage, the compact Hebrew language takes on for Reznikoff
and his character, David (named after the preeminent Jewish king and
poet), the combined physical, social, and spiritual attributes of the Jewish
people. At the spiritual level, Hebrew becomes here, as it does in a differ-

ent way in the Kabbalah, the core of Judaism. Reaffirming his identity in
the face of pogroms, David seeks to recapture the lost sacred quality of
Hebrew, which Reznikoff had noted in an earlier short poem:

> I have learnt the Hebrew blessing before eating bread;
> is there no blessing before reading Hebrew?
>
> (*CP* 1.72)

This poem is instructive, though, not just for its reverence toward Hebrew
but also for what it says about the issue of mediation. Far from being a
direct, immediately apprehensible language, Hebrew is portrayed here by
Reznikoff as so material that it requires a blessing before being employed.
Like Benjamin, Reznikoff seems to locate the "purity" of Hebrew in
terms not of immediacy but rather of infinite translatability—as though
"Hebrew" were the *ability* to bless rather than the specific words used in
a natural language for blessing. Reznikoff presents Hebrew as the language
in which the material world is said to be sacred. This characterization echoes Benjamin's understanding of "pure language": for Benjamin, a pure
language is not a mimetic language that ties words directly to things—
as Ezra Pound sought in Chinese, for example—but rather an abstract
language of structuration that makes meaning and communication and
blessing possible.

In the passage just quoted from *The Lionhearted,* the materiality of Hebrew is infused with a desperate sensuality during a time of persecution.
First, the words become a physiological necessity, "thirsted for" like the
few drops of water capable of reviving a wounded man. Beyond this image, though, in something like a wounded man's hallucination, Hebrew
flashes forth as the desirable woman, whose "full sounds and tight sentences" contain a palpably eroticized promise of "pleasure."[11] With his
Hebrew (bride), the poet dreams of drumming up a primitive fertility rite
"as a savage can out of sticks and a hide," invoking, with the help of an-
thropologists like Sir James Frazer, the "primitive" social underpinnings of
religion.[12] This anthropological gesture represents another way of making
material and erotic the generative functions of Hebrew. Finally, through
his lips, in the material act of reading, Reznikoff's character David hopes
to embody and unite "the speech of his fathers" with the "full sounds
and tight sentences" of the mother's Hebrew—as though the *langue* (the
structure) of Hebrew were masculine and the *parole* (the utterances) feminine.

In the opening poem of *Jerusalem the Golden* (1934), Reznikoff uses similar images to tie the hurt of persecution with the desire for erotic fulfill-
ment in the pure language of Hebrew:

The Hebrew of your poets, Zion,
is like oil upon a burn,
cool as oil;
after work,
the smell in the street at night
of the hedge in flower.
Like Solomon,
I have married and married the speech of strangers;
none are like you, Shulamite.
(*CP* 1.107)

Like a balm, Hebrew poetry's coolness heals and compensates for the wound caused by burning hatred (or by the drudgery of "work"). And again, as in *The Lionhearted,* the healing quality of Hebrew is conflated with the erotic—in the "smell in the street at night / of the hedge in flower." By a comparison with Solomon, the cosmopolitan poet accuses himself not of adultery but of polygamy and exogamy, having "married and married the speech of strangers." Like Solomon, too, in the Song of Songs, he returns (incestuously) to the Hebrew beloved (mother) as to an original or pure language, from whom he expects a perfect homecoming. In the phrase "none are like you, Shulamite," Reznikoff again sacralizes the Hebrew language, this time by echoing not only the sacred eroticism of the Song of Songs but also the common liturgical expression, "None are like you, O Lord."

For the later Jewish poet, Paul Celan, in his most famous poem about the Holocaust, *Todesfuge, Shulamite* also functions as an image for the Hebrew beloved and the beloved Hebrew language. Like Reznikoff, Celan contrasts Hebrew with the cosmopolitan language, in this case German, by placing *Shulamite* alongside Goethe's Margareta, tragic heroine of *Faust,* juxtaposing the now-ashen hair of the former with the golden hair of the latter:

> dein goldenes Haar Margarete
> dein aschenes Haar Sulamith

In the ironic poetic economy of Paul Celan, a parallelism such as this actually emphasizes differences rather than similarities: although he invokes the hair of two beautiful women, Celan places the shadow of the Final Solution between the German and the Hebrew beloveds, as John Felstiner demonstrates (22–41). In his masterful commentary, *Paul Celan: Poet, Survivor, Jew,* Felstiner gathers the relevant Jewish associations with *Shulamite* in order to show how much distance separates the two beloveds:

Shulamith is no ash blond but the "black and comely" maiden in the Song of Songs, a princess "the hair of whose head is like purple" and whose dancing feet are beautiful in sandals. Akin to *shalom* ("peace") or *Yerushalayim* (Jerusalem), her name guards its identity, occurring only once in the Bible. . . . Shulamith is the beloved par excellence and is seen as the Jewish people itself: "Return, return, O Shulamite; return, return, that we may look upon thee" (Song 7:1). Since the Song is read at Passover, she figures as a promise of return to Zion, and mystical tradition interprets her as the Shechinah, who wanders with the community of Israel. When "Deathfugue" twins Shulamith with *Faust's* devout, ruined Margareta, nothing can reconcile them. Celan's word *aschenes* tells why.
(38)

As Reznikoff asserts in *The Lionhearted,* the Hebrew language takes on a powerful erotic presence in a time of extremity. In Celan's poem, Hebrew becomes literally embodied in the word of desire, "Shulamith," which holds out against the fatally tainted German language by serving as the last word of *Todesfuge* (Felstiner 41). For Reznikoff, Hebrew seems to hold out the promise of the perfect marriage, both erotic and sacred; learning to read the language would allow him to redeem the promise:

> I began to pick it up when I was in my twenties. And I may be mistaken, but it seemed to me that in Hebrew as *I* read it, I found an affinity. I found that emphatic language, as *I* read it, in the vowels. My father was then alive, and he heard me read it as I had picked it up and he was shocked. He said, "That's Arabic!" because they were using different vowel sounds, but I found a lot of pleasure in reading it.
> (*MP* 121)

Like an immigrant to Israel, Reznikoff "picks up" the new Sephardic Hebrew (which offends the Ashkenazic ears of his father), as though undoing the Diaspora, returning to the mother tongue, to the best wife, who fulfills all her husband's desires. Representing Hebrew as feminine, Reznikoff goes against the grain of the Jewish gendering of languages: for most Jews, Yiddish is feminine (the *mame loshn*) and Hebrew is masculine (the *loshn koydesh,* "holy tongue"); when he idealizes Hebrew and shuns Yiddish, though, he reverts to type.[13] His own wife, Marie Syrkin, who was not content with the role of a new Shulamite, noted approvingly that he remained faithfully wedded to the Hebrew he "picked up" in a bedtime ritual that persisted to the end of his life: "Each evening he read a few pages of the Old Testament in the original Hebrew and in two translations, English and Luther's German" (*MP* 59). From this testimony it appears that in Reznikoff's daily practice the purest Hebrew acted, finally, not as utopian escape from the rigors of exile but instead as what Benjamin calls the "unconditionally translatable" medium of a poet's reading.

"HERE'S A MAN'S LIFE"

The complex gender relations inscribed in Reznikoff's negotiations with Hebrew have their ramifications in not only his childhood but also his adult life, particularly his marriage. Conversely, his attitudes toward marriage and children bear directly upon his stance as a writer, and these attitudes are intimately intertwined with his use of Hebrew as a generative factor in the writing. When he married Marie Syrkin in 1930, Reznikoff was thirty-six and Syrkin was thirty-one. Both had lived with disappointments and drudgery for many years. After an elopement at sixteen that was annulled by her father, Nahman Syrkin, founder of Labor Zionism, Marie had married a young biochemistry instructor, Aaron Bodansky, in 1919, at the end of her freshman year at Cornell. She continued there as a student, receiving bachelor's and master's degrees in English. Carole Kessner sums up the salient points of Syrkin's personal and professional life during the decade before she met Reznikoff:

> Throughout the 1920s, Marie Syrkin's professional activities were restricted primarily to poetry, journalism, and teaching. Her personal situation—the tragic death of her first son, the birth a few months later of her second son, the death of her father, her separation and subsequent divorce from Bodansky, and her return to New York with her surviving child—necessitated self-support, which she accomplished by teaching English at Textile High School in Manhattan. This was a job that she utterly detested, but which she kept out of economic necessity until 1948.
> (58)

Before she could marry Reznikoff, Marie had to travel from New York to Reno to obtain a divorce. In the touching letters he wrote to her during this time, Reznikoff appears straitjacketed by language, trapped in his job of writing legal definitions: he needs the money to free him to write his own work, but he takes so long to craft the definitions in his meticulous fashion that he has no time left. And looking at Syrkin, he sees that she, too, has been trapped for many years—in a failed marriage, as a single mother, and in teaching high school. He writes to her in Reno, "Listen, honey, we are like two wild animals—despite our—at least my—pacific appearance; we have never been completely house-broken or harness broken, and I do not intend to be, nor that you should be. Now, I am one wild animal explaining to my mate how I expect to evade the traps set for me" (UCSD 9.25.2). In the letters, he presents her not only with the promise of a weekly box of chocolates from Macy's, but with compulsive calculations about how long it will take to finish his current batch of definitions, what his chances are of persuading his boss to let him work half-time, or how long it might take to find a new job. In this particular letter, after an unintentionally Chaplinesque juggling act consisting of rationalizations and calculations, this "wild animal" finds himself reduced to a mouse or a deer, and concludes, "So I will work on—not trapped at all, my dear, but in a trap, nibbling at the cheese, with one eye on the door, or like a deer that come [sic] to town to nibble at a garden and hopes to dash away before it is too late. Well, dearest, I see the road clear before us, a rocky road, but it leads to freedom—for both of us together. Dear wife, in a few days you will have hurdled one obstacle [divorce], I hope; with patience, courage, and love we shall reach Jerusalem together."

Judging from this letter, chances are slim that these lovers will turn the "rocky road" into a "clear road" and "reach Jerusalem together." Nor does Reznikoff's fantasy of the perfect Jewish wife, enunciated in another letter from this time, seem very realistic: "Darling, won't you like to keep an orthodox Jewish home? Bless candles on Friday, keep all the holidays? I like to think of you blessing the candles in our home. I kiss you a hundred times. Good night until tomorrow" (*Letters* 119). This fantasy of orthodox Jewish coziness, in which the husband kisses the sacred words on the lips of his wife—again the erotic linguistic conjunction, this time in the form of bless/kiss—never materialized.[14] Although she became a highly influential and indefatigable Zionist, Syrkin was not about to assume the role of female guarantor of Jewishness, regardless of the sacred/sexual rewards accompanying that role. As she puts it dryly in her memoir of her husband, "Ours was the typical home of an emancipated American Jew periodically moved by sentiment and ancestral memories. On Passover we conducted our own, unorthodox, wilful seder; that was the extent of our bow to tradition" (*MP* 55).

Syrkin not only made things difficult for Reznikoff by deflating his wishes in religious matters, she also denied him "material" benefits. Instead of tending the hearth, she taught high school, which she referred to as "drudgery," and yet she refused to support him financially. His own work history testifies to a constant struggle to maintain at all costs his freedom as a writer: although he completed a law degree at New York University (1912–15) and was admitted to the bar (1916), he did not practice

law, but chose instead to earn an extremely modest living selling hats for
the family's millinery business, writing definitions for the legal encyclope-
dia, working as an assistant to a Hollywood producer, and later doing editorial work. Marie's skeptical reception of his endless calculations—regarding such things as how much work would be needed to supply him
with a specified amount of time for writing or how many pages of fiction
he would have to write before his talent and industry would earn them a
living—caused friction in their relationship. Lacking enthusiasm for his
impractical schemes to earn money as a writer, she felt herself unfairly
contrasted and compared to the traditional images of the long-suffering
Jewish wife or the shrewish spouse of the wise philosopher:

> Though not precisely Xantippe I always felt that the lady had gotten a
> bad press. Equally irritating was the image of the Hebraic "woman
> of valor," the perfect wife extolled in the Psalms who spins, weaves,
> looks after her household and burgeoning family while her spouse
> sits at the city gate discussing public affairs with his peers—surely
> one of the earliest though most revered exemplars of male chauvinism!
> Actually Charles' expectations had a long Jewish tradition according
> to which a true scholar might spend his days in pious study while his
> barely literate wife uncomplainingly ran the store. . . . Charles remem-
> bered a grandfather who wanted to write Hebrew poetry and an ener-
> getic grandmother, and he too viewed his poetic vocation as a sacred
> study.
> (MP 51)

During the forties, their difficult relationship floundered, and they experienced what Syrkin calls "a growing estrangement." She says that in
spite of their distance, though, "neither of us wanted a divorce." Several
of Reznikoff's poems of the forties reflect this unhappy state of affairs. In
one, he delivers some bitter reflections upon his place in her life:

> I remember very well when I asked you—
> as if you were a friend—whether or not
> I should go somewhere or other,
> you answered: "It does not matter:
> you are not at all important."
>
> That was true. But I wonder
> whom you thought important.
> He who has been in his grave
> these ten years or more?
> Or he who is wearing out a path

in the carpet of his room
as he paces it
like a shabby coyote in a cage,
an old man hopelessly mad?

Yourself, no doubt:
looking like one
who has been a great beauty.
(*CP* 2.81)

Based on personal knowledge of Reznikoff and Syrkin, Milton Hindus surmises that Reznikoff wrote this poem about his wife, her deceased father, and her first husband, Maurice Samuel ("Charles Reznikoff" 258– 59). The first stanza records a stinging slight, whose force must have remained with Reznikoff for many years, since he had already recorded it approximately ten years earlier in his "Autobiography: New York" (*CP* 2.36). In the second stanza, he accepts her belittling gesture, and then asks, sarcastically, who else deserves a greater stature—a dead father? or a mad lover? In the third stanza he strikes back more directly, accusing her of valuing herself above others and of a laughable vanity regarding her fading beauty. The latter point he also makes in a short poem in "Autobiography: New York" that is worthy of Villon: "Holding the stem of the / beauty she had / as if it were still / a rose" (36). In another poem reflecting on their marriage, Reznikoff complains about her lack of sympathy for his struggle as a writer—"I know you did not approve of the struggle at all— / sure that I could not possibly win"—and accuses her of betraying him by not making any sacrifices for his art. He ends the poem leaving their marriage hanging in the balance: "Now stay if you like / but, if you want to, go" (77).

Syrkin did go in 1950, accepting a professorial appointment at Brandeis University. Reznikoff remained in New York, and so they spent the next seventeen years living apart, although maintaining contact. In fact, it was during this time that she was finally able to relieve his constant anxieties over money by offering him the managing editorship of *Jewish Frontier*. Largely hiding from her his feelings of emotional abandonment during these years apart, Reznikoff poured them into a novel, *The Manner "Music,"* which was discovered among his papers after his death. Syrkin's description of finding the novel stresses her outrage, sorrow, and even surprise: "The wife of the main character, a composer, is a petulant, pretty, notably unsympathetic female, a Zionist, a high school teacher who tactlessly keeps complaining about her fatigue and lets her talented, unappreciated husband end his poverty-stricken quest in Bellevue. A *roman à clef* with a vengeance! I read Charles' novel in 1976 in sorrow at the intensity of the suffering revealed" (*MP* 52). The novel's dénouement turns on the startling revelation that the protagonist, Jude Dalsimer, a talented, avant-garde composer, had destroyed all of his music—his sole passion in life—just before he was committed to Bellevue.[15] The narrator, Jude's friend, finds this out when he speaks to Jude's wife in the hospital. Referring to the composer's music, his wife asks:

> "Truthfully, now, did you like it?"
> "I did not like it," I said slowly. "But then I know little about music. It will be for others to judge."
> "No one will ever judge," said Lucy.
> "What do you mean? Have you destroyed it?"
> "Jude has. There is nothing to judge. He tore up everything. Everything he has ever written and burnt it. They found the heap of ashes near him when they took him to the hospital. That's what brought the police. The fire, you know. He left nothing with me of his music when he went away from"—she hesitated a moment at using the word Jude might not have used—"home. And they found nothing in his pockets or the bundle he had with him. All his music was burnt," she repeated, and there was something so childlike and helpless in the way she spoke I was a little sorry for her.
> (*Manner* 128–29)

Reznikoff's own sense of betrayal at what he saw as Syrkin's abandonment of "home" resonates through this passage. More remarkable, though, is the extreme to which Jude, the "talented, unappreciated husband" (in Syrkin's words), arrives during his unsuccessful attempt to live a life that would support his musical vocation: not only does he go mad, but his madness results in the burning of the music to which he devoted himself. This particular tragic outcome did not come arbitrarily to Reznikoff: something similar actually happened to his grandfather Ezekiel. The man after whom Reznikoff's mother had wanted to name her son was a poet who wrote in Hebrew—a poet who had *only* his name, for when he died in Russia, his wife burned all of his poetry. In the novel *By the Waters of Manhattan* (1930)—the "name" Reznikoff used for three of his books and for a number of the groups of poems he published in journals—he describes the incineration of his grandfather's poetry this way:

> He brought Ezekiel's baggage. Hannah opened it, and on top she found a bundle of long sheets of paper, carefully wrapped. They were covered with verse in Hebrew, and Abram was the only one of them who could

read it at all. Ezekiel had been somewhat free in his speech, and Hannah was afraid there might be something Nihilistic in his writing that would get them all into trouble. She was afraid to ask an outsider what the writing was about. In those days it was enough to say of a family, "They are Nihilists," to have them arrested at once; the police investigated at their leisure. There was too much to burn at one time, so she burnt a few sheets every morning until all were gone. As she put the first into the fire she said, "Here's a man's life."

(83)

Here is the primal scene of poetry for Charles Reznikoff. His grandfather's lifework, his secret self, written in Hebrew, language of the Torah—not Yiddish, language of the Diaspora, or Russian, the cosmopolitan language—is destroyed out of fear and ignorance.[16] Ezekiel dies not once but twice, first as a traveling sales agent who succumbs to influenza on the road and then as a carefully wrapped bundle of sheets that must be cremated. Why? Because the sheets may be tainted with "Nihilism," with a Jewish-inspired, metaphysical influenza so potent it has spread into the political sphere and threatens to overthrow the Czarist regime. "It was this sad story," says Milton Hindus, "that prompted Reznikoff's decision to see to it that his own work was printed, even if he had to do it himself. He was not going to leave his brain-children (the only ones he had in his life) to the care of his family or friends" (*MP* 17). This "sad story" was related by Reznikoff obsessively in interviews and in the family histories he wrote in prose and verse. Unquestionably, "Charles" identifies directly with "Ezekiel." In an interview he argues, "the fact that a man could spend his life or a good portion of his life writing Hebrew poetry that wasn't even published, would show an inclination that might crop up, and I think, perhaps did crop up in me" (125–26). In his own poetry, Reznikoff expresses his identification even more directly:

> My grandfather, dead long before I was born,
> died among strangers; and all the verse he wrote
> was lost—
> except for what
> still speaks through me
> as mine.
> (*CP* 2.91)

A desire to embody the grandfather's lost legacy appears in the possessive terms "my grandfather" and "mine," as well as in the parallel disyllabic lines "was lost" and "as mine." Making manifest his inheritance, Reznikoff's poems are the great-grandchildren—as though the dead, cremated manuscript had produced, through the intermediary of Charles's mother, this new brood of American Jewish poems. The equation of poetry with children occurs even more explicitly in another poem:

> At night, after the day's work, he wrote. Year after year he had
>   written,
> but the right words were still not all there, the right rhythms not
> always used. He corrected the old and added new.
> While away on a business trip he died. His children playing about the
> house, left home by the widow out at work, found the manuscript
> so carefully written and rewritten.
> The paper was good to scribble on. Then they tore it into bits. At
>   night
> the mother came home and swept it out.
> (*CP* 1.58)

Although published in 1921, years before his marriage, this poem conflates the destruction of an unsuccessful poet's verse with betrayal by wife and children. The wife is at work, leaving both the children and the poems at home to fend for themselves, unprotected. The children assert their own wills by scribbling over the poetry, substituting themselves for what Ezekiel's wife had called "a man's life." In this poem, Reznikoff lays bare what must have been a central element of conflict in his marriage with Syrkin: he portrays the responsibility he feels for his poetry as being directly at odds with a bond to wife or children.

Having suffered the immeasurable loss of Ezekiel's poetry—and the name Ezekiel as well—Charles vows to ensure the survival of his only progeny and his "name" by publishing his poetry at all costs. His sacred duty, as he sees it, is *publication,* the ushering of his poems into the physical world; whether, or when, the poems find a readership is another matter. In an argument with Harriet Monroe over revisions to a group of his early poems, for example, Reznikoff asked for them back and printed them himself, instead of letting them appear in an adulterated form in *Poetry,* the most prestigious venue of the day (*MP* 24). Although Reznikoff published extensively in journals, he protected his poetry by printing nearly all of his books privately, rather than leave any of it in manuscript or at the mercy of editors who, while they might secure him a larger audience, had their own ideas about what worked and how to present it. By publishing his poetry—even typesetting and printing it—Reznikoff treats it like a loving father (saving it from the traitorous wife?), lavishing all of the care and attention he can upon it before sending it into the world. In this way,

Charles revives Ezekiel, seeking to repair the damage done by anti-Semitism in Russia through the dissemination of a new Jewish poetry in America. The disseminative quality of Ezekiel's burnt book needs to be thought through even further, though, for its loss proves both tragic and productive. The burnt book acts as a precious absence, drawing forth and, in a sense, "underwriting" the creation of Reznikoff's poetry; having been consigned to fire, a manuscript of poetry that may have been, after all, quite ordinary acquires a sacred aura. In this way, it joins the library of burnt books that accompanies the Jews through their turbulent history as "the people of the book."

The Jewish book most commonly consigned to the flames is the Talmud, a book that so represents the Jewish people—especially through its lifelong study by men—that it would be appropriate to announce at its burning, in the words of Ezekiel's wife, "Here's a man's life." In a fascinating meditation, *The Burnt Book: Reading the Talmud,* Rabbi Marc-Alain Ouaknin presents the burnt book as a central image for the place of Talmud in Jewish history. In Ouaknin's reading, however, the "burning" of the book is not primarily a tragic sign of anti-Semitism but rather a necessary sacrifice for the continuity of interpretation. Ouaknin chooses as a symbol a book written by Rabbi Nahman of Bratslav, the most enigmatic Hasidic Master of the late eighteenth century, who ordered one of his manuscripts burned and later gave it the title *The Burnt Book.* Although he had read the manuscript to his disciples and prepared it for publication, Rabbi Nahman seems to have consigned it to the flames because of the dangerous power of its esoteric teachings and also because of a tradition that holds that books must be burnt or lost to make room for future books. Based upon this example and upon a series of talmudic readings inspired by contemporary French thinkers Emmanuel Levinas, Edmond Jabès, Maurice Blanchot, and Jacques Derrida, Ouaknin discerns a tradition of Jewish reading in which "burning the book" forms a necessary stage. For new interpretations that speak to the present to come forth, older interpretations must go up in smoke—even if, as Rabbi Nahman and others intimate, the old may be much more powerful and revelatory than the new. The burnt book, by virtue of its precious absence, opens a tremendously charged space that demands to be filled by new writing.

The book in the flames calls forth Reznikoff's poetry in a variety of ways. In the poem "Samuel," for instance, which ends his self-published 1927 collection, *Five Groups of Verse,* Reznikoff ties his vocation as writer to the purifying effects of fire. In this poem he dons the mask of the prophet Samuel to speak as a Jewish poet in America:

Samuel

All day I am before the altar
and at night sleep beside it;
I think in psalms, my mind a psalter.
I sit in the temple. From inside it
I see the smoke eddy in the wind;
now and then a leaf will ride it
upward and when the leaf has spinned
its moment, the winds hide it.
Against their hurly-burly
I shut the window of my mind,
and the world at the winds' will,
find myself calm and still.

The days in this room become precious to others also,
as the seed hidden in the earth becomes a tree,
as the secret joy of the bride and her husband becomes a man.

The altar blazes. I bring
my thoughts to heap upon it.
The smoke of my breath
is an offering.

Whatever unfriendly stars and comets do,
whatever stormy heavens are unfurled,
my spirit be like fire in this, too,
that all the straws and rubbish of the world
only feed its flame.

The seasons change.
That is change enough.
Chance planted me beside a stream of water;
content, I serve the land,
whoever lives here and whoever passes.
(*CP* 1.73 + variant)

Tending the altar fire, the prophetic poet remains sequestered within the temple, where the spell of the fire calls forth psalms. The striking rhyme of "altar" with "psalter" emphasizes the connection between the sacrificial fire and the production of poems. Observing worldly events as floating leaves, Samuel rebuffs the winds that control them and collects himself in meditation. To do so is not to turn his back on the world, however, but to excavate an internal space from which new ideas can emerge; this creative self-entry results in new social growth, for the prophetic poetry that arises from it acts like the planting of a seed that "becomes a tree" or like the sexual ecstasy that "becomes a man." Although this is a masculine fantasy, the mother remains implicit in the imagery, for the new man arises out of the joy of the "*bride* and *her* husband." In the third stanza the poet acknowledges that the sacrificial fire requires the immolation of cherished thoughts and the offering up of one's very breath, if the new psalms are to arrive.[17] Then, identifying for once with the terrible force of the fire itself, the poet wills himself capable of consuming and transmuting all of the "straws and rubbish" (like "the long shadows of clods") that stand against him. This stanza, with its fierce determination, was chosen (presumably by the editor, Seamus Cooney) for an epitaph, printed on the first page of Reznikoff's posthumously published *Poems 1918–1975;* but when the stanza is separated from its context the fire is no longer confined to the altar and becomes an unbounded conflagration. In the context of the poem, however, this stanza and the one preceding it show Reznikoff extending the metaphor of the burnt book. Beyond its ritual role in the revelation and concealment of the divine, as in Ouaknin's interpretation, the fire of Jewish commentary is invoked by Reznikoff to purify the endlessly stormy social life around him.[18]

In the last stanza, asserting a stoic resignation, Reznikoff tacitly accepts the unlikelihood of revolutionary change or definitive social amelioration, conceding that seasonal change "is change enough." Finally, refusing to claim that God has appointed him to the prophetic role, he speaks explicitly about his position as Jewish-American psalmist in New York City: "Chance planted me beside a stream of water; / content, I serve the land, / whoever lives here and whoever passes." In a world of social strife and blind contingency, in a country where divine law has been superseded, in an era when the languages and the genders are incommensurable, the self-divided Charles Reznikoff vows to persist as the self-enclosed prophet, whose devotions blaze up to consume our endless "straws and rubbish" and thus to "serve the entire land." Call him Samuel or Ezekiel, this poet will offer the precious crucible of the burnt book to "whoever lives here and whoever passes," to countryman and stranger alike.

The burnt book functions as a generative trauma in similar ways in a recent work of Jewish-American literature. In *Maus,* Art Spiegelman's masterful cartoon depiction of his parents' survival of the Holocaust, there is a climactic moment at the end of book 1 in which Artie discovers that Vladek, his father, has burnt the autobiographical journal of his dead mother, Anja. Having recounted his parents' life story up to their parting at the gates of Auschwitz, Artie (as character) says, "This is where Mom's diaries will be especially useful. They'll give me some idea of what she went through while you were apart" (158). At this point, Vladek confesses that in a fit of depression following Anja's suicide he burned the notebooks that had been intended for his son's reading. Artie is devastated and angered by the loss of his mother's chronicle, and the volume ends with him walking away, muttering to himself, "Murderer" (159). In an interview, though, Spiegelman (as writer) acknowledges that the burnt book provided a creative opportunity:

> The fact that he'd destroyed that autobiographical journal of hers . . . meant that the story forcibly became increasingly *his* story, which at first seemed like a terrible, almost fatal, problem. The absence of my mother left me with—well, not with an antihero, but at any rate not a pure hero. But in retrospect that seems like one of the strengths of *Maus*. If only admirable people were shown to have survived, then the implicit moral would have been that only admirable people deserved to survive, as opposed to the fact that people deserved to survive as people. Anyway, I'm left with the story I've got, my shoehorn with which to squeeze myself back into history.
> (Weschler 78)

Once again in Jewish literature, a burnt book has presented a creative thinker with a seemingly insoluble dilemma whose brilliant solution determines the quality of the work. There are two gifts of the burnt book in this instance: first, it provides unity of viewpoint by making Vladek the sole narrator of the story of Vladek and Anja's Holocaust survival; second, by forcing us to identify with Vladek, a character whose annoying habits and compromised morality make us uncomfortable, it draws attention to the "ordinary" qualities of Holocaust victims and stymies any attempt to distance ourselves through hero worship or condemnation.

Like Spiegelman, Reznikoff portrays nonheroic people in his writing, people who deserve not only survival but also respect merely because they are human. Reznikoff accords such respect throughout his work, but in two books in particular, *Testimony: The United States (1885–1915),* more than five hundred pages long, and the much shorter *Holocaust,* he dedicates entire volumes to documentary histories that perform the remarkable feat of allowing the Other access to the page. Taking the examples of Reznikoff and Spiegelman, let us speculate that there is a Jewish form of witnessing, whose early models might be Lamentations and Job, that eschews a narrative of redemption. This witnessing occasionally has become capable of letting the Other speak for him- or herself—as opposed to the dominant Christian mode of witnessing, which often claims to speak for the Other and wants to draw his or her testimony into a redemptive narrative.[19] In *Testimony* and *Holocaust,* Reznikoff does not give himself a narrative voice, so that his witnessing the sufferings of others produces a shock in his readers: there is a sense of confronting the raw voice or materiality of the Other, without the filter of an actual or implied narrative voice. Because of this, both of these books are almost unbearably difficult to read. Any poem taken at random can serve as an example:

> A band was playing
> on the excursion train;
> Joe heard it
> on his way home from school
> and boarded the train with other boys.
>
> A crowd waiting
> to board the train.
> While it was moving towards the passengers,
> a man with a lantern
> in one hand and a stick in the other
> came through the cars,
> shouting at the boys
> to get off
> and striking at them with the stick.
>
> Trying to get off while the train was running,
> Joe fell between the cars.
> (*Testimony* 1.26)

Culled from a law book and told in the barest possible detail, this is a simple but profoundly disturbing story that offers no hope for a future, no understanding, no transcendence, no escape.[20] By presenting the blind contingency of accident, this poem leaves its reader in a similar condition to "Joe": because the poet provides us with no interpretive frames whatsoever with which to make sense of this occurrence, we are in free fall between concepts, in an ungrounded condition likely to be fatal—especially to illusions about the meaningfulness of reality. As an inspection of his working papers at the library of the University of California at San Diego makes evident, Reznikoff worked long and diligently to pare away every inessential detail and rationalization from the legal testimony he gathered, leaving the reader with virtually unframed, finally inassimilable human experience—experience as dictated by an all-powerful Chance. For

Reznikoff, this artful, concentrated telling of an actual event, without interpretation, acts to ground history, and it must be given precedence whenever we try to come to terms with the past. Reznikoff's strength lies in his ability to look directly at the language of human experience, to render it cleanly and potently, without embellishment; and to hand it to his readers with the confidence that we, too, are capable of grasping this molten material. Not only *Holocaust* and *Testimony,* but all of Reznikoff's works emerge and take shape out of the crucible of the burnt book, revealing incandescent glimpses of Otherness that rarely breach the filtering mind of another writer.

IMMANENCE AND DIASPORA

FALLING BETWEEN TWO STOOLS

As was mentioned in the introduction, Reznikoff's contributions of works and ideas to the *Menorah Journal* were substantial and in many ways sustaining to him. It is not surprising, therefore, that he was asked to review *The Menorah Treasury* (1964), an anthology that appeared after the journal ceased publication in 1962. In the course of his review, he hints at the push-pull quality of American Jewish identity by using an odd cliché, "falling between two stools":

> On one point, I must differ from the editor of *The Menorah Treasury*.
> Mr. Schwarz in his foreword says: ". . . by 1930 the Great Depression
> had taken its toll. Both the Menorah movement and *The Journal* received
> a body blow from which they never recovered" (p. viii). I do not doubt
> that the depression was a contributing cause, but *The Menorah Journal*
> fell between two stools as it were—Communism and Zionism. The
> average Jewish young man of that time who was both intelligent and
> idealistic was often attracted to one or the other, sometimes passionately
> and single-mindedly.
> (UCSD 9.18.9)

In this passage, Reznikoff identifies not with the young men of the time who committed themselves to one of the political ideologies, but with the afflicted *Menorah Journal,* which refused to choose between the two positions and thus lost currency. His description of the unfortunate outcome of the journal's unwillingness to take a political stand initially caught my attention because I had previously seen the same cliché used in a

review of *The Menorah Treasury* by Robert Alter. Alter invokes the phrase
when remarking on the Jewish self-hatred exhibited in the young Lionel
Trilling's discussion of Isaac Nathan, a Jewish contemporary of Lord By-
ron's. Since Reznikoff's unpublished review resides among his papers in
a folder alongside a clipping of Alter's essay sent by the soliciting editor,
it appears that Reznikoff subconsciously borrowed the cliché from Alter—but why? Although Alter and Reznikoff use this phrase in different
contexts, somehow it must answer a shared necessity: whether Alter is
describing Trilling's Isaac Nathan as suffering "a painful fall between two
cultural stools," the Jewish and the British, or Reznikoff is arguing that
the *Menorah Journal* was not overtly a victim of the Great Depression but
rather fell between the two stools of Communism and Zionism, these
writers are, in the end, characterizing a larger double-bind situation and its
outcome—as though an inevitable pratfall awaited the passionate cultural
aspirations of Jews in the English-speaking world. The phrase paints at
once a painful and a humorous picture, contributing to what we might
think of as a Marx Brothers version of cultural history.[1]

According to *The Dictionary of Cliches,* "falling between two stools" has
a long pedigree in the slapstick representation of betweenness or undecid-
ability:

> *Fall Between Two Stools.* To fail or not act because of indecision over
> two choices (said often of a problem that lands between two people or
> agencies that might be expected to deal with it). One can imagine a
> person so absentminded or distracted as to miss each of two nearby seats,
> landing between them. An old form of the saying is "Between two stools
> one goes [or falls] to the ground." The Romans had a similar expression.
> In English it was recognized as familiar by 1390, when it appeared in
> John Gower's *Confessio Amantis:* "Bot it is seid . . . Between two stoles
> lyth the fal." In 1536 it appeared in a book of proverbs as "Betwen two
> stolis, the ars goth to grwnd."
> (82)

The Harpo Marxes of the world have convulsed us with this routine for
a long time. It's exactly the sort of prank that Harpo and Chico rejoice in
playing, not only to expose stuffed shirts but especially to embarrass Jewish
pretenders. In this way, they join in the same tactics of embarrassment that
Trilling employs in his merciless exposé of the pretenses of Isaac Nathan:
Nathan may have been a fine rabbi, but, according to Trilling, his envy
of the Gentiles made him "a bad critic [who] could quote Rashi, Jonathan,
son of Huziel, and David Kimhi to support his opinions of English verse"
(Alter, "Epitaph" 52). Under the sign It Takes One to Know One, such
Jewish "critics" reach to pull the chair out from under their confrères,

thereby baring the condition of betweenness in which they all reside. A good example of such embarrassing exposure of what Alter calls "the culturally aspiring Jew" occurs in *Animal Crackers* (1930), where Harpo and Chico identify Roscoe W. Chandler, a suave art connoisseur in possession of a great masterwork, as a former peddler from the Old Country. While the unmasked millionaire frantically tries to silence them with bribes, the Marx Brothers shame him and render him absurd, chanting, "Abie the fish man! Abie the fish man!"[2]

To fall between two stools is to plunge into a kind of cultural void. Out of this vertiginous experience comes the pretension-exploding, slapstick hilarity for which Jewish comedians are renowned. Modern Yiddish folklore even has a name for the hapless occupants of this void: *luftmenschen,* "people of the air." As Benjamin Harshav explains, *luftmenschen* are portrayed in Yiddish storytelling and literature as "people who have no income from productive work and live 'on air' as well as 'in the air,' with no ground under their feet, unlike a healthy nation rooted in its own soil. This expression became a key image of self-criticism of the Jewish Diaspora existence in most Jewish ideologies, from Zionist to Socialist, as well as by Western Jews in Berlin or New York vis-à-vis their Eastern brethren" (Harshav, "Texts and Subtexts" 59). Aware of feeling precarious and sometimes absurd—even of living a groundless existence—modern Jewish writers and artists have used this bizarre image of life in midair as a device for exploring a world fraught with cultural contradictions. Harshav offers as examples the portraits of *luftmenschen* in the writings of Scholem Aleichem (the inspiration, too, for *Fiddler on the Roof*), Kafka's "Investigations of a Dog," and the floating Jews of Chagall's paintings (59–63). If Christian iconography makes soaring a divine attribute, the soaring Jews of modern art are, by contrast, groundless occupants of the air between established social locations.

This awkward condition entails both liabilities and benefits for Jewish intellectuals such as Reznikoff and his *Menorah* colleagues. In theoretical terms, "falling between two stools" can be seen as a way of occupying what Homi Bhabha calls "the interstices—the overlap and displacement of domains of difference" (2). Bhabha thinks of interstices as "spaces that are produced in the articulation of cultural differences," and he values "these 'in-between' spaces" because they "provide the terrain for elaborating strategies of selfhood—singular or communal—that initiate new signs of identity" (1)—that is, hybrid identity. During the past century, the evolving forms of Jewish-American identity provide rich examples of such hybridity arising out of betweenness. The specifically postmodern forms of hybridity that Bhabha celebrates in *The Location of Culture* are

new, however, in that they purposely draw attention to the signs of difference among the "identities" they gather. Prior to the postmodern moment, hybridity had been employed by outsider groups largely as a strategy
for minimizing an awareness of differences; this is certainly true for the
Jewish intellectuals around the *Menorah Journal,* who sought ways to make
"Jewish" and "American" look like natural partners.

In a fascinating article written in 1919, after the Balfour Declaration
excited new interest in Zionism, Thorstein Veblen speaks admiringly
about the hybrid quality of Jewish culture and assigns to this hybridity
the responsibility for producing renegade Jews who advance Western
knowledge through their restless skepticism. Veblen argues for "The Intellectual Pre-Eminence of Jews in Modern Europe" in order to point out
that if the just Zionist cause of securing a national homeland were to suc-
ceed and the Jews were to be segregated in Zion, it would deprive both
Europe and the Jews of mutual intellectual stimulation. In the course of
the article, Veblen makes acute observations about the effects of betweenness on Jewish intellectuals. Noting that "men of this Jewish extrac-
tion count for more than their proportionate share in the intellectual life
of western civilization; and they count particularly among the vanguard,
the pioneers, the uneasy guild of pathfinders and iconoclasts in science,
scholarship and institutional change and growth" (36), Veblen contends
that the Jewish thinker, having left the security of his traditional culture
behind, becomes a wandering skeptic and is thus able to participate in the
modern "intellectual enterprise that . . . presupposes a degree of exemp-
tion from hard-and-fast preconceptions, a skeptical animus, *Unbefangen-
heit,* release from the dead hand of conventional finality" (39). By stepping
outside of traditional Judaism but not succumbing to Christianity, the "in-
tellectually gifted Jew" preserves an

> immunity from the inhibitions of intellectual quietism. But he can come
> in for such immunity only at the cost of losing his secure place in the
> scheme of conventions into which he has been born, and at the cost,
> also, of finding no similarly secure place in that scheme of gentile con-
> ventions into which he is thrown. . . . He becomes a disturber of the
> intellectual peace, but only at the cost of becoming an intellectual way-
> faring man . . . seeking another place to rest, farther along the road,
> somewhere over the horizon.
> (39)

In his somewhat lyrical portrait of intellectual Jews without a homeland,
Veblen carefully points out that this wandering does not completely sever
one's attachment to Jewishness. Although one may venture far beyond

the intellectual confines of traditional Judaism, one does not easily leave behind the condition of being a Jew, "for the heart-strings of affection and consuetude are tied early, and they are not readily retied in after life." Similarly, the intellectual Jew seldom turns to Christianity, for

> the animus with which the community of safe and sane gentiles is wont to meet him [does not] conduce at all to his personal incorporation in that community. . . . Their people need not become his people nor their gods his gods, and indeed the provocation is forever and irritably present all over the place to turn back from following after them. . . . One who goes away from home will come to see many unfamiliar things, and to take note of them; but it does not follow that he will swear by all the strange gods whom he meets along the road.
> (41–42)

This modern image of the skeptical Jew, who, because of his hybrid identity as an "intellectual wayfaring man," feels free to walk beyond the bounds of convention, has a long and fruitful lineage, which includes such seminal modern figures as Spinoza, Heine, Marx, Freud, and Einstein.

American intellectual Jews who fit the profile described by Veblen often found themselves forcefully addressed by the *Menorah Journal*'s attempt to turn hybridity into an asset. As someone who came of age during the rise of the Menorah movement, Reznikoff naturally looked to the *Journal* as a primary outlet for his writing, especially his works that examine Jewish history and the condition of betweenness. The first four pieces he published there, in 1924 and 1925, comprise plays dramatizing climactic moments in Jewish history. In all, he wrote nine short, historical plays— six on Jewish themes, two on American themes, and one on the role of the writer—which he collected in *Nine Plays* (1927), now out of print. In her memoir, Marie Syrkin speaks of *Nine Plays* as a poignant example of Reznikoff's care in the production of his writing: "All nine plays came to 113 pages of verse. Four hundred copies had been printed. Charles had set the type by hand and done all the work on a press he had acquired and kept in the basement of his parents' home. It was the work of a meticulous craftsman, as meticulous as his typed manuscripts or as the page proofs whose neatly indicated corrections would sometimes elicit more admiration than the text" (*MP* 39). Like a parent whose concern for his child's welfare translates into an obsessive attention to the child's appearance, Reznikoff made sure that his texts were "presentable" and "on their best behavior." Such "fussy" attention to detail does not usually accompany the broad strokes of expressionist musical theater—which is what Reznikoff felt he was writing: the plays, he says, "are really libretti and should be accompanied by music. They really require staging and dancing. When I wrote them, I was very much under the influence of German expressionist drama, particularly that of Georg Kaiser. I was also interested in *The Dybbuk,* which had a lot of music and dancing" (*MP* 106).[3]

One of Reznikoff's most extensive depictions of a brilliant *luftmensch* occurs in the early play, *Uriel Acosta,* which appeared not only in the *Menorah Journal* (1925) and *Nine Plays* (1927) but also earlier in *Uriel Accosta* [sic]: *A Play and A Fourth Group of Verse* (1921). In this play Reznikoff interrogates both Jewish and American identities by voicing objections to Jewish tradition and expressing concerns about the antinomian American self. By these means, he succeeds in exposing some of the anxieties inherent in Jewish secularism. Uriel Acosta (Da Costa), a famous early seventeenth-century Jewish apostate whose life seems to fall literally between the two stools of Christianity and Judaism, makes a particularly appropriate figure to symbolize the religious and cultural ambivalence of modern Jews. Employing such a compelling protagonist and conscious of the prior success of *The Dybbuk,* Reznikoff must have had high hopes for the staging of this play and its relevance for a sizable American Jewish audience.

The play opens in Portugal at the close of the sixteenth century. Uriel Acosta, a *converso* (a Christian of Jewish descent), is mourning the death of his father and confessing to his brother his intent to renounce Christianity by escaping to Amsterdam, where Jews are allowed to practice their faith freely. His brother, representing as he does throughout the play the conventional views of those around him, counsels against this course of action. At the end of the scene, after learning that a Jewess and a Moor are about to be burned in the square, he has the shutters closed, and then sits down to read; "Uriel's brother reads until a shriek is heard. He presses his palms against his ears" (*Nine Plays* 4).

Notwithstanding this experience of Christian intolerance, Uriel's brother sides with his father's friends when they come to dissuade the two from leaving Portugal, but ultimately he emigrates with Uriel to Holland. In the first scene in Amsterdam, Uriel listens impatiently to a rabbi explaining the rules for keeping kosher. Uriel complains, in disbelief and disdain, "Must I spend my life in mummeries that common sense / Tells me at once are frippery and rigmarole?" (7). Rejecting the "wisdom" of his elders, he observes, "I have fallen among another pack that says, / Do as we do, do and be still!" (8). At this the rabbi pronounces a ban on Uriel, forbidding members of his congregation from speaking with, trading with, or coming near the apostate. Uriel's subsequent torments include his arrest, a fine, the burning of his treatise on religious relativism, and stones flung at his windows.

After fifteen years of isolation, Uriel learns from his brother that the rabbis have forgiven him. He contemplates joining the congregation, musing ruefully to himself, "So I become at last a monkey among monkeys" (13). He meets with a rabbi, who advises him to live with his brother, in whose house he can practice the rituals of Jewish religious life and "learn the happiness in a Jewish home" (14). After Uriel moves into his house, Uriel's brother tries to bring him into his mercantile investments, but Uriel is more interested in two young students who have read a surviving copy of his book and want his advice about whether to convert to Judaism. In an ironic allusion to Esau's trading away his birthright, Uriel asks them why they would want to incur the wrath of the powerful Christian majority in exchange for "a mass of prayer and petty regulation?" (16). The crowd in the street hears of his advice and shouts "Unbeliever!" at him (17); then the rabbi arrives and imposes a strict penance: Uriel is banished from Jewish company until he appears in the synagogue, confesses his errors to the congregation, and stretches across the threshold to be trod upon. Uriel's defiance renews itself, however, and he walks away unreconciled. Seven years later, a broken man, he gives voice in a final soliloquy to fear and loneliness, endeavoring to persuade himself anew to undergo the penance, if only to be able to "have friends about to distract the mind from pain, dying and living" (19).

Reznikoff presents in his Acosta a tragic hero of conscience, a lone voice of authenticity in a hypocritical and torturous world, who suffers from both Christian and Jewish persecution. Interestingly, Reznikoff omits in this portrait two major features of the Acosta story: that Acosta reconverted to Judaism while still in Portugal by reading the Torah and then was dismayed, after his move to Amsterdam, to find that the rabbis had perverted the "pure" religion he had read about; and that he died a shattered suicide, leaving behind his autobiographical *Exemplar humanae vitae*. By not including the original and climactic moments of this well-known Jewish legend, Reznikoff gives us a more "existential" hero, whose battle between his conscience and his fellow-feeling for other Jews forms the basis of the drama. This antimelodramatic treatment of Acosta can be explained, to a certain extent, as a reaction against an earlier portrait: "*Uriel Acosta* started with my dissatisfaction with a German play by that name. It was very romantic; the hero wasn't bothered by any theological questions except incidentally—he was in love. That explained all his troubles" (*MP* 105). Reznikoff's Acosta is a man torn by theological and social questions,

who does not belong in either the Jewish or the Christian worlds—who
is unable either to be Jewish or to stop being Jewish—and the play focuses
exclusively upon these dilemmas.

Although theological questions bother Reznikoff's Acosta a good deal,
he does not enter the age-old debate over which is the "true religion,"
Christianity or Judaism. Theologically, Acosta sides completely with Judaism and has nothing but contempt for Christianity. At the beginning of
the play, for instance, he offers his brother a sarcastic rendition of the Cath-
olic welcome given to seekers after truth:

> Here in Oporto Mother Church takes those who grope too far,
> Gently by the hands and hangs them by those hands, hangs stones
>   upon their feet,
> To lengthen their reach that, groping and groping,
> They catch hold of truth at last.
> (*Nine Plays* 1–2)

Acosta's theological dilemma, then, is not one of *choosing* the true religion
but one of *belonging* to any religion at all. When he falls between the two
stools of Christianity and Judaism, he becomes a kind of *luftmensch,* floating completely out of the social world that has been apportioned primarily
along religious lines. The imagery of Reznikoff's play presents this socio-
religious issue of belonging in highly corporeal terms of alimentation. If
the religious community is perceived as a body, then ingestion symbolizes
the introduction of foreign substances into the body; and digestion, the
incorporation of these substances into the body's own structure. Uriel
Acosta is an indigestible figure who resists incorporation within either
Christianity or Judaism. To a certain extent, though, the entire issue of
incorporation is a Christian one: traditionally, the corporate body of the
Church is the only vehicle of salvation; at the time, Judaism and Islam
represented external substances to be both ingested and digested into the
body of the Church through conversion.

In the first scene, Uriel exhorts his brother, a believing Christian ("for
whom the only son of God has died, / Who takes his flesh in wafers in
your mouth" [2]), to understand that Christ's passion was nothing more
than a fable and that all a Christian prays to is a "gilt Jesus and Madonna"
(3). Here Acosta denies the reality of communion, the primary act of incorporation in Christianity, claiming that this form of ingestion does not
result in an authentic spiritual digestion into the body of Christ. To point
up further the Church's hypocrisy and corruption of the truth, Uriel gives
his brother two examples of indigestibility caused by the Church. If a man
is "thirsty" for truth, he argues,

Mother Church lifts his head
And down his nostrils drips drop by drop. He chokes—
But if he gulped too much would he not choke?—
Until he would swallow, like you and me, enough.
(2)

Acosta compares the "truth" administered by the Church to a form of
water torture; those who are really avid for truth must cry "Enough!"
and ultimately refuse to swallow any more. Conversely, in the succeeding
three lines, Acosta notes how the Church itself will not incorporate into
the body of Christ anyone who retains Jewish characteristics:

They have burnt a woman with a queasy intestine
That could not put up with bacon on Mondays,
For having Jewish villi.
(2)

This distasteful image depicts the subtlety and pervasiveness of Iberian racism, which imagines it can see "Jew" imprinted indelibly upon every inch
of a *converso*—down to the tiny hairs of the intestine. And from a Jewish
perspective, Christianity, with its abnegation of the Jewish laws of righteousness, is as indigestible as pork. Uriel ends his exhortation by asking,
"What must be done to cure a queasy mind?" (2), a mind that cannot
"stomach" Christianity.

Uriel's mind is not just queasy about Christian sustenance, however, for
the kosher laws also evoke his disgust. When Acosta and his brother arrive
in Amsterdam, the first scene takes place in a synagogue, where a rabbi
explains to them the reason for keeping meat and milk dishes separate.
Upon hearing this, Uriel "makes a gesture of impatience," to which the
rabbi replies:

You must unlearn the uncleanliness of Christians.
The rabbis have considered each thought and action;
Troublesome to plan each step oneself,
How much better to do what wise men have thought out,
And the generations found good.

To this traditional counsel, Uriel responds sarcastically:

And become a mechanism, not a man.
Nothing is true unless true for myself, by myself tested,
And then true or false only for myself.
What wisdom is such that I must
Shut eyes and gulp it, like a child medicine?
(6–7)

Again, alimentary terms frame the issue of belonging to a religion: the rabbi's first instructions in Judaism concern prohibitions about eating; in response, Acosta offers an ironic simile, comparing the unthinking ingestion of proscriptive wisdom to a child's blind acceptance of unpleasant medicine. Uriel sees the kosher laws as another attempt by a religious orthodoxy to incorporate its members through blind obedience. Defiant, he refuses to accept the symbolic connection between food and spirituality that underlies both religions, quoting from Jesus (Matt. 15.11), "not that which goeth into the mouth defileth" (7). In direct contradiction to this attempt by Acosta to separate alimentation from religion, another rabbi steps in to reaffirm an immediate connection between the (social) body and the spirit: "As if what harms the body with which we are entrusted, / Does not hurt the soul whose machine it is" (7). In lines quoted previously, Uriel denounces this unthinking acceptance of symbolic prohibitions in the kosher laws as a misidentification of playacting for reality: "Must I spend my life in mummeries," he asks incredulously, "that common sense / Tells me at once are frippery and rigmarole?" (7).

Reznikoff presents Acosta's reaction to both the Christian and the Jewish notions of symbolic alimentation as one of self-reliant, antinomian resistance; by doing so, he invokes one of the ideological hallmarks of American culture. During the course of the drama, the playwright fashions for his character a kind of American antinomian self who will say with figures like Ralph Waldo Emerson, Henry David Thoreau, and Walt Whitman, "Nothing is true unless true for myself, by myself tested, / And then true or false only for myself" (6–7)—as if the correct response to finding oneself between the two stools of Christianity and Judaism were to acquire an American, resolutely individualistic self. In keeping with this response, Reznikoff's rebellious character seems to be alluding to passages such as Emerson's denunciation of conformity in "Self-Reliance" and the disparagement of tradition in "Nature" when he says of the Jews of Amsterdam, "I have fallen among another pack that says, / Do as we do, do and be still!" (8). Similarly, in the chief rabbi's reply to this objection, Reznikoff encrypts Thoreau's famous saying, "If a man does not keep pace with his companions, perhaps it is because he hears a different drummer. Let him step to the music which he hears, however measured or far away" (Thoreau 215). The rabbi warns that

> . . . the young and foolish, always with us,
> Turn and listen,
> Whoever pounds a drum and mounts

A stool:
Follow him into the marshes of his thoughts.
(*Nine Plays* 8)

To this Uriel responds, "Perhaps he is the sanest of you all" (8). While
Acosta, like Thoreau, sides with the resistant man of integrity who inspires
by example, the chief rabbi worries that the resistant man will become
a skeptical pied piper, leading others "into the marshes of his thoughts."

Along with depicting Acosta as an American antinomian—who, like
Thoreau, dismisses tradition as mere hearsay and dedicates his efforts to
finding out the truth for himself—Reznikoff, like Nathaniel Hawthorne,
also demonstrates that a willful rejection of the social world makes a person, however well intentioned, prone to delusion as well as insight. Living
outside society and bearing a social stigma, his Uriel Acosta resembles Hester Prynne; and, like the heroine of *The Scarlet Letter,* Uriel's estrangement
from his community makes him not only perspicacious with regard to
hypocrisy, but also susceptible to delusory speculations. Just as Hester's
lack of belonging, signaled by the stigma upon her chest that is meant
to restrain her, gives her instead the freedom for wide-ranging mental
conjecture, so Acosta says of himself: "Free as a tethered goat, I must feed /
On truth and falsehood, although it gives me colic" (10). Again, in a climactic moment of the play, the imagery turns to alimentation. Recognizing that his freedom of thought has been bought at the price of social
ostracism, Uriel knows, as an outsider, that he will inevitably ingest falsehood along with truth, that reason's "truth" may lead to social "falsehood." Like the woman whose villi could not tolerate nonkosher food,
his irritated intestines reveal his distress; this time it is not a religion that
proves indigestible but Acosta's own speculations in isolation—as though
remaining for too long between chairs disrupts the alimentary process and
brings on a painful attack of colic.

The paradoxical terms in Uriel's self-description—freedom and re-
straint, truth and falsehood, nourishment and indigestion—are echoed by
a compelling paradox later in the play. By means of a rhetorical question,
Acosta signals the crisis of belonging that infuses his theological resistance:
"We who hold out against the world, was I not most the Jew, / When I
held out also against my fellow Jews?" (15). If over the course of their
existence the Jews have acquired a collective identity among the nations
as a "stiff-necked," resistant people, then doesn't Uriel affirm his identity
as a Jew by resisting Jewish tradition?[4] Yes and no. Yes, he takes the demythologizing and rationalistic qualities of Jewish thought to new heights;
in turning these qualities upon Judaism, however, he cuts his ties with

the Jewish world and journeys out beyond the realm of religion. In this statement by Acosta, Reznikoff encapsulates the contradictions in the Jewish secularism that formed a major component of the *Menorah Journal* and its audience: the secular Jew displays pride in being Jewish by resisting all authority, including Jewish authority, and practices righteousness by testing every religious statement against his or her own reason. As a legendary example of Jewish secularism, Uriel Acosta provides Reznikoff and the *Menorah Journal* with a chilling model of the dilemmas facing the modern Jew. In a note that was intended for publication alongside his plays in the *Journal*, Reznikoff spells out the representative quality of figures like Acosta: "Perhaps in the last analysis I am only projecting these plays because they seem symbolic of myself, and you, reader, if you are interested in them, are only interested because they seem symbolic of your struggles" (Sharp, "*Nine Plays*" 272).[5]

URIEL DA COSTA, BARUCH SPINOZA, AND SECULAR JUDAISM

In order to understand the background of the dilemmas facing secular Jews, it will be useful to explore the social and philosophical responses of the historical Uriel Da Costa (as he is now more commonly known) and of his near-contemporary Baruch Spinoza to the situation of betweenness. When Da Costa shot himself in Amsterdam in 1640, Spinoza was eight years old. To many historians, Da Costa represents a direct precursor to one of the founding philosophers of modernity; over the past three hundred years, "he has been seen as a martyr of religious bigotry, the spiritual father of Spinoza (there is a nineteenth century painting showing the young Spinoza sitting on Da Costa's lap), and the father of modern unbelief" (Popkin, "Epicureanism" 351). Endeavoring to understand the conditions enabling people like Da Costa and Spinoza to break with revealed religion, recent scholarly attention has focused microscopically upon the Marrano community of sixteenth- and seventeenth-century Amsterdam, in which both thinkers lived. In this unsettled social milieu an acute crisis of Jewish belonging occurred, one whose effects are still being felt by secular Jews and by Western culture in general.

The Marranos (also called *conversos*) were former Jews who were converted to Christianity, usually against their wishes, in Spain and Portugal. Many of them observed Judaism in secret and, like Da Costa, returned to their faith when they moved to Amsterdam and other areas promoting religious freedom. A deep-seated Iberian racism developed against the enterprising Marranos (the term itself is derogatory, meaning "piglet"), who were able to infiltrate the higher levels of Spanish and Portuguese society, including the Church and the Court. By referring to Marranos as "New Christians," the "Old Christians" gave them both religious approval and an indelible social stigma. When, following expulsions and inquisitions, life became untenable for Jews in Spain and Portugal and caused many to move to the relative freedom of Amsterdam, large numbers reconverted publicly to Judaism—sometimes even after their family had been Christian for generations—and thereby earned the doubly ironic title of "New Jews." Whipsawed back and forth, these Jews experienced an identity crisis of major proportions:

> Wherever he turns, the Marrano is an outsider and someone "new" (he is a New Christian or a New Jew). He does not belong to any cultural context simply or naturally, and feels both inside and outside any one of them. If he seems to have solved his problem and found an identity for himself (through assimilation into Christian society or by returning to the Jewish fold), this identity does not adhere to him simply or directly, for he must constantly struggle to engender and preserve it, overcoming the internal contradictions it entails.
> (Yovel 1.49)

For many people, this simultaneous occupancy of both insider and outsider positions led to "a life of mental ferment and upheaval, to manifestations of doubt," and ultimately to ruptures with self, memory, and future. According to the Israeli historian of philosophy Yirmiyahu Yovel, the alienated Marrano "is the true wandering Jew, roaming between Christianity and Judaism and drifting between the two and universalism." Such an experience of radical betweenness places the Marrano "among the precursors of modernity, with its skepticism and its breakdown of traditional structures." As a Marrano thinker, Uriel Da Costa lived, "in the words of his own book, an *exemplar humanae vitae* . . . in conditions of deracinating ferment" (1.49–50).

In his two-volume study, *Spinoza and Other Heretics,* Yovel makes a compelling case that the Marrano condition has profoundly influenced modern culture, most particularly contemporary Jewish thought and literature.[6] He demonstrates, first, how the double binds experienced by Iberian Marranos, with regard to religious and social identity, produced in response a "dual" language of dissimulation used both for hiding (from outsiders) and for revealing (to insiders) the disaffection caused by these double binds. As in any situation of prolonged political or social oppression, the resourceful victims develop symbolic ways to express their dissatisfaction so that it will be apparent to their peers yet overlooked by their oppressors. Yovel further explores how the double binds and the

dual language gave rise to habits of thought and expression that were inherited by later generations. These dissimulating habits eventually had the
unintended effect of denaturalizing both Jewish and Christian cultures in
the eyes of Marrano descendents, so that ultimately thinkers like Da Costa
and Spinoza found themselves standing apart from the only cultural perspectives then available to them. Richard Popkin observes that "Da Costa
was perhaps the first modern man to step outside the Judeo-Christian tradition, and to proclaim himself a *man* rather than a Jew or a Christian.
'These are the men who are continually vaunting, I am a *Jew,* or I am a
Christian. . . . He who pretends to be neither of these and only calls himself
a man, is far preferable'" ("Epicureanism" 353). Although Da Costa calls
for a universalism that will shortly be answered philosophically by deism,
he might be seen more properly, given his vacillations and ultimate despair, in the light in which Reznikoff places him: as a *luftmensch* between
rather than outside religions; seeking to ground his thought in "universal"
reason rather than in tradition, but finding himself with no place to stand;
lacking a secure identity and a sense of belonging. As Yovel trenchantly
puts it, "it was precisely because Da Costa strove to identify directly with
mankind in general that he ended his days estranged from himself and
from all other men" (1.49).

Yovel presents Da Costa's tragedy as an illustrative enactment of the
tensions inherent in the Marrano condition. Like many Marranos, Da
Costa hoped to create a stable identity by imagining an ideal religion—
which could be either Christianity or Judaism. From the Christian side,
Saint Teresa of Ávila was the most prominent of the Spanish mystics
whose *converso* backgrounds drove them to seek ever purer and more ideal
forms of religion (1.26). Characterizing the "purifying reform in the original direction of the Bible" (1.48) that Da Costa endeavored to introduce
into Jewish Amsterdam as an "idealized object of yearning," Yovel discusses the consequences for Marranos of trying to base a stable identity
upon such an ideal:

> The Marrano living in an alien culture projects an idealized object of
> yearning, with which he has no real contact—either by his life or by his
> knowledge—and yet he attempts to gain by this object a new identity
> and sense of belonging. In effect, therefore, he lives divorced from both
> his natural environment and his idealized object of yearning. And when
> he perceives the discrepancy between that idealized object and the his-
> torical reality that is supposed to achieve it, he is liable to lose his footing
> altogether and, like Da Costa, fall outside all spheres of identity and be-
> longing.
> (1.49)

For Yovel as for Reznikoff, Da Costa exemplifies, in his tortured vacilla-tion between yearning for the ideal religion and despairing of finding it among human beings, the unbearable condition of falling between two stools; in the end he achieves neither a stable identity nor a sense of belong-ing. Historically, Da Costa's double bind was irresolvable, for there was not yet an "outside" (a defined cultural space) for him to occupy: "To exist, he had to be in a religious community. To be himself, he could not so live" (Popkin, "Epicureanism" 353).

Although he, too, was excommunicated by the rabbis, Baruch Spinoza, a generation later, was able to leave behind both his religious belief and his affiliation with the Jewish community; within an emerging secular space, he proceeded to develop an entire philosophy out of the condi-tion of betweenness. Spinoza's alienation was only slightly less extreme than Da Costa's, however, with repercussions that were not only social but linguistic. In light of the issues treated in chapter 1, Spinoza's negotia-tions with language provide another fascinating instance of the multi-lingual dilemmas of Jewish culture. Born into the Jewish-Portuguese enclave of Amsterdam, Spinoza acquired a number of languages for a variety of uses:

> As a child, he evidently spoke Portuguese at home; at the same time he learned Spanish, which as an adult he liked to use for his casual reading (travels, drama, history, etc.). He later learned Latin, which he adopted for his philosophical studies. He knew Hebrew from an early age, but as the scholarly language of the classroom and the *Yeshiva,* not as a living tongue; and he seems to have picked up Dutch "by osmosis," enough for all practical purposes but without making it his truly active language. (Yovel 1.173)

This shifting among languages, each with its particular sphere of compe-tence, was replicated by his wandering between Jewish and Dutch socie-ties. Although Spinoza had access to many different worlds, he did not belong in any of them—and in this respect he resembles Da Costa most closely (174).

Yovel argues that Spinoza's Marrano background made possible his ma-jor innovations in philosophy, which Yovel summarizes as being the reli-gion of reason and the doctrine of absolute immanence. These innova-tions influenced both directly and indirectly such seminal Enlightenment and post-Enlightenment thinkers as Kant, Hegel, Heine, Feuerbach, Marx, Nietzsche, and Freud, as well as the English Romantic poets be-ginning with Samuel Taylor Coleridge and William Wordsworth. Yovel makes grand claims for Spinoza's contributions to philosophy:

His philosophical revolution anticipated major trends in European
modernization, including secularization, biblical criticism, the rise of
natural science, the Enlightenment, and the liberal-democratic state.
Above all, he put forward a radically new philosophical principle that I
call the philosophy of immanence. It views this-worldly existence as all
there is, as the only actual being and the sole source of ethical value.
God himself is identical with the totality of nature, and God's decrees
are written not in the Bible but in the laws of nature and reason.
(1.ix)

The philosophical shift from a conception of God as wholly transcendent (Judaism) or as transcendent/incarnate (Christianity) to one that sees
God as, in Spinoza's words, "the immanent, not the transitive, cause of all
things" (Spinoza 100) resonates deeply in literature as well. For someone
attuned to literary history, the significance of a philosophy of immanence
to the entire field of Romantic and post-Romantic poetry cannot be over-
estimated. Major critics such as M. H. Abrams, in *Natural Supernaturalism;*
J. Hillis Miller, in *Poets of Reality;* and Charles Altieri, in *Enlarging the Temple,* have traced the development of immanentist thought in Romantic
poetry and its successors. In the twentieth century, the philosophy of immanence has become so dominant in poetry that Altieri can distinguish
two opposing kinds of poetry, "symbolist" and "immanentist," *within* the
ongoing tradition of immanentist thought. Using Coleridge as the model
for a symbolist poetry of structuration and Wordsworth as the model for
an immanentist poetry of discovery, Altieri delineates the Wordsworthian
side, to which the Objectivists belong, as follows: "Here poetic creation
is conceived more as the discovery and the disclosure of numinous relationships within nature than as the creation of containing and structuring
forms. Hence its basic commitment is to recovering familiar realities in
such a way that they appear dynamically present and invigorate the mind
with a sense of powers and objective values available to it" (17). The Objectivists represent the most dedicated application of these principles in
American poetry—so much so that critics have come to denote the immanentist strain in American poetry as "objectivist."

Reznikoff's own unswerving commitment to "recovering familiar realities in such a way that they appear dynamically present and invigorate
the mind" makes him the model Objectivist. In his conception, divinity
can only be recovered immanently, by an ethical immersion in the details
of mundane existence. Looking to figures such as Da Costa and Spinoza,
Reznikoff plumbs the sources of immanentist thought in Jewish history
and brings them into an American context that weds Judaism and natural
supernaturalism. In "Jerusalem the Golden," the title poem of the 1934

book he published with the Objectivist Press, Reznikoff places Spinoza within a genealogy of immanentist thought in Jewish culture. The four sections of the poem, respectively titled "the Lion of Judah," "The Shield of David," "Spinoza," and "Karl Marx," move from biblical scenes to modern philosophy, stressing the progressive influx of the divine into ethical acts of daily life. In "The Lion of Judah," the setting is war, and everyone—the soldiers, the prophet Samuel, and King David himself—seems driven by bloodlust. In the final lines of the section, though, the prophet Nathan insists that even the king of Israel, who has arranged the death of Bathsheba's husband, must submit to justice; he will not be the one to build the Temple because of his excessive recourse to bloodshed:

> But Nathan said to the king, even David, the great king,
> You have dealt deceitfully with the Hittite, your faithful servant;
> and you shall not build the Lord's house,
> because your hands have shed much blood.
> (*CP* 1.127)

"The Shield of David" continues the theme of righteousness in daily life, depicting God as preferring to be worshipped "in kindness to the poor and weak, / in justice to the orphan, the widow, the stranger among you, / and in justice to him who takes his hire from your hand" (1.128), rather than honored through ritual correctness in sacrifices, festivals, feasts, and fasts. This preference is similar to Reznikoff's opting in "Kaddish" for direct communion with his dead mother over the "trifles" of "prayers and words and lights" (2.56). After narrating the two biblical scenes in "Jerusalem the Golden," he speaks in the voice of Spinoza, suggesting that the philosopher, like a new prophet, makes the next major step in bringing God into the mundane world:

> *Spinoza*
> He is the stars,
> multitudinous as the drops of rain,
> and the worm at our feet,
> leaving only a blot on the stone;
> except God there is nothing.
>
> God neither hates nor loves, has neither pleasure nor pain;
> were God to hate or love, He would not be God;
> He is not a hero to fight our enemies,
> nor like a king to be angry or pleased at us,
> nor even a father to give us our daily bread, forgive us our trespasses;

nothing is but as He wishes,
nothing was but as He willed it;
as He wills it, so it will be.
(1.128)

The Deity who says in "The Shield of David," "I am the God of Justice,
I am the God of Righteousness," has become the God of nature, who no
longer speaks through Scripture but rather inhabits the entire created universe. Spinoza's God has lost his anthropomorphic qualities but retains his
ability to be everywhere and to make everything happen: "Whatever is, is
in God, and nothing can be or be conceived without God" (Spinoza 94).
As Reznikoff interprets it, this marks the ultimate expression of the sanctity of the ordinary: no matter where we turn—toward the stars, the rain,
or the worm passing underfoot—there is nothing but God anywhere.

Yovel designates Spinoza's conception of God's immanence as his most
radical contribution to philosophy, a contribution expressing a rejection
of both conventional Christianity (represented in Reznikoff's poem by
echoes of The Lord's Prayer: "a father to give us our daily bread, forgive
us out trespasses") and conventional Judaism (whose images of God as
hero and king are also negated in the poem). Such a rejection, Yovel argues, could have been made at this time only by a Jewish thinker. Although Descartes, Leibniz, and the skeptical deists all postulated a "God
of the philosophers" in their rational systems, they placed his metaphysical
role as Creator and First Cause outside creation. Spinoza was the only
philosopher who refused God any particular role, seeing God instead as
the totality of the universe:

> The identification of God with the world implies a more profound re-
> jection of Judaism and Christianity than ordinary atheism. Spinoza does
> not contend that there is no God, only the inferior natural world. Such
> a contention is itself steeped in a Christian world view. Spinoza con-
> tends, on the contrary, that by virtue of identifying the world with God,
> immanent reality itself acquires divine status.
> (Yovel 1.175)

Like many Jewish intellectuals of the past two centuries, Reznikoff is
drawn to Spinoza for the way he shifts the religious categories of sanctity, justice, mercy, and righteousness into the mundane world, where
the poet believes the deepest religious obligations reside. Milton Hindus confirms this reading of Reznikoff's religious position, noting, "His
God, except in direct translations from the Bible, is perhaps nearer to the
God of Spinoza and of Whitman than He is to the God of Jewish tradition" (Hindus, *Charles Reznikoff* 20). Discounting the personal God of the

Bible, Reznikoff himself says, "To me God is not a human being, that is, talking of putting his hand over anyone" (*MP* 120). In his rejection of a personal God, Reznikoff follows a tradition established by Spinoza in his *Theological-Political Treatise,* where he argues that our "personal" relationship to God is a matter wholly of superstition, based upon our desires and fears (Spinoza 6–10). If God is not personal, then the modern Jew can focus personal relations not outwardly toward the transcendent realm but inwardly toward the immanent realm of other human beings and nature.

In "Karl Marx," the final section of "Jerusalem the Golden," Reznikoff speaks entirely from within the immanent realm, as one of the workers for whom Marx's vision of justice has become operative. Sharing Marx's wholly immanentist philosophy, Reznikoff's speaker anticipates an end to alienated labor, war, hatred, hunger, drudgery, and private property, reaching a prophetic climax with a central communist dictum:

> Proclaim to the seed of man
> throughout the length and breadth of the continents,
> From each according to his strength,
> to each according to his need.
> (*CP* 1.129)

These final lines of "Jerusalem the Golden" (and of the volume bearing its name) carry Reznikoff's historical vision of the evolving understanding of justice in Jewish thought into the era of the Great Depression, when the desire for work was a palpable need and the possibility of revolution was a mounting hope. By its placement after "Spinoza," "Karl Marx" also ties the contemporary revolutionary movement to the tradition of Jewish secularism, with its central emphases upon justice and social belonging.

Reznikoff is not the only Jewish-American intellectual to link Spinoza and Marx to a chain of Jewish revolutionaries. Isaac Deutscher (1907–67), author of the famous essay "The non-Jewish Jew," also constructs a secular Jewish tradition running through these two major figures. A child prodigy, ordained at thirteen as a rabbi in his native Poland, Deutscher became in succession a poet, a communist, and an anti-Stalinist. His "non-Jewish Jew" has gone beyond local identifications and embraces universal liberation, following in the footsteps of Spinoza, Heine, Marx, Rosa Luxemburg, Trotsky, and Freud: "They all found Jewry too narrow, too archaic, and too constricting. They all looked for ideals and fulfilment beyond it, and they represent the sum and substance of . . . the most profound upheavals that have taken place in philosophy, sociology, eco-

nomics, and politics in the last three centuries" (26). Taking a position
similar to Veblen's, Deutscher contends that because of their abiding in
a state of betweenness, these Jewish figures were able to break free from
ethnocentrism and other cultural restrictions: "as Jews they dwelt on the
borderlines of various civilizations, religions, and national cultures. . . .
They lived on the margins or in the nooks and crannies of their respective nations. Each of them was in society and yet not in it, of it and yet
not of it. It was this that enabled them to rise in thought above their societies, above their nations, above their times and generations, and to strike
out mentally into wide new horizons and far into the future" (27). Although these figures surpassed Judaism, they did not cease being Jews;
Deutscher, like Yovel and like Reznikoff's Acosta, contends that "[t]he
Jewish heretic who transcends Jewry belongs to a Jewish tradition" (26)
and that the philosophical and political inventions of these figures exemplify a Jewish way of coping with modernity.

The heretical "Jewish tradition" of Spinoza and Marx also had a profound impact upon Louis Zukofsky. When the Great Depression hit, Zukofsky was one of those Jewish young men for whom the *Menorah Journal*
lost its appeal in the face of the greater urgency represented by communism. In his poetry of the 1930s, especially "Song 27" ("Song—3/4 time
[pleasantly drunk]"; *Complete Short Poetry* 58–61) and *"A"*-8 and the first
half of *"A"*-9 (*"A"* 43–108), Zukofsky dedicates himself to reproducing
Marx's labor theory of value in poetic form. Although Spinoza remains
important to Zukofsky throughout his career, appearing as early as "Poem
beginning 'The'" (1926), he doesn't step in to take the place of Marx as
central philosopher until 1948, after the ravages of World War II and the
revelations of the brutality of Stalinism; at this time, Spinoza replaces Marx
in the second half of *"A"*-9 and becomes a central theoretical touchstone
for Zukofsky's contemporaneous work of criticism, *Bottom: On Shakespeare* (first published 1963). When Zukofsky makes the turn from Marx
to Spinoza in *"A"*-9, however, the shift marks more of a continuity than
a break, as Michael Davidson explains:

> In *"A"*-9, Spinoza reaffirms unities of subject and object, God and
> nature, much as Marx reaffirms the identity of laborer and product. In
> both seventeenth-century philosopher and nineteenth-century econo-
> mist, reification begins with the invention of unattainable things-in-
> themselves, divorced from human action and separated from the sensual
> body. Zukofsky modulated the thought of each by rephrasing Marx
> through Spinoza in the second half, thus illustrating the inseparability
> of intellectual labor and material value.
> (132–33)[7]

Like Reznikoff, Zukofsky sees an intimate connection between the two Jewish philosophers on the basis of their rigorous antitranscendentalism: Spinoza's demystification of religion and insistence that nothing resides outside of nature becomes the foundation for Marx's materialism. This point of agreement between the two philosophers also gives us a means for contrasting the two poets by observing how they enact the ethics of immanence. Deeply theoretical in both his poetry and prose, Zukofsky relentlessly derives theories from each delineation he makes of the interactions among things and people, no matter how concrete or personal the scene he depicts. When Zukofsky switches from Marx to Spinoza in the second half of "*A*"-9, for instance, he signals the metamorphosis by rewriting Marx's master term *labor* as Spinoza's master term *love*. The first half of the poem condenses passages from Marx about how labor is reified into commodities, beginning with these lines:

> An impulse to action sings of a semblance
> Of things related as equated values,
> The measure all use in time congealed labor
> In which abstraction things keep no resemblance
> To goods created
> (*"A"* 106)

In the second half of the poem, Zukofsky opposes commodification by invoking the restorative notion Spinoza develops of sight purified by love. Basing the entire poem formally upon Guido Cavalcanti's canzone "Donna mi priegha" (and inspired by Ezra Pound's translation of it), Zukofsky replicates in the second half of his poem many of the words and all of the line endings of the first half. This portion begins,

> An eye to action sees love bear the semblance
> Of things, related is equated,—values
> The measure all use who conceive love, labor
> Men see, abstraction they feel, the resemblance
> (108)

Drawing upon Marx and Spinoza and asserting a relationship between them in far different ways than Reznikoff does, Zukofsky typically works with many overlapping textual frames: in this poem he orchestrates Cavalcanti, Pound, Marx, Spinoza, and a number of other figures, tying them together by equating the "notes" struck by their ideas, images, words, et cetera. This elaborate counterpoint makes apparent why Zukofsky claims Bach's *Art of the Fugue* as a major formal inspiration. Just as significant, though, he employs his fugal form to synthesize theoretical statements that speak to the concerns of every figure he invokes. Reznikoff, on the other hand, eschews this kind of formal intricacy and refuses to wax theoretical in his poetry, returning again and again to irresolvable moments of ethical crisis. When Reznikoff invokes figures from the past, he does so in order to reanimate their historical dilemmas, rather than to use them largely as touchstones for thought. To compare the poets' conceptions of the figure of Spinoza, we could say that he stands primarily as the philosopher of intellectual love for Zukofsky, while for Reznikoff he represents the "natural" basis of ethical obligation.

"NOT THE ACTUAL LAND OF ISRAEL BUT A SPIRITUAL ISRAEL"

In the poem "Jerusalem the Golden," Reznikoff invokes Marx as one figure in the Jewish tradition of thought about justice, rather than asking him, as Zukofsky does in *"A"*-8 and the first half of *"A"*-9, to provide an absolute scale for social and intellectual measurement. In the same way, Reznikoff gestures toward Zionism, that other "chair" that lured intellectuals away from the *Menorah Journal* in the thirties, without ever becoming himself a Zionist. In his review of *The Menorah Treasury,* for instance, he notes how the journal constituted an alternative Zion, particularly for Jews who found a home neither in prayer nor in Palestine:

> Let us say it offered a land: not the actual land of Israel but a spiritual Israel, at least the Israel that could be translated into English. But it was a land which those of us who joined a Menorah society at school or read the *Journal* afterwards entered gladly: a land where we were welcomed as Jews and felt at home, even if we had little Jewish learning and knew no Hebrew nor the prayers which our fathers had repeated since they were children. The articles and stories in the *Journal* interested us, for they reflected, directly or indirectly, our own Jewishness, and here our own verse and prose would, so at least some of us hoped, find a place: not in spite of the fact that we were Jewish but just because we were Jews and perhaps had something to say as Jews.
> (UCSD 9.18.9)

Reznikoff presents the *Menorah Journal* as a Land of In-Between, where Jews with any or with no relationship to Judaism could meet in an American context; from this position they could lobby for acceptance into the cultural elite of America and of the world. The journal's purpose was not to reinforce a particular strand of normative Judaism, but rather to provide a space for translating "Israel" (that is, Jewish culture) into English, a space where Jewish writers could invent a form of American intellectualism. A 1929 statement by Reznikoff sums up beautifully how the *Menorah Journal* brought a "spiritual Israel" to American Jews: "The land that we Jews hold in common—free of any mandatory power—is ideas expressed in words: this is the only land of Israel. We have been in possession three thousand years and are a people only because of it. I think of The Menorah Journal as a colony" (*Letters* 69).[8] Although at the time of this testimonial he was shortly to marry the indefatigable Zionist Marie Syrkin, Reznikoff was not himself politically active. In the aforementioned statement, for instance, he adapts the terms of contemporary Zionism, with its hopes focused upon the British mandate in Palestine, praising the *Journal* by converting the political passion into a more broadly intellectual one. As a significant mouthpiece of "the only land of Israel," a land of free thought without geographical boundaries, the *Menorah Journal* won Reznikoff's lifelong allegiance.

Reznikoff's symbolic invocation of Zionism in his statements about the journal resonates with a number of references to Zion and Jerusalem quoted in the previous chapter. When he exclaims in the poem recounting his difficulty with Hebrew, "How far have I been exiled, Zion" (*CP* 1.72), or when, in "Samuel," he sits down by the water in a land of exile, like the poet who weeps "by the waters of Babylon" in Psalm 137, Reznikoff invokes the age-old Jewish desire to return to the Promised Land. As the classic formulation of the exile's yearning for a homeland, Psalm 137 figures in the last stanza of "Samuel," though in a distinctly un-Zionist manner:

> The seasons change.
> That is change enough.
> Chance planted me beside a stream of water;
> content, I serve the land,
> whoever lives here and whoever passes.
> (*CP* 1.73)

This verse espouses what Nietzsche called *amor fati,* affirming contingency and historical reality rather than advocating either a return to an earlier perfection or the struggle for a new state. Instead of yearning for a supernatural or political order, the poet accepts the natural world, with its seasonal order, and, like Nietzsche, he even raises "Chance" to something like a deity (Nietzsche 223–24).[9] In his acceptance of self and world as they are, however, Reznikoff seems a much more wholehearted practitioner of *amor fati* than does Nietzsche. In contrast to the poet of Psalm 137, who, when he sat weeping beside the waters of Babylon, refused to

sing a song of Zion for his captors and instead uttered curses, Reznikoff
calls himself "content" in his exile and vows to "serve the land," its inhabitants, and even its strangers. The poem "Samuel" does not condemn
the Diaspora, nor is there such an impulse anywhere in Reznikoff's work.
Symbolically, Zion functions for him in the same way as the Hebrew
language does—offering a primary image of linkage to generations in the
past; as such, it has a strong appeal. Instead of invoking "Zion" as a means
of indulging in nostalgia or as the basis for a Zionist politics, Reznikoff
sees his job as making the condition of exile habitable. As Burton Hatlen suggests, "rather than seeking to recover the lost homeland, Reznikoff would embrace diaspora itself as the fundamental condition of Jewish existence" (166).

A critique of Zionism and advocacy of diasporism has been mounted
in recent years from a number of quarters, most prominently in a contro-
versial essay by Daniel and Jonathan Boyarin, "Diaspora: Generation and
the Ground of Jewish Identity." Wishing to avoid an imperialist model
for Jewish culture and, like Reznikoff and the *Menorah* writers, wishing
to affirm the value of the entire span of Jewish history (not merely that
part of it recorded in the Bible), the Boyarins argue that in many ways
Zionism is not a particularly "Jewish" approach to political identity: "The
solution of Zionism—that is, Jewish state hegemony, except insofar as it
represented an emergency and temporary rescue operation—seems to us
the subversion of Jewish culture and not its culmination. It represents the
substitution of a European, Western cultural-political formation for a traditional Jewish one that has been based on a sharing, at best, of political
power with others and that takes on entirely other meanings when combined with political hegemony" (324). Like Philip Roth in his dazzling
novel, *Operation Shylock* (1993), the Boyarins advocate "an Israel that re-
imports diasporic consciousness" (325)—although for the Boyarins this
would mean "a consciousness of a Jewish collective as one sharing space
with others, devoid of exclusivist and dominating power," while in
Roth's multileveled satiric fiction, a man named Philip Roth advocates a
return of the Jews to their "true homeland," Europe, in order to save
them from a Holocaust in the Middle East. If, as the Boyarins suggest, the
Promised Land was in some senses always an ideal, even during ancient
periods when Jews ruled the land of Israel, then the notion of Zion as a
cultural lodestone must be seen, paradoxically, as a central feature of a
diasporic, or nomadic, Jewish identity.

These lines of reasoning have been perceived as threatening by many
Jews having a deep attachment to the religious ideal of Zion or to the
political desirability of a Jewish state. Although strong arguments can be

marshaled for both sides of the Zionist/diasporist debate, diasporism has
for the present study the heuristic value of throwing into relief the position
of betweenness Charles Reznikoff shared with other American Jewish
intellectuals in the first half of the twentieth century. Concerned to preserve Jewish identity, as are the *Menorah* writers and the Boyarins, Reznikoff makes Zion a site of yearning, but he never calls explicitly for a return to the Land. Giving no weight to the usual modern underpinnings
of identity, such as autochthony, nationalism, or hegemonic power, he
cares passionately about cultural survival and ethnic identity. Celebrating
the survival of Jewish identity in poem after poem, he seems to accept
scatteredness as the essential human destiny. Amid what must have been
extremely loud appeals, particularly in the thirties, for commitment to
Zionism (especially by his wife) or to Communism (especially by friends
such as Louis Zukofsky and George and Mary Oppen), Reznikoff, though
demonstrably sympathetic to any and all victims of injustice, preserved an
attachment to Diaspora rather than embracing any form of utopia. In her
memoir of their life together, Marie Syrkin describes his response to an
actual invitation to visit Zion:

> In 1933 my Zionist interests called for a trip to Palestine. Charles, as his
> poems attest, was deeply Jewish, but when I urged a trip together during
> my summer vacation he assured me in all gravity that he was too busy;
> he had not yet explored Central Park to the full. In due time, he prom-
> ised, he would set out on a walking tour of England, Wales and Ireland;
> then he would go to Paris, Rome, Jerusalem—all in some indefinite
> future. I did not wait and he did not object.
> (*MP* 44)

In his somewhat comic refusal to leave New York City, Reznikoff sounds
like the archetypal New Yorker who does not really believe that the world
holds anything of interest beyond the metropolis. Lest we imagine that
Reznikoff was actually so self-enclosed, however, Marie includes in her
memoir an excerpt from a letter he wrote during her visit:

> I feel a compulsion, which I shall not resist, to write my lament for Israel.
> I am thinking of nothing else in my spare time, and though nothing may
> come of it, I must do what I can. . . . I wish you to see everything and
> enjoy everything slowly, unhurriedly, to soak in as much as possible.
> Somehow, I feel as if I as well as you am in Palestine, that is that you are
> my alter ego, and so I know that we have really become one flesh.
> (44)

Although he did let himself join Marie imaginatively in Palestine,
his commitment to exploring the local world of Central Park during his

long daily walks was quite real. He walked, on average, twenty miles through New York City, stopping occasionally at an Automat for coffee or a baked apple, observing the inhabitants of the urban world as though he were an anthropologist, always ready to engage in conversation anyone he encountered, but able also to step back and place the ordinary scenes of the city within his highly disciplined, often epigrammatic verse. In his earnest exploration of the local world, Reznikoff resembles Thoreau, who likewise wrote epigrammatically and refused invitations from friends to travel to exotic places. Thoreau's characteristic dismissal of such invitations, partaking of a sense of humor similar to Reznikoff's, appears near the beginning of *Walden,* when he boasts, "I have travelled a good deal in Concord" (2). Through their fervent dedication to walking, both writers became "natural historians," observing closely the flora and fauna (including human beings) to be found in their native locales. Reznikoff's avid attention to the physical world, to the individual creature or person, and to the existential moment—to that which survives into the present— acted against the desire to undertake a pilgrimage or endorse a redemptive ideology. Since there has never been a utopia, a point of safety and secure control, in Jewish history—nor, as he argues by example in *Testimony,* has there been such a paradise in American history—why put one's energies into building an illusion? We might summarize Reznikoff's diasporic ethics this way: wherever one finds oneself, there are ample opportunities to care for self, neighbors, and surroundings; *here* is the most demanding and rewarding outlet for impulses to "save the world." From a diasporic perspective, the world is a realm of multiple identities and affiliations where one remains at home not in a Sacred Land but in a Land of In-Between.

Reznikoff's diasporic ethics makes an explicit appearance in two poems from *Inscriptions: 1944–1956* (1959). In the first, he clarifies the exact location of Paradise:

As I was wandering with my unhappy thoughts,
I looked and saw
that I had come to a sunny place
familiar and yet strange.
"Where am I?" I asked a stranger. "Paradise."
"Can this be Paradise?" I asked surprised,
for there were motor-cars and factories.
"It is," he answered. "This is the sun that shone on Adam once;
the very wind that blew upon him, too."
(*CP* 2.75)

Paradise exists wherever one finds oneself, among the exigencies of daily life. Only "unhappy thoughts" cloud the vision of Paradise, and Reznikoff contrasts such thoughts forcefully, by his use of line break, with looking and seeing. If Diaspora has its kabbalistic equivalent in "The Breaking of the Vessels" (the scattering that takes place in Creation when the divine vessels of light are shattered), then the act of seeing depicted in this poem effects a *tikkun,* a restoration of the divine context to a particular experience. In this humorous recounting of what others might portray as a mystical or conversion experience, Reznikoff keeps the focus resolutely upon the everyday and the commonplace. Invoking the sun and wind that Adam felt produces not an apotheosis but an affirmation of immanence, experienced uncannily as the "familiar and yet strange."

In the subsequent poem, Reznikoff makes explicit his commitment to the commonplace:

> *Te Deum*
>
> Not because of victories
> I sing,
> having none,
> but for the common sunshine,
> the breeze,
> the largess of the spring.
>
> Not for victory
> but for the day's work done
> as well as I was able;
> not for a seat upon the dais
> but at the common table.
> (2.75)

"Victories" pertain to the realm of "causes," to political and military struggles; the distinctly nonaggressive sentiments voiced render inappropriate, or maybe hyperbolic, the poem's title. Pitted against the value of "victory" is that of the "common," and these terms are significantly repeated in this short poem. "Victory" implies hierarchies—chains of command, not to speak of winners and losers—and so victories are celebrated by raising up victorious leaders, as upon a dais. In the "common" world, which includes both the abundance of nature and the ubiquity of work, one celebrates doing "as well as I was able" by joining the democratic fellowship of the table. And to complete the conquest of "victory" by the "common," this poem, like the previous one, recognizes the immanent forces of divinity in the mundane influences of the sun and wind.

Reznikoff's celebration of a democratic, diasporic identity pertains not just to moments in which sun and wind prevail. In a poem that was first printed in the *Menorah Journal* in 1940, he affirms the continuity of a diasporic identity in the midst of Hitler's persecution of the Jews:

> Despite this and despite this,
> Despite this and despite this, too;
> for we are a stubborn people.
>
> The bulls of
> Assyria gored and trampled us
> and the jackals and hawks of Egypt tore us to bits
> and the eagles of Rome feasted upon us,
> and yet despite that and despite that—
> why not, Israel,
> despite this and despite this, too?
> (2.20–21)

In the *Menorah Journal*, Reznikoff published this poem as the second of a group of six entitled "A Short History of Israel." The first poem, in five pages, gives a capsule history of the persecution and dispersal of the Jews throughout the ages, ending with the admonition to "stand up to plead— / in every language— / for the poor / and wronged, / teach by formula and picture, / speech and music— / heal and save!" (2.20). The second poem, then, concentrates on the moral fiber needed for sheer survival. The mild indirection of "Despite this and despite this," spoken possibly in a Yiddish accent of incredulity and resignation, enacts a verbal overcoming of the horrors to which it alludes by not mentioning them. This strategy ensures that rather than succumb to hopelessness one will remain fortified in the stubborn tenacity that has enabled survival thus far.

The next poem in this series is a marvelously ironic paean to Jewish survival as seen from the point of view of Christianity:

> Wouldn't they have been surprised, Saint Louis and his knights,
> still bleeding from the scimitars,
> if, crowding forward to greet the Queen of Heaven,
> she were to turn from them and say, pointing to a wretched Jew,
> "The bravest of you all is he,
> who alone,
> hedged in by monks and knights, by staves and swords,
> in answer to your question
> still denied me!"
> (2.21)

This is the ultimate wish-fulfillment, in which Reznikoff imagines proving the Christians wrong at their own highest court, giving the victory again not to the warrior but to the "wretched Jew," whose virtue is resistance. As presented by both Reznikoff and the Boyarins, a diasporic identity, for all its being "a notion of identity in which there are only slaves but no masters" (Boyarins 323), represents not weakness but a holding fast to a sense of difference through the vicissitudes of millennia. This poem illustrates wonderfully the hybrid nature of such an identity by imagining the resistant Jew's triumph taking place within a Christian heaven.

Like the other *Menorah* writers and, indeed, like all of the Jews who have entered modernity since Uriel Da Costa, Reznikoff lives in a world between Judaism and Christianity—even when that world is called "secular." For some modern Jews, this sense of betweenness has prompted a commitment to one of the many forms of universalism, such as communism or socialism, which results in leaving Judaism (and Christianity) completely behind; for others, it has prompted an adaptation of Jewish culture to the ideology of the modern nation-state, in the form of Zionism; for others, such as Reznikoff, it has prompted the formation of a new diasporic Jewish identity. And these are not, of course, the only positions inhabited by modern Jews. Reznikoff's writing gives evidence that he thought long and hard about the meaning of a Jewish identity in the modern world, wishing both to maintain his affiliation with past generations and to espouse modern democratic ideals: he determined that a contemporary Jewish identity founded on the groundless but stubborn condition of Diaspora answers best to both the present and to the entire history of the Jewish people.

Born fourteen years after Reznikoff into a wealthy, assimilated, non-religious German-Jewish family, George Oppen, the youngest Objectivist, had a very different relationship with Judaism and Jewishness than Reznikoff or Zukofsky. With no religious education and no experience of *Yiddishkeit* (eastern European Jewish culture), Oppen found Jewish identity a lifelong conundrum rather than something from which to draw sustenance or against which to rebel. As John Taggart points out in his remarkable essay on Jewish issues in Oppen's work, "Walk Out," the situations in his own life and thought that Oppen considered most "Jewish" involved two qualities: resistance and betweenness. With these responses to modernity as his only touchstones of Jewishness, Oppen experienced a dilemma of belonging much more acute than that of Reznikoff or Zukofsky. Although Zukofsky rejected Judaism outright and aspired, through his astonishing erudition and unrivaled poetic virtuosity, to place himself at the center of Western culture, there is still no question that he grew up speaking Yiddish in New York City, the son of pious

Reb Pinchos Zukofsky. A non-Jewish Jew *par excellence,* Oppen was never
sure how to conceive of himself as Jewish; the issue of identity remained
unsettled. Even so, he shared with Reznikoff a powerful Jewish experience: by maintaining twenty-four years of silence as a writer, Oppen composed, in a sense, his own burnt book. Choosing to become a communist
in response to the misery caused by the Great Depression, Oppen put aside
his poetry in order to organize and work in manual labor. After World
War II he paid for his communist affiliation by years of exile in Mexico.
As challenging and often dispiriting as these experiences were, his combat
service in Europe during the war added trauma and guilt. The book he
lived through rather than wrote during the years between 1934 and 1958
has the uncanny presence of a central text in Oppen's oeuvre, a text whose
voluntary effacement may have been a source of the flood of writing let
loose in the twenty years that followed.[10]

When trying to understand his Jewish identity, Oppen, like many assimilated American Jews, looked to the Holocaust and the State of Israel
as monumental occurrences that call for some kind of active identification.
Through his abhorrence of fascism and anti-Semitism as well as his combat
service, especially his participation in liberating a concentration camp,
Oppen had an active sympathy for victims of the Holocaust and a guilty
conviction that he must try to allay suffering such as this in any way possible. His feelings about the Jewish state were much less certain, but he had
an opportunity to test them during a two-month stay in Israel in 1975,
which provoked a crisis in Oppen's Jewish identity. In conversation about
the stay with the poet's daughter and niece, Taggart learns that Oppen
considered himself a "self-chosen" Jew ("choosing" to be one of the
"chosen people") who could not identify with a Jewish society that was
establishing itself as a nationalist power; what is more, he "returned from
Israel a shaken man" because of this inability to identify (31–32). In a
journal entry he speaks about this plainly: "I cannot see a place for myself,
an identity, in Israel—and I cannot think at all of going through a conversion, of going through religious instruction—etc.—I am a stiff-necked
people—we—Mary and I, are a stiff-necked people" (quoted in Taggart
33). Like Uriel Da Costa and Isaac Deutscher, Oppen implies that what is
most Jewish about himself is his resistance to institutions, including Jewish
ones. In fact, as Taggart notes, he refers to himself in a letter as "antinomian" (39–40). The danger inherent in this antinomian stance has been
memorably thematized by Oppen as "the shipwreck of the singular" in
his greatest poem, "Of Being Numerous," which investigates the conflicting but irrefutable demands of individuality and of "being numerous."
For Oppen, a Jewish identity would fit strangely in between existential

consciousness and human solidarity—the two entities whose relationship he has devoted his life to illuminating—and thus he doesn't know exactly what to make of it, other than to note its betweenness: "somewhere half-way between the fact of being singular and the fact of being numerous is the fact of being Jewish" (quoted in Taggart 41). Between universal humanity and the individual would lie collective identities, such as extended family or tribe, which Jews have held on to fiercely throughout millennia of dispossession; this is the dimension of human identity whose loss Oppen's poetry grapples with.

In a late poem that concerns Jewish identity, "Semite," he speaks of the "distances" brought about by his antinomianism: "my distances neither Roman / nor barbarian" (*Collected Poems* 246). Oppen identifies neither with the distance of "Roman" imperial hauteur nor with those "barbarians" whose distance from the imperium signals active resistance. In this way, he differs from Reznikoff, who, in "Hellenist," refers to himself as "I, barbarian" (*CP* 1.107), identifying directly with the outsiders who wish to preserve a collective identity in the face of a triumphant culture. Oppen's resistance has a second-order quality to it: he would resist not only the conquerors but also those who circle around to preserve their identity in response to being conquered. Discussing Oppen's reaction to his visit to Israel in a gloss of the lines *"it is dreary / to descend // and be a stranger"* (Schwartz 570), Taggart explains this second-order quality further:[11]

> It is dreary to descend and be a stranger because the poet, as an invited guest in his ancestral homeland, must become an other to the others, a "traitorous" stranger reinscribed as stranger to the no longer strangers (Jews) in a no longer strange land (Israel). An exile among the exiled. He has been invited, "called" back to this homeland, but he has chosen to hear this calling as an invitation to go away from that homeland, to loosen his bonds with Judaism.
> (61)

Oppen's diasporism, then, is also of a second order: he not only refuses to identify with the nationalist enterprise of Zionism, he also realizes that he will never feel "at home" as a Jew, either. If Reznikoff's diasporism refers to a collective condition, from within which individual Jews must learn how to find "Zion" in everyday life in a strange land, then Oppen's diasporism includes a further exile from Jewish identity itself. Like the most extreme dilemmas that plague the Marrano condition, Oppen's alienation can be expressed in the terms Yovel uses to describe the Jew who flees Spain or Portugal for Amsterdam: "He does not belong to any cultural context simply or naturally, and feels both inside and outside any one of them. If he seems to have solved his problem and found an identity for himself (through assimilation into Christian society or by returning to the Jewish fold), this identity does not adhere to him simply or directly, for he must constantly struggle to engender and preserve it, overcoming the internal contradictions it entails" (1.49). In the lines that end the poem "If It All Went Up in Smoke," Oppen's contribution to *Voices within the Ark: The Modern Jewish Poets,* he cries out in anguished supplication from within such internal contradictions:

> help me I am
>
> of that people the grass
> blades touch
>
> and touch the small
>
> distances   the poem
> begins
> (573)

Speaking of distances again, as in "Semite," he seems to writhe within an untenable strangeness: finding himself, as one of the (Whitmanian) blades of grass, "touched" by his participation within the collective identity of being Jewish, he must nonetheless recognize a "small" but unbridgeable gap between himself and other Jews. Out of this minute but nonetheless abject experience of distance within identity within strangeness, of difference within belonging within betweenness, arises the anguished prophetic tone that drives so much of his poetry. For Oppen, these Jewish dilemmas make up the inaugural "distances" in which "the poem / begins."

THREE

HEBRAISM AND HELLENISM

HISTORY AND JEWISH IDENTITY

Reconfiguring the past was one of the main strategies used by Jewish intellectuals of the first half of the twentieth century to find a place in American culture. Indeed, if the perception of the dominant society is that one represents an atavistic strain in human culture—something long superseded by the progress of Christian civilization—then an effective way to counter this idea would be to rearticulate one's place in history. Reznikoff and a number of other *Menorah* writers did so in two related ways: they became "objective" historians, seeking to dispel the many myths about the Jewish past by giving a historically accurate account of that past; and they took on the central myth of Western civilization—that it unites two opposing impulses, Hebraism and Hellenism—and either rewrote or deconstructed the myth to make Jews legitimate heirs to both strains.

For modern Jews the subject of history has become something of an obsession, forming a primary ingredient in attempts to reconstitute Jewish identity. In the past, Jewish movements would ground themselves in new interpretations of Scripture; in the modern era, every ideological position (including Zionism and diasporism) grounds itself in an interpretation of history. In keeping with this emphasis, the *Menorah Journal* numbered historians among its most distinguished writers, and the recourse to history in the *Journal* reinforced a central concept of the publication, Jewish humanism. In his review of *The Menorah Treasury,* Robert Alter singles out for high praise the writing of historians such as Salo Baron, Cecil Roth, and Harry Wolfson during the first fifteen years of the *Journal:* "The his-

torical essays published in the *Journal* during this period are particularly
remarkable. . . . Without insight-hunting or tendentiousness, the historical writers manage to make palpable their own sense of the relevance of
their subjects. . . . [O]ne of the implicit intentions of the writer is to startle
the reader into a realization that the Jewish past is more complex and certainly more interesting than his cherished stereotypes of it" (53). In the
context of the *Menorah Journal,* this recognition of the complexity and
variety of the Jewish past gives rise to "humanistic" values, such as perspectivism, tolerance, and compassion, cultivated at the expense of values
such as exclusivism and exceptionalism.

For Reznikoff in particular, history comprised a central strand in a complex weave of identity and vocation—which included the following professional roles, not all of which could otherwise be harmonized: poet,
playwright, novelist, historian, lawyer, translator, and editor. Milton Hindus notes that Reznikoff "considered the idea of taking a doctorate in
history and becoming a professional historian. If he did not realize this
ambition, he still managed to do work which professional historians could
respect" (*Reznikoff* 10). Indeed, history pervades Reznikoff's poetry, novels, plays, memoirs, and the extensive range of his nonfiction writing. In
verse, *Testimony* and *Holocaust* are constructed wholly from archival materials, and many of his individual poems recount historical events ranging
from biblical times to the twentieth century. All of his *Nine Plays* portray
historical figures, if we count the biblical characters as historical. His novel
The Lionhearted treats the Jews of medieval England, and he wrote two
books based on his family's history, *By the Waters of Manhattan* (1930) and
Family Chronicle (1963). As a "professional" historian, Reznikoff produced
a surprising variety of work: he translated from German I. J. Benjamin's
My Three Years in the United States: 1859–1862 (1956); edited two volumes of the papers of jurist Louis Marshall (1957); wrote five historical
sketches about Jews in American history for the *Menorah Journal,* which
he called "Scenes and Characters from the American Epic" (1943–48);
published reviews of books on Jewish-American history along with historical articles about Jews in colonial America and the Jewish communities
in New Haven, Boston, and New York City, all for *Commentary;* and
wrote, with the collaboration of Uriah Engelman, *The Jews of Charleston:
A History of an American Jewish Community* (1950).

In the introduction to the latter book, commissioned to celebrate the
bicentenary of the Jewish community in Charleston, South Carolina,
Reznikoff argues for the contemporary relevance of history, noting that
it provides consolation for present hardships and positive examples for
emulation:

History, as such, is of little value to most of us except as a guide to the present. Whether we who are Jews in this country belong to congregations that are called Orthodox, Conservative, or Reform, or to no congregation at all but consider ourselves Jews and find strength in the knowledge of what our ancestors survived as well as daily sustenance in the essentials of their faith, it is of no little importance to us to see how Jews at other times lived and adjusted themselves to their environment: particularly so when that environment was, like ours, American. It is the purpose of this history to show how the Jews of Charleston became Americans of their region, and remained Jews.

(x)

Ultimately, Reznikoff thinks of historiography as a means of creating and preserving identity. In his own case, although *The Jews of Charleston* was written on commission, he must have felt an identification with the Jewish population of a city that was first known as "Charles Town." Later, he became fascinated with aspects of Charleston's history and began a novel, which he called *Charles Town: A Historical Novel* (UCSD 9.19.21–23). In more broadly social terms, by demonstrating in *The Jews of Charleston* the early success of Sephardic Jews in establishing a hybrid American identity, Reznikoff can argue implicitly that twentieth-century Ashkenazic Jewish immigrants can also "become Americans" and "remain Jews."

During the twentieth century tensions necessarily arose, however, between the projects of becoming American and remaining Jewish, and the rich historiographical activity by modern Jews takes place in the midst of such tensions. According to the contemporary historian Y. H. Yerushalmi, the very turn to history constitutes an important aspect of the modern break with traditional Judaism. In his view, the Jewish historian becomes an illustrative figure of betweenness, caught in a peculiar double bind: by achieving a fuller, more objective understanding of Judaism in its historical contexts, the historian tacitly betrays the sacred tradition that is based upon the memory of a covenant with God and of divine interventions in history:

> There is an inherent tension in modern Jewish historiography even though most often it is not felt on the surface nor even acknowledged. To the degree that this historiography is indeed "modern" and demands to be taken seriously, it must at least functionally repudiate premises that were basic to all Jewish conceptions of history in the past. In effect, it must stand in sharp opposition to its own subject matter, not on this or that detail, but concerning the vital core: the belief that divine providence is not only an ultimate but an active causal factor in Jewish history, and the related belief in the uniqueness of Jewish history itself.
> (89)

Another Jewish historian, Amos Funkenstein, has challenged Yeru-shalmi's influential contention that Jewish historiography marks a break from collective memory. In his *Perceptions of Jewish History,* Funkenstein argues that historical consciousness has been a constant fixture of Jewish culture, consonant with the unending need to assert uniqueness. Because Jewish culture did not, from biblical times onward, "view its existence and distinctive features as a matter of course or as a given part of the furniture of the world," it must be seen as, "by definition, a self-reflexive culture," in which "[h]istorical consciousness became the mode of . . . self-reflection" (2). Funkenstein further asserts, "The very emergence of Israel as a young culture among older cultures within 'historical' times needed explana-tion—the biblical account of history . . . provided it. The conquest of a land already inhabited by others likewise needed a justification. . . . Every further turn in the history of Israel had to be explained, none seemed self-evident—neither in times of prosperity nor, indeed, in times of need" (2). Because the Jews have never been able to take for granted "their identity, existence, and fate" (3), they have always used historiography as a means of self-understanding. In Funkenstein's view, Jews have engaged continu-ally in historical reflection in order to locate "the grounding of their uniqueness in an understanding of history" (21). In the final analysis, it may be that Funkenstein and Yerushalmi have different notions of what history is, for each of the processes they discuss seems valid. Both as a sign of the modern rupture with traditional Judaism (Yerushalmi) and as a manifestation of a deeper continuity with Jewish self-conceptions (Fun-kenstein), history has provided an effective tool for thinking about Jewish identity in the modern world.

In the Menorah movement, which began among Harvard students in 1906 as a means to promote the study of Jewish culture, historiography was not only a widely practiced art but a matter of great symbolic impor-tance. By 1913, when the movement had grown so large that an Intercol-legiate Menorah Association was founded, one of the first texts distributed to its member societies was an essay by the eminent Russian Jewish histo-rian Simon Dubnow (1860–1941)—an essay that seeks to convert history into an object of religious devotion.[1] Intent upon elevating Jewish history by ascertaining its "essence," Dubnow's *Jewish History* (1893; trans. 1903) employs a broadly Hegelian approach. In considering the two major pe-riods of Jewish history—before and after the collapse of the Jewish state in 70 C.E.—Dubnow claims that the history of both periods chronicles the achievements of "a spiritual people" (13). To become "a spiritual peo-ple," he explains, the Jews were elected by God as a nation of priests; then the prophets instilled spiritual ideals "into the very pith and marrow of the national consciousness" (16), so that these ideals were not only the possession of a priestly caste. Dubnow points out that these ideals gave birth to Christianity, too: "Out of the bosom of Judaism went forth the religion that in a short time ran its triumphant course through the whole ancient world, transforming races of barbarians into civilized beings. It was the fulfilment of the Prophetical promise—that the nations would walk in the light of Israel" (17). By subsuming Christianity within Judaism, Dubnow finesses the Greek (Roman)/barbarian (Jewish) dichotomy that later troubled Reznikoff and Oppen.

According to Dubnow, at the outset of the Diaspora the Jews developed a spiritual discipline that would preserve their virtues: "'To think and to suffer' became the watchword of the Jewish people," for whom "the spiritual discipline of the school came to mean . . . what military discipline is for other nations" (19). In keeping with this discipline, the entire second half of Jewish history "gives heartrending expression to the spiritual strivings of a nation whose brow is resplendent with the thorny crown of martyrdom. It breathes heroism of mind that conquers bodily pain. In a word, Jewish history is history sublimated" (21). By endowing the Jewish nation with "the thorny crown of martyrdom," Dubnow makes it symbolically equivalent to Jesus. He thus turns Jewish history itself into an object of worship, urging Jews to a new religious duty, the developing of a "historical consciousness." Acknowledging the religious burden he was placing upon history, Dubnow states in a diary in 1892, the year before he wrote *Jewish History,* "I have, as it were, become a missionary for history" (Frankel 11). If the Jewish people had been held together in antiquity by "state, race, and religion" and later on "it was chiefly religious consciousness that cemented Jewry into a whole" (26–27), he reasoned, then in the present age of enlightenment and schism "the keystone of national unity seems to be the historical consciousness" (27). In the place of talmudic study, Dubnow substitutes historical study, converting the binding force of Judaism from law *(halakhah)* to a historical principle. Dubnow himself was aware of the analogy between historical study and talmudic study. Reflecting in his autobiography upon his early determination, in the words of Robert Seltzer, to "master universal knowledge and become a full member of the cosmopolitan brotherhood that would liberate mankind from its intellectual fetters," Dubnow "points out the similarity between this undertaking and his grandfather's devotion to talmudic study" (290).

In addition to binding Jews "fast to one another" politically and socially through a renewed "national consciousness," the study of history, according to Dubnow, also has a moral impact upon individual Jews. "Jewish history admonishes the Jews: '*Noblesse oblige.* The privilege of belonging to a people whom the honorable title of the 'veteran of history' has been conceded, puts serious responsibilities on your shoulders'"

(179–81). The tone of moral uplift sounds more Christian than Jewish, with its rhetoric of martyrdom, moral perfection, and the extirpation of faults. In a contiguous passage, in fact, Dubnow cites approvingly Paul's Epistle to the Hebrews, noting that "[h]istory speaks to [the suffering Jewish soul] constantly through the mouth of the great apostle who went forth from the midst of Israel eighteen hundred years ago" (179).[2] Dubnow's moral exhortation regarding Jewish history also contains the curious non-Jewish term *noblesse oblige*. Two of the leaders of the Menorah movement, Henry Hurwitz and Leo Sharfman, used this same phrase in their rationale for a Jewish student organization. Speaking of young Jewish collegians, they proclaimed, "If theirs is the fortune of the Jewish tradition, theirs is equally the obligation to carry on the spirit and ideals of that tradition in the modern world. *Noblesse oblige!*" (Hurwitz and Sharfman 12). The Menorah founders seem to have borrowed this aristocratic byword from Dubnow, bringing with it a defensive/aggressive tone of Jewish cultural superiority, as in their claim that "a knowledge of the history and culture which are their own heritage must stir young men with red Jewish blood in their veins to endeavor to be worthy of that heritage"(12). *Noblesse oblige* seems such an unlikely standard to apply to the Jewish people, for whom its aristocratic (and imperialistic) overtones could have, in most cases, nothing but an unfortunate ring. On the other hand, the notion of the Jews as a "spiritual aristocracy" is an ancient one, which can be invoked to screen the fact that Jews in America at the beginning of the twentieth century—or the eastern European Jews whom Dubnow was addressing—had as yet virtually no opportunity for exercising *noblesse oblige* in the social and political climates in which they lived.

Addressing its own time and place, the Menorah movement sought to promote a "healthy" relation between Jews and a largely hostile American society. Jews from eastern Europe entered American colleges so quickly and in such great numbers that they caused consternation among their classmates:

> Overnight, or so it must have seemed to contemporaries, the campus was being swamped with an unfamiliar type of Jew. Frequently ill-mannered, speaking bad English and, worst of all, hailing from the lower classes, the Jewish immigrant student, willy-nilly, appeared to shake the foundations upon which America's prestigious colleges rested. His arrival introduced notes of discord onto the campus as its shared vocabulary and homogeneity seemed to vanish in the face of "Polish Jews with anemic faces . . . watching with envious curiosity the courteous indifference of the superior race."
> (Joselit, "Without Ghettoism" 135)[3]

Afraid of *appearing* defensive by speaking out against anti-Semitism, the Menorah movement hoped instead to develop more "manly" and "noble" images and ideals for American Jewry. From this perspective, it is not surprising that Dubnow's cultural nationalism, with its heavy-handed adoption of Christian and imperialist rhetoric, would have a strong appeal as a positive approach to "the Jewish Question."

This approach became a point of departure from the Menorah movement for Charles Reznikoff, for he entertained no sympathy whatsoever with the notion of a Jewish *noblesse oblige*. From beginning to end, his sights were focused upon the "little" people of New York and of Jewish history, rather than upon such qualities as "honor," "manliness," and "nobility." With his lifelong study of Jewish history and with the poems, articles, and books he wrote that themselves contribute to Jewish historiography, Reznikoff certainly followed Dubnow and the Menorah movement in dedicating himself to maintaining a "historical consciousness," but the Romantic celebration of martyrdom and sublimation—which Salo Baron deplored (in the pages of the *Menorah Journal*) as the "lachrymose" conception of Jewish history (63)—was inimical to him. Reznikoff's historiography is too disillusioned and too ironic to succumb to the kind of idealism that attracted Dubnow and the founders of the Menorah movement.

A telling example of Reznikoff's more stoical, less Romantic treatment of Jewish history can be found in his poem "In Memoriam: 1933," which was first printed in its entirety in an issue of the *Menorah Journal* and then published as a book by the Objectivist Press (1934). Adopting the method of his earlier plays, Reznikoff casts as dialogues seven critical moments in the history of the Jews, presenting this series of tableaux as a response to the Nazi accession to power in Germany.[4] In a review of the book in *Poetry*, H. R. Hays comments, "Hitler's rise to power and subsequent persecution of the Jews has stimulated race consciousness in many ways. We shall probably have no better expression of it in literary form than Reznikoff's poem, *In Memoriam, 1933*" (230–31).[5] What Hays dubs "race consciousness" Dubnow might call "historical consciousness," but Reznikoff's portrayal of major disasters in the history of the Jews depends on neither "the mystico-religious conception of race" (Hays 231) nor a sublimation of Jewish suffering, as in Dubnow. Instead, Reznikoff emphasizes Jewish survival as an end in itself, celebrating virtues of tenacity and adaptability that have enabled Jews to confront manifold historical crises by both changing and remaining the same. He implies that the greatness of the Jewish people depends not on "nobility" but on a resilience that is nearly inexhaustible; disasters of the magnitude of those he recounts would obliterate many social groups, but the Jews have developed an ethos that values both tradition and change and that allows the group, when confronted with exile or decimation, to adapt and continue.

The poem consists of seven parts, each presenting a historical crisis of the first magnitude. "Samaria Fallen: 722 B.C.E." concerns the demise of the Northern Kingdom (Israel) and the deportation of Jews by the Assyrians. "Babylon, 539 B.C.E." takes place in the wake of the fall of Judah, the destruction of the Temple (587 B.C.E.), and the exile of the Jews to Babylon. There is a hopeful quality to this section, in that a messenger from Cyrus arrives to tell the Jews that Babylon is about to fall and that they will be allowed to return to Judah and rebuild the Temple. At the end of the section an imaginary character, The Prince of the Captivity, declares:

> Let other people come as streams
> that overflow a valley
> and leave dead bodies, uprooted trees and fields of sand;
> We Jews are as the dew,
> on every blade of grass,
> trodden under foot today
> and here tomorrow morning.
> (*CP* 1.141)

Rather than prevailing like conquering rivers among the dynasties of the Near East, the Jews, in this Whitmanian passage, reappear perpetually like resilient drops of dew, vulnerable but persistent. Where Oppen will later portray the Jews as grass blades that "touch // and touch the small // distances," emphasizing a palpable alienation within the social body, Reznikoff calls attention to the regenerative quality of Jewish social cohesion.

The third section, "The Academy at Jamnia: *Anno* 70," takes place just before the destruction of the Second Temple. Again, as in the previous section, Reznikoff chooses not to depict the climactic moment; instead, he presents a group of rabbis anticipating the inevitable, planning to perpetuate Judaism through a school of sages, since the current constitutive ritual of priestly sacrifice will become impossible without the Temple. Reznikoff portrays this fundamental reorientation of Judaism through a speech given by the primary sage at Yavneh (Jamnia), Johanan ben Zaccai, which ends with the verses, "only a school / will float our cargo" (146). At this juncture in their history, the Jews must entrust themselves completely to the watery element and learn to navigate the "streams / that overflow a valley," since there is not, as in the previous section, an opportunity to return to a grassy Jerusalem as "dew." Earlier in his speech, Johanan prophesies that, although the legions may "trample down" the

grass of Jerusalem, the Jews will outlast the Romans. Reznikoff clearly
aims his version of this prophecy at the Nazis:

> these Romans,
> all the legions of the East
> from Egypt and Syria,
> the islands of the sea and the rivers of Parthia,
> gathered here
> to trample down Jerusalem,
> when they have become a legend
> and Rome a fable,
> that old men will tell of in the city's gate,
> the tellers will be Jews and their speech Hebrew.
> (145)

Again, as in the texts discussed in chapter 1, Reznikoff affirms the power
of Hebrew to overcome the physical subjugation of the Jews. The virtue
on display here is not martyrdom, as in Dubnow, but creative survival,
aided decisively by the perpetuation of the Hebrew language. In the next
three sections of the poem, "4. The Synagogue Defeated: *Anno* 1096,"
"5. Spain: *Anno* 1492," and "6. Poland: *Anno* 1700," Reznikoff portrays
the European history of anti-Semitism, first in the slaughter of Rhineland
Jews at the start of the First Crusade, next in the Inquisition, and then in
the Cossack uprising in the Polish Ukraine under Chmielnicki. The year
1700, which saw the birth of the Baal Shem Tov, founder of Hasidism,
makes an intriguing setting for the sixth section. It begins with an old Jew
remembering the Cossack massacres of a half century earlier; then another
Jew recalls the comforts of the Talmud: "Unravel this world / with your
nervous fingers / and reweave the knotted thread / on the loom of the
Talmud" (158). Finally, a young Jew expresses his impatience with these
reflections on history and the law, invoking instead a mystical awareness
to be found in the commonplace:

> only the joy in God has no end—
> this it is that in the wind
> showers the petals upon the grass,
> whirls up the glistening snow,
> or sweeps the dust along the streets before the storm;
> it shines upon me
> as the sun upon a tree in winter
> after rain.
> (159)

These verses express a kind of particulate mysticism in which "the joy in God" appears in petals, snowflakes, dust, and rain. This imagery of particles of water or dust harks back to the image of the Jews as dew on grass, making a characteristically rich collocation of survival, ecstasy, and the commonplace.

This celebration of the divine in the mundane, with its Hasidic (or Spinozistic) overtones, represents a perspective that Reznikoff cherished; he refuses, however, to end his history of the Jews on this note. The final section, "Russia: *Anno* 1905," comprises a single speech by a young Jew confronted with the pogroms of revolutionary Russia. In response to threats of murder or persecution, he considers three alternatives—alternatives that mirror those facing a German Jew in 1933: either he can immigrate to America ("nation whose founders were not leaders of legions or regiments, / or masters of the long ships of war, of bowmen or artillery, / but farmers, who spoke of liberty and justice for all / and planted these abstractions in the soil" [161]); make the pilgrimage to "the land of rock and sand, mountain and marsh, / where the sun still woos Delilah / and the night entraps Samson, / Palestine— / and your speech shall be Hebrew" (162); or stay put in Russia, telling himself,

> These are my people,
> Russian and Ukrainian, Cossack and Tartar, my brothers—
> even Ishmael and Esau;
> know myself a stitch, a nail, a word
> printed in its place, a bulb screwed in its socket,
> alight by the same current as the others
> in the letters of this sign—*Russia.*
> Or better still,
> there is no Russia;
> there are no peoples, only man!
> (163)

Although both the nationalistic and the universalistic rhetoric in this passage sound seductive, Reznikoff rejects the false idealism that arises from such desperate rationalizing: no matter how much one feels "screwed in" place in a hostile world, he or she must not clutch at a utopian ideal—whether in the form of martyrdom for the faith or revolution for the masses—that blinds him or her to the necessity of making the changes that will ensure survival. If Jewish history records many apocalyptic events and many radical reconfigurations of Jewish culture, then the lesson to learn, the poem suggests, is that creative adaptation—not martyrdom—saves the faith. In one passage of the poem, Reznikoff gives the reader the opportunity to make explicit the poet's own position on willful stasis: when the Russian Jew asks, "Should I, like Abraham, become the Hebrew, / leave Ur of the Chaldees, the accident of place, / and go to other pastures, from well to well; / or, the Jew, stay" (163), the presumed answer must be "become the Hebrew"—where "Hebrew" means etymologically the "crossover" people.[6] "[L]ike Abraham," make flexibility and adaptability your watchwords, Reznikoff counsels, rather than become fixed in your conception of "the Jew." There is something suicidal about the martyrdom that Dubnow touts as the essence of Jewish history, as if Jewish identity consisted in doggedly remaining in place as the murderous forces mass to attack. Reznikoff, who continued to write about contemporary attacks upon European Jews throughout the prewar and war years and made it the subject of his last book, urges Jews to embrace change as the only proven way to survive.

"A COMPASSIONATE PEOPLE"

Reznikoff's mistrust of ideology and of high-sounding rhetoric and his corresponding care for the quiet virtues of the commonplace provide a telling contrast to the tone adopted from Dubnow by the leaders of the Menorah movement, with its rhetoric of nobility and defensive/aggressive assertion of Jewish cultural superiority. This tone can be heard even in an avowedly open-minded statement in the inaugural issue (January 1915) of the *Menorah Journal,* a statement that sets a broad agenda for this groundbreaking publication:

> *The Menorah Journal* is under compulsion to be absolutely non-partisan, an expression of all that is best in Judaism and not merely of some particular sect or school or locality or group of special interests; fearless in telling the truth; promoting constructive thought rather than aimless controversy; animated with the vitality and enthusiasm of youth; harking back to the past that we may deal more wisely with the present and the future; recording and appreciating Jewish achievement, not to brag, but to bestir ourselves to emulation and to deepen the consciousness of *noblesse oblige;* striving always to be sane and level-headed; offering no opinions of its own, but providing an orderly platform for the discussion of mooted questions that really matter; dedicated first and foremost to the fostering of the Jewish "humanities" and the furthering of their influence as a spur to human service.
> (Schwarz vii)

From this statement, we can see what the Menorah movement hoped to offer its members by sponsoring a journal. In regard to behavior, if the "pushy" Jews invading American higher education were known for the often bitter, seemingly unmotivated aggression in their argumentation, then the *Menorah Journal* would not encourage *that* sort of Jewish activity; instead, it would inculcate a more "English," "sane and level-headed" attitude, taking pains not to appear opinionated; the journal would not engage in talmudic hairsplitting but would promote "the discussion of mooted questions that really matter." To balance this sort of self-policing, the journal would be "animated with the vitality and enthusiasm of youth" and thus would bring its readers in tune with the more general temper of the times. Because of the journal's youthful outlook, it was singled out by Waldo Frank, in *The New Republic* of December 23, 1925, as "the most promising Jewish activity in the United States. It corroborates the feeling that America is indeed coming of age. For it is very close to the self-critical and creative temper of the American youth everywhere, confronted as we all are with an inherited chaos of deformed and misapplied ideals from which we must make order and on which we must ineluctably build our future" (Schwarz viii). During the 1920s, the journal fulfilled the potential Frank saw in it, cultivating a stable of young writers, Reznikoff included, who engaged in the contemporary American quest for "a usable past," seeking, in this case, a past within Jewish history and offering it to American culture at large. As youthful intellectuals, they were, as Elinor Grumet puts it, "fired by the contemporary American work of traditionmaking, not tradition-retrieval; the past was of interest to them only insofar as it was accessible and usable for the present" (Grumet 59).[7] This statement provides a context for the claim about the efficacy of history made years later in the introduction to Reznikoff's *The Jews of Charleston:* "History, as such, is of little value to most of us except as a guide to the present" (x).

In addition to the youthful high spirits cultivated by the journal and its goal of "normalizing" Jewish intellectual behavior, there are three more specific proposals in the statement of intent that spell out its anticipated direction: it would be nonpartisan with respect to Jewish religious and political positions; it would "deepen the consciousness of *noblesse oblige*"; and it would foster the Jewish "humanities." As it quickly emerged from a limited role as house organ of a collegiate movement into a national Jewish intellectual forum, the *Menorah Journal*'s commitment to nonpartisanship bore immediate fruit: it became *the* venue both for chronicling the relations among factions within the Jewish community and for discussing the interactions of the American Jews with the nation and the world. Robert Alter spots this dual focus in the journal's advertisements: "The various theological seminaries enumerate the attractions of their programs beneath suitably grim-looking photographs of their buildings; and, on facing pages, *The Dial* announces the first American publication of *The Waste Land,* or the *Yale Review* lists the distinguished critics and writers of fiction among its contributors." These unlikely juxtapositions attest to the journal's unique success in opening its pages to all topics of interest to Jewish intellectuals of the time: "certainly there has been no journal since whose readership has had an equally keen interest both in what was happening within the seminary walls and on the advanced fronts of creative writing" (54).

Beyond the journal's maintenance of a nonpartisan stance lies its intent toward those more loaded terms, *noblesse oblige* and the Jewish "humanities." In practice the terms complement each other, so that the tone of moral uplift in the notion of *noblesse oblige* works in tandem with the broader concept of Jewish humanism to define the basis of the *Menorah* platform. To the founders of the Harvard Menorah Society, cultural humanism, as defined by Victorians such as Matthew Arnold and John Ruskin and as exemplified in many of their own Harvard professors, was a supreme value. They strove, accordingly, to Americanize themselves by demonstrating the humanistic values in Jewish history. This goal contributed to the bourgeois tone and style of the Menorah enterprise and removed it from the concerns of many Yiddishist intellectuals, who inclined much more toward radical political action than did the majority of *Menorah* writers. In this sense, these contributors "present us with the first glimpse of what the American-Jewish amalgamation would be like—less ideological, and motivated by a cerebral interest in things Jewish rather than an emotional one" (Feingold 77).

Imitating the cultured tones of American humanists, the *Menorah* writers unavoidably turned for their self-definition to Arnold's *Culture and Anarchy,* with its argument that culture is based upon a dialectic between Hebraism and Hellenism. Ironically, the dichotomy itself has a Jewish provenance, since Arnold borrowed these terms (as well as the term *Philistine*) from the Jewish poet of the nineteenth century, Heinrich Heine (Super 5.435); he developed his thinking about the terms through discussion with Lady de Rothschild and response to the works and actions of Benjamin Disraeli.[8] With regard to Heine, an aversion to certain aspects of his character tempered Arnold's great admiration for his thought and his poetry. Summing up his views of Heine, Arnold first judges from the perspective of middle-class values: "Not only was he not one of Mr. Carlyle's 'respectable' people, he was profoundly *dis*respectable; and not even the merit of not being a Philistine can make up for a man's being that" (3.131–32). Heine had something vital missing from his character, something

that sounds, ironically, a lot like the moral imperative of "Hebraism":
"that something else was something immense; the old-fashioned, labori-
ous, eternally needful moral deliverance. . . . [Heine had] a deficiency
in self-respect, in true dignity of character" (132). Having lived a "dis-
sipated" life in France and spurned organized religion and middle-class
values, the apostate Jewish poet does not deserve to represent the puritanical outlook that Arnold associates with Hebraism. In the last sentence
of this particular paragraph, though, Arnold switches gears, judging
Heine a supreme poet: "But, such as he is, he is (and posterity too, I am
quite sure, will say this), in the European poetry of that quarter of a century
which follows the death of Goethe, incomparably the most important
figure" (131–32). Joseph Carroll suggests that Arnold's ambivalent evaluation of Heine stems from an anxiety of influence: "Arnold's ultimate
repudiation of Heine frees him from the burden of conscious intellectual dependence and alleviates his fear of suffering under the anguish of
Heine's spiritual suspension. Heine remains, nonetheless, the primary formative influence on Arnold's cultural theory" (Carroll 232–33). By alluding to the "anguish of Heine's spiritual suspension," Carroll also points
up the Jewish experience of betweenness that Arnold would have avoided
instinctively.

In the course of discussing Heine's "Jewish element," Arnold delineates
his predecessor's relationship to Hebraism and Hellenism. First, he notes
that Heine "has excellently pointed out how in the sixteenth century
there was a double renascence,—a Hellenic renascence and a Hebrew
renascence,—and how both have been great powers ever since" (Super 3.127). Then Arnold proceeds to differentiate these two strands in
Heine's own character: "He himself had in him both the spirit of Greece
and the spirit of Judaea; both these spirits reach the infinite, which is the
true goal of all poetry and all art,—the Greek spirit by beauty, the Hebrew spirit by sublimity. By his perfection of literary form, by his love
of clearness, by his love of beauty, Heine is Greek; by his intensity, by his
untamableness, by his 'longing which cannot be uttered,' he is Hebrew"
(127–28). Arnold is right, of course, to read Heine's dichotomy of Hebraism and Hellenism back into his own character, but Arnold idealizes
the interaction between the two terms, thereby pacifying a bitter struggle that for Heine was irresolvable. As Sander Gilman puts it, Heine invoked "a classical world which mirrors the basic human desires and faults
of the poet. The masks that Heine created in search of the classical myth,
those of Hellene and Hebrew, of the exile and death of the gods, are but
extensions of the sick poet's ego" (*Inscribing* 118). When Heine probes
the relationship between Hebraism and Hellenism, he presents it in more
conflictual terms than Arnold is wont to do. In an essay on Shakespeare,

for instance, Heine posits "the enmity that has existed for eighteen centuries between two completely heterogeneous manners of perceiving the world, one of which stemmed from the dry earth of Judea, the other from flowering Greece. Yes, this resentment between Jerusalem and Athens, between the Holy Sepulcher and the cradle of art, between the life in spirit and the spirit in life has lasted eighteen centuries" (cited in *Inscribing* 129).

As a famous man of letters, Heine became another primary figure of Jewish betweenness, inventing from the grounds of his own ambivalence the conflicting images of Hebraism and Hellenism that Jews had to contend with for the subsequent century. Like Spinoza, Heine has held a place in the tiny pantheon of enlightened Jewish figures who have achieved a measure of centrality in Western secular culture; for American Jewish intellectuals, reading (and even translating) Heine became a significant act of self-definition—as major volumes by figures such as Emma Lazarus (1881) and Louis Untermeyer (1937) suggest. As a cultural hero, Heine provided a decisive example for Reznikoff, he reports, in helping him resolve to study law (*MP* 128). Heine remained a compelling figure for later Jews, though, not only because of his success but also because of his failure; like Spinoza's influence, Heine's stems both from his writing and from the double-bind quality of his existential predicament: "Heine not only perceived himself as the absolute outsider but was socially isolated. Unable to assume a position within the dominant society, he removed himself from it. . . . In no little measure his being labeled as a 'Jew,' indeed, in the course of the nineteenth century as "'the Jew,' was the cause of his sense of isolation" (Gilman, *Inscribing* 129). In this sense, Heine was a much more public figure than Reznikoff; likewise, Heine's bitter awareness of his untenable social position informs the many changes of tone in his poetry, while Reznikoff's more private role corresponds to his more modulated tone. Theodor Adorno gives a trenchant account of Heine's alienation and of what Gilman calls his "contaminated pen" in an essay, "Heine the Wound." Calling Heine's poetry "an attempt to draw estrangement itself into the sphere of intimate existence," Adorno contends that, after the triumph of capitalism and the Holocaust, such estrangement has become ubiquitous: "Now that the destiny which Heine sensed has been fulfilled literally, however, the homelessness has also become everyone's homelessness; all human beings have been as badly injured in their beings and their language as Heine the outcast was" (85).[9]

From within his chilling social isolation, Heine turned, like many another modern Jew, toward the patron saint of betweenness, Spinoza. Yovel points out the telling fact that when Heine speaks of Spinoza, his "customary scoffing and mockery, which spared neither himself nor

most of those he admired or agreed with, totally evaporates" (Yovel 2.58).
Heine's worshipful tone shows up in a portrait of Spinoza that Yovel
quotes and paraphrases: "'the spirit of the ancient Hebrew prophets seems
to hover over this distant offspring of theirs' who, in personal purity and
in the crown of thorns he wore on his head, also resembled another divine
parent of his, Jesus Christ" (58). Heine's sarcasm returns, though, when
he describes Spinoza's fall between two stools: "The rabbis, Heine says,
declared Spinoza 'undeserving to carry the name Jew,' yet 'his enemies
were magnanimous enough to leave this name to him.' Heine knows this
experience all too well. Spinoza heralds for him the lot of the modern Jew
who, projected beyond Judaism and Christianity alike, still carries over
with him a new creed, a new earthly route to something resembling redemption" (58–59). Even beyond the arresting image he offers of the
modern Jew, Spinoza's revolutionary philosophy has penetrated to the
heart of Western culture: as Heine claims, "All our contemporary philosophers, perhaps without knowing it, are looking through the eyeglasses
that Baruch Spinoza polished" (52).

   This same image of looking through eyeglasses is used by Marvin Lowenthal, the managing editor of the *Menorah Journal,* to speak of the impact of the Hebraism/Hellenism antinomy on modern Jews.[10] In a searching essay, "On a Jewish Humanism" (1924), he points out that "Western
Jews, whether they have read Arnold or not, look at Judaism through his
bi-focal glasses" (Schwarz 66–67). This dichotomous vision of a culture
split between religion and science, action and art, Jew and Greek, entered
modern Jewish history with the Marrano background of Spinoza and at-
tained memorable formulation in Heine. It becomes in turn a dominant
way of constructing a self-image for modern American Jews, who received it, somewhat ironically, from the pen of Matthew Arnold. In order
to identify humanistic elements in Jewish culture, Lowenthal must turn
to the troubling term *Hebraism* and its *locus classicus* in Arnold's *Culture and
Anarchy.* Rather than quibble about the particulars of Arnold's definition
of "Hebraism," Lowenthal makes a more radical rhetorical move, in effect
deconstructing Arnold's binary opposition by showing how significant
aspects of Jewish experience slip through its grasp: "I discovered that what
I had in mind as a Jewish humanism was rather similar to what Arnold
meant by Hellenism. And I also discovered that the greatest obstacle to
understanding—and what is equally important, to employing—what I
mean by Jewish humanism is Arnold's own conception of Hebraism accepted, as it is, by great bodies of western Jews" (65). Rather than dispute
with Arnold, Lowenthal directs his critique primarily at Western Jews
who acquiesce in embodying Arnold's characterizations. To make these

characterizations explicit, Lowenthal invokes Arnold's succinct formulations: Hellenism is "to get rid of one's ignorance, to see things as they are, and by seeing them as they are to see them in their beauty," while Hebraism is devoted to "strictness of conscience" and is always "aiming at self-conquest and rescue from the thrall of vile affections"; Hellenism is a matter of understanding, Hebraism of action. Although these opposing terms presumably are of equal importance, their disparity comes into view when Lowenthal comments that "Hebraism . . . sounds in Arnold's definition like an old-fashioned medicine—something bitter, unpleasant, but good for one" (66).

Continuing his analysis, Lowenthal shrewdly notes how influential Arnold's formulation of Hebraism has been upon the modern Jewish self-conception, how Jews have accepted as "natural" the traits ascribed to them: "Arnold somewhere makes a point of England's affinity with this Hebraic spirit; one can, with perhaps even closer accuracy, speak of a modern Jewish affinity with this English notion of Hebraism. Western Jews, whether they have read Arnold or not, look at Judaism through his bi-focal glasses" (66–67). Whether looking back toward the *mitzvot,* the duties required of a religious Jew, or forward toward the contemporary Zionist or socialist plans to build a better world, Western Jews have confined themselves to conceiving of Jewish culture along Arnoldian lines as solely "a recipe for action" (67). Contesting this limited definition, a Jewish humanism would change the prescription on Arnold's bifocals by teaching a new "attitude of mind": "This humanism, leisurely acquired and slowly matured, flowers—not, as I have said, in a program, a formula, an enterprise, but—in an attitude of mind. This attitude is at once critical, appreciative, and fructifying. It rises, to begin with, through a disinterested but enthusiastic absorption in Jewish culture, and ultimately from the confrontation of this culture with a series of alien worlds, including the world of today" (68).

Lowenthal's program for Jewish humanism sounds something like the anthropological model of participation-observation in fieldwork, in which the "critical, appreciative" anthropologist endeavors to maintain a "disinterested but enthusiastic absorption" in a foreign culture; ultimately, through ethnography, the foreign culture is placed in a larger perspective that arises from "the confrontation of this culture with a series of alien worlds, including the world of today." In the case of Jewish humanism, the "field" of the participant-observer's investigation is constituted historically rather than geographically. In the nineteenth century, Jewish history loomed as a "new world," whose exploration began with the great European historians of Judaism, such as Leopold Zunz, Heinrich Graetz, and

Simon Dubnow. In Lowenthal's time, the stellar group of historians publishing in the *Menorah Journal* pushed ahead on this heroic work of exploration. If Jewish humanism involves, as I am arguing, a sort of ethnographic
discipline, then its purpose is to cultivate "an attitude of mind . . . at once
critical, appreciative, and fructifying"; in other words, Jewish humanism
becomes a form of perspectivism that teaches one, in Arnold's formulation
of Hellenism, "to see things as they are" by constructing more-inclusive
contexts. Another way of putting this would be to think of Jewish humanism as a form of ethnographic self-regard, in which the "other" is oneself,
and in which identity is achieved only by recognizing the alterity of those
with whom one identifies. This complex self-construction accounts for
many Jewish contributions to modern culture, from the ethnography of
Franz Boas to the ethnopoetics of Jerome Rothenberg.

Lowenthal contends that serious study of Jewish history dispels many
illusions about "Hebraism" as an essence of Jewish experience (69): "This
destruction of habitual notions under the shock of facts is itself a humaniz-
ing process. It is a spiritual calisthenics and limbers not only the mind, but
that dim seat of our deepest instincts, the core of impulse and prejudice
we call the soul" (70). He argues against an "essence" of Judaism or even,
as we saw in Dubnow, an "essence of Jewish history," preferring, like
Reznikoff, to emphasize the huge capacity for change. As Reznikoff will
later do in "Jerusalem the Golden," Lowenthal notes that the very core
of the Jewish religion—the conception of God—has been transformed
over the course of history: "Although Jews in their temples and syna-
gogues today may repeat the same phrases with regard to the unity of God
as their ancestors in the wilderness, even a superficial glance at the records
will reveal a vast and ever-changing difference in what the phrases mean"
(71). And against Dubnow's notion of an essential Jewish history, Lowenthal points out that Jewish history is a record not of the preservation of a
primordial "purity" throughout time but of an ever-changing hybridity.
Furthermore, making a similar point to Veblen's, Lowenthal argues that
this hybridity has benefited Jews by making them into "natural" critics of
the larger worlds in which their communal life has taken place (72–73).

What is "Hebraism," then? Arnold's definition derives from a Jewish
culture he imagines as having exerted its primary influence in the ancient
past; in his own usage, the term refers primarily to the puritanical qualities
of modern British culture. For Lowenthal, conversely, Hebraism represents not merely an ancient ingredient, long dissolved, in the stew that has
simmered for many centuries to form modern Western culture; instead,
it has had a more dynamic existence, developing both inside and outside
Western culture during the latter's entire history: "unlike the Greek and

Roman, [the Jew] has not only been a cultural ancestor, but he has persisted in being a contemporary. He has everywhere been a native—with
a foreign past and the possibility of a foreign future. . . . Because of this
continuous presence yet separation, similarity yet difference, coincidence
yet tangency, his culture becomes for Europe a basis of measurement and
appreciation" (73).

Historically, this "humanistic" appreciation of the merits of a social position both inside and outside Western culture has not been a popular one
and often has taken a large degree of intellectual courage to sustain. In
the nineteenth century, in particular, many prominent thinkers drew the
opposite conclusion from the historical experience of the Jews. Richard
Wagner's infamous remarks in "Judaism in Music" (1850), for instance,
constitute exactly the sort of anti-Semitic slander that Lowenthal seems
intent on refuting. Speaking like the Norman knight in Reznikoff's novel
The Lionhearted, Wagner argues that Jews can never produce great music
or poetry because they will always be foreigners: "The Jew speaks the
language of the nation in whose midst he dwells from generation to generation, but he speaks it always as an alien" (Wagner 84). For Wagner, language expresses the historical development of a nation, a development in
which the Jew cannot take part:

> A language, with its expression and its evolution, is not the work of
> scattered units, but of an historical community: only he who has uncon-
> sciously grown up within the bond of this community, takes also any
> share in its creation. But the Jew has stood outside the pale of any such
> community, stood solitarily with his Jehova in a splintered, soilless stock,
> to which all self-sprung evolution must stay denied, just as even the pe-
> culiar (Hebraic) language of that stock has been preserved for him
> merely as a thing defunct. Now, to make poetry in a foreign tongue has
> hitherto been impossible, even to geniuses of highest rank. Our whole
> European art and civilization, however, have remained to the Jew a for-
> eign tongue; for, just as he has taken no part in the evolution of the one,
> so has he taken none in that of the other; but at most the homeless wight
> has been a cold, nay more, a hostile looker-on.
> (84–85)

Participating in the esthetic upheavals of modernism, Jewish writers
have proven Wagner both right and wrong. It is true that there is something foreign or strange in the language of many of the early twentieth-
century Jewish writers who wrote in European tongues. However, since
one of the major thrusts of modernism has been to undo the fiction of a
"natural" relationship to language such as Wagner assumes, Jewish writers
such as Franz Kafka, Bruno Schulz, and Gertrude Stein have capitalized

upon the marginal positions they occupy within their cultures to create influential models of modernist practice. If the primary experience of the twentieth century has been an oftentimes shocking recognition that each one of us is a "foreigner" in societies that no longer function as self-reinforcing wholes, then Jewish writers have not only contributed important linguistic experiments to modern culture, but have also made their texts represent with great acuity this uncanny perception of being both at home and a stranger within Western culture.

Lowenthal's declaration that "because of this continuous presence yet separation, similarity yet difference, coincidence yet tangency, [Jewish] culture becomes for Europe a basis of measurement and appreciation" has added resonance today because, post–cold war, issues of foreignness and otherness arise with great urgency as we become painfully aware of the shortcomings of nationalism. In *Figures of Conversion: "The Jewish Question" and English National Identity,* Michael Ragussis makes explicit how Jewish culture became such a basis of measurement. He does this by showing that English national identity in the nineteenth century was constructed, in part, through novels featuring Jewish characters, whose conversions or attempted conversions constituted a symbolic narrative of "English" relations to those inside and outside the nation. In addition to being a point of reference for the construction of European nationality, the long Jewish experience of being a nation within another nation, which has made for the conjunctions and disjunctions noted by Lowenthal, can provide historical understanding for other groups whose cultural experience of "similarity yet difference" parallels that of the Jews.[11] For example, a new field of inquiry, diaspora studies, bases its investigations of minority cultures deriving from places such as Africa and India upon terms that were first applied to the Jewish experience. Similarly, in books such as *Insider / Outsider: American Jews and Multiculturalism,* scholars have recently presented the Jewish experience in twentieth-century America as a complex illustration of the difficulties and promise of multiculturalism. Where Wagner boasts that "we good-natured Humanists" have "cast upon" the Jew "a darkness" in order "to make him look less loathly" (82), Lowenthal wants to bring Jewish experience out of obscurity and into the light; for him, the knowledge gained by studying the often difficult adjustments Jews have made to historical contingencies constitutes the very core of humanism:

> It is not, I believe, too much to say that out of reliving this experience, there is born in one an attitude toward these questions today that, in its understanding of what any minority—individual or group—is seeking and suffering, in its sympathy for the claims of the majority, in its knowl-

edge of the many and intricate forms the conflict has taken throughout the centuries, and in its intimate recognition of all the human factors entering the problem, may best be called humanistic. And one will have seen the problem assume so many labels, appeal to so many superhuman sanctions, justify itself with such a diversity of reasons, that a genial skepticism toward the modern equivalents of these ancient dodges is certain to color this new attitude. And this is humanism.
(74)

Reznikoff shares this skepticism toward "superhuman sanctions" and utopian solutions to the "Jewish Question." Beyond this shared attitude, Lowenthal's vision of Jewish humanism as the fruit of a study of Jewish history—and of wisdom, justice, and compassion as the virtues of that humanism—coincides with the burden of a major public poem by Reznikoff, "A Compassionate People" (*CP* 2.59–61), composed in 1944 to commemorate the thirtieth year of the *Menorah Journal*. With their declamatory cadences, the seven stanzas of the poem gather force when read aloud; likewise, the formalized blessing at the end of each stanza gives the poem a liturgical quality that has made it easy to adapt for use in the synagogue as a responsive reading.[12] The first two stanzas begin with a question, "Where is that mountain of which we read in the Bible— / Sinai—on which the Torah was given to Israel?" In the second stanza, Reznikoff hints that the physical location of the mountain cannot be ascertained because

> Sinai was built out of the skeletons
> of much suffering,
> in which the lives of the Israelites
> were like the sands—
> that become in the centuries rock, ledges of rock,
> a mountain, and at last
> the Law,
> cut into tables of stone.
> (2.59)

In this version of Jewish history, written during the Holocaust, the stone tables of the Law can only be found atop the mountain of Jewish suffering; that suffering must be accepted as providing the foundation, and even the height, from which a viable religious vision can be received. From this perspective, it is not surprising that the first four stanzas end in variations on a blessing that thanks God not for wisdom or justice, but for survival: *"Blessed are You, God, King of the Universe, / Who has kept Israel alive."*

Reiterating the contention of the first half of the poem—that the Scriptures arise from exile and persecution—the third stanza asks:

> Where was the Bible written?
> Some of it in Babylon
> where the Jews wept when they remembered Zion;
> exiles among the hosts of Persia,
> to be given away by a nod of a drunken king
> to a Haman for slaughter,
> or, in another whim of the king,
> to be saved by an Esther and a Mordecai.
> Yes, they sang the songs of Zion
> in a strange land,
> even in the land of their captivity.
> *Blessed are You, Lord, God of the Universe,*
> *Who has kept Israel alive.*
> (59)

Here, as we have seen him do before, Reznikoff invokes the weeping exiles of Psalm 137, but he does so in two remarkable ways. First, he calls up the supremely nihilistic Holocaust experience of absolute arbitrariness regarding who is slaughtered and who is saved. Reznikoff does not subscribe to a tragic view of life and death or even to the view that can be inferred from the Book of Job that the arbitrariness of fate still has a divine backing; instead, he portrays a world in which the "whim" of a ruler, rather than either destiny or divine intervention, decides without "reason" between life and death. In such a world, as many Holocaust survivors attest, it is as terrible to be spared as to be annihilated, for both conditions affirm the state of meaninglessness in which life and death wait at the mercy of human whim. Reznikoff gives a second surprising response to Psalm 137 by contradicting it: "Yes, they sang the songs of Zion / in a strange land, / even in the land of their captivity." Again, as in earlier stanzas, he makes the point that the sacred writings of Judaism arise not from an attachment to a sacred land but from exile and suffering. Even out of the terrible experiences of witnessing unprovoked slaughter or of being preserved arbitrarily, the healing quality of the Scriptures takes shape.

In keeping with the emphasis upon cultural survival as an ultimate value, the fifth and sixth stanzas speak of the scattering that follows the decimation of Jewish populations, a scattering that brings new insemination. In the fifth stanza, Reznikoff compares the twin diasporas that occurred after the destruction of the Temple and after the Inquisition to the felling of a great tree, which, when cut down, sends forth its seeds onto the winds and the waves, so that it blossoms and bears fruit "a hundred and a thousandfold" (60). Analogously, the sixth stanza portrays a single man escaping from the Warsaw Ghetto,

> in his heart the word *Jew* burning
> as it burned once in Jeremiah
> when he saw the remnant of Judah
> led captive to Babylon
> or fugitives in Egypt,
> from that man
> shall spring again a people
> as the sands of the sea for number,
> as the stars of the sky.
> *Blessed are You, God of the Universe,*
> *delighting in life.*
> (61)

As before in this poem, Reznikoff places the contemporary experience in the context of Jewish history, comparing the survivor of the Warsaw Ghetto to a prophet and making the same promise to him that God made to Abraham, Isaac, and Jacob.

The last stanza, which ends without the italicized blessing, shows that the sort of survival Reznikoff has in mind entails not mere physical continuity but a transmuting of the suffering undergone through persecution into a form of spiritual wealth:

> Out of the strong, sweetness;
> and out of the dead body of the lion of Judah,
> the prophecies and the psalms;
> out of the slaves in Egypt,
> out of the wandering tribesmen of the deserts
> and the peasants of Palestine,
> out of the slaves of Babylon and Rome,
> out of the ghettos of Spain and Portugal, Germany and Poland,
> the Torah and the prophecies,
> the Talmud and the sacred studies, the hymns and songs of the Jews;
> and out of the Jewish dead
> of Belgium and Holland, of Rumania, Hungary, and Bulgaria,
> of France and Italy and Yugoslavia,
> of Lithuania and Latvia, White Russia and Ukrainia,
> of Czechoslovakia and Austria,

Poland and Germany,
out of the greatly wronged
a people teaching and doing justice;
out of the plundered
a generous people;
out of the wounded a people of physicians;
and out of those who met only with hate,
a people of love, a compassionate people.
(61)

Borrowing the form of a litany of prepositional phrases from the opening section of Walt Whitman's "Out of the Cradle Endlessly Rocking,"
Reznikoff uses it to intone the sites of Jewish disaster and to enumerate
the spiritual treasures that have been converted alchemically from Jewish
suffering. The roll call of nations, particularly in the World War II list,
constitutes both a ritual condemnation and a memorial recollection; from
those sites of distress emerge the precious treasures: the sweetness of the
strong; prophecies and psalms; the Torah and the Talmud and the commentaries; hymns and songs; the teaching and practice of justice; generosity; an abundance of physicians; love and compassion.

Intriguingly, the poem ends not with praise for God but for the variety
of exemplary human virtues, texts, and practices that have been culled
from Jewish history. If Jewish history has an "essence" for Reznikoff, it
can be found here; these praiseworthy goods also overlap significantly
with the "Hebraic" virtues of humanism that Lowenthal celebrates. In
answering the question of why he writes Jewish history, Reznikoff makes
explicit his veneration for such hard-won virtues: "I do not think it sufficient to answer, Because I am one. But because I am one, I am at home
among my people, I think I understand their thoughts and speech better
than those of another people. Nor is this sufficient. The Jews typify, perhaps more than any other people, constant and often victorious struggle
against a hostile environment and hostile elements within itself, a struggle
which has constantly evolved Jews that are symbols of the admirable"
(Sharp, "Reznikoff's *Nine Plays*" 272–73).

Reznikoff's commitment to Jewish history was a central feature he
shared with the humanism of the *Menorah* writers. By engaging in historiography, they began to discover the tremendous variety of situations in
which Jews have lived, and with that discovery came a salutary perspectivism. Likewise, as Reznikoff shows, an immersion in Jewish history can
have a consolatory value, creating a hedge against despair. Speaking specifically of Lowenthal's essay, Alter notes, "A Jewish humanism, then,

would break down all of our petrified reductionist conceptions of the nature of Jewishness; the inquiring Jew would discover a collective history that was immensely richer than any simple program of commitment or rejection could possibly conceive" (53). Upon the basis of such historical discoveries, Jewish humanists could argue for a vision not only of a heterogeneous Jewish culture but also, by analogy, of a heterogeneous American culture in which a Jewish culture might flourish. Such a historical project formed the background of the cultural pluralism enunciated in the pages of the journal by Horace Kallen, Randolph Bourne, and John Dewey.

It is worthwhile to think in larger terms about the signal recourse to history by Reznikoff and the other *Menorah* writers. To extend Dubnow's idea that studying Jewish history ought to replace the study of Talmud, we could assert that writing history became for these intellectuals something akin to an alternative form of commentary. The classic way of reconciling the Jewish past with the present involves commenting upon earlier Jewish texts—pulling a thread from the fabric of tradition and embroidering it in such a way that it speaks to present concerns. In poems such as *In Memoriam: 1933* and "A Compassionate People," Reznikoff reverses the hermeneutic ratio; he uses Jewish history to comment upon contemporary events, making the "proof texts" be first the Nazi accession to power and initial persecution of German Jews and then the broader experience of the Holocaust. In *Zakhor: Jewish History and Jewish Memory,* cited at the beginning of this chapter, Yerushalmi sums up the crucial role that history has come to play for modern Jews:

> The modern effort to reconstruct the Jewish past begins at a time that witnesses a sharp break in the continuity of Jewish living and hence also an ever-growing decay of Jewish group memory. In this sense, if for no other, history becomes what it had never been before—the faith of fallen Jews. For the first time history, not a sacred text, becomes the arbiter of Judaism. Virtually all nineteenth-century Jewish ideologies, from Reform to Zionism, would feel a need to appeal to history for validation. Predictably, "history" yielded the most varied conclusions to the appellants.
> (86)

The ability of history to answer, as Scripture does, to multiple interpretations makes it receptive to inventive commentary—which modern Jews have performed on their collective past for a wide variety of purposes. Over and over during the course of his career, Reznikoff returned to major events in Jewish history in the way that a midrashic commentator recurs to passages of Scripture, hoping to weave an identity for modern Jews by knotting present events—especially calamities—to earlier moments. As a body, the *Menorah* writers used history to help establish an American group identity in two general ways: they shed a new, "objective" light upon events that still remained in the collective memory—thus reauthorizing them; and they set Jewish actors and populations in direct relation to other agents and peoples that have received extensive historiographical treatment. Both results of the turn to history depend upon the fundamental discursive claim that historiography makes: its subjects have a *place* in history. In other words, writing history represents an active response to finding oneself between two stools. As the *Menorah* writers probed many of the fascinating and long-forgotten avenues of Jewish history, an underlying vision emerged, which might be articulated as follows: having occurred in every time, place, and cultural situation imaginable, Jewish history is boundlessly heterogeneous; therefore, an America that is beginning to recognize itself as culturally plural can turn to the Jews for the premier example of living under culturally plural conditions. Deep down, *Menorah* writers such as Horace Kallen believed that if America would fully embrace its cultural pluralism, it would come to see the Jews as representative Americans.

HEBRAISM AND AMERICANISM

Like many *Menorah* figures, Horace Kallen (1882–1974) gravitated instinctively toward the Hebraism/Hellenism dichotomy in his attempt to articulate a space for Jews in American culture. For Kallen, who referred to himself as an "atheistic humanist" (Schmidt, "Zionism" 36), Hebraism represents Jewish culture minus the "Judaist" religion; his form of Jewish humanism is among the most radically secular of those enunciated in the *Menorah Journal.* To overturn the implicit hierarchy of Hellenism over Hebraism, Kallen pursues a different course from that taken by Lowenthal; rather than deconstructing the dichotomy, Kallen reconfigures Hebraism to align it with the philosophy of pluralism invented by his teacher, William James. Out of this union of Hebraism with pluralism, Kallen develops the concept of cultural pluralism, a concept that has had greatly renewed influence in the past thirty years. Arising from a conflation of the American ideals of equality and self-determination with a reconfigured Hebraism, Kallen's philosophy was an attempt not to essentialize Jewish history but to essentialize the experience of betweenness itself.

Born in 1882 in Berenstadt, a town in Silesia (then Germany, now Poland), Horace Kallen was the eldest son of Berenstadt's assistant rabbi. When Horace was about five years old, his father took the family to Bos-

ton, where he became rabbi of a German-speaking Orthodox congregation. Home-schooled in an Orthodox manner by his father until he was
eight or nine, Kallen also attended Hebrew schools (Konvitz 16–17). His
stringent Orthodox upbringing initiated him into a culture from which
he would continue to draw support and against which he would cease-
lessly rebel. As he himself notes, normative Judaism provided a template
for his later formulations of Americanism: "It is upon the foundation and
against the background of my Jewish cultural milieu that my vision of
America was grown" (Schmidt, "Zionism" 33). In his father's view, however, Horace's adaptations to America were not only unnecessary but
counterproductive, for the Jewish world was all that mattered; he intended for his son to become a rabbi. At this the son rebelled, running
away from home several times. In later life, Kallen recalls the conflict: "I
never could make my devout and learned and very snobbish father . . .
[—] too powerful, too demanding, to be idealized, to be anything but
feared and dodged and hated—understand the why of these truancies"
(34–35). Summing up his attitude toward his father, he states, "My father
was a strict man; I didn't like him" (Konvitz 17).

What took the place of his father's restrictive Orthodoxy in the young
Kallen's mind was a romantic panorama of American history, itself fraught
with ideological suppositions of which the eager "convert" was unaware:
"I saw a pious and heroic generation of Puritans making their righteous
and providential way . . . against devilish and blood-thirsty redskins. . . . I
saw their descendants, a heroic and embattled handful of lovers of liberty"
(Schmidt, "Zionism" 33). Looking back on this time, Kallen notes with
irony how easily, under the influence of the public school, his allegiance
to Jewish ideals was transferred to American ones:

> In our household the suffering and slavery of Israel were commonplaces
> of conversation; from Passover to Passover, freedom was an ideal cere-
> monially reverenced, religiously aspired to. The textbook story of the
> Declaration of Independence came upon me, nurtured upon the deliv-
> erance from Egypt and the bondage of exile, like the clangor of trum-
> pets, like a sudden light. What a resounding battle cry of freedom! And
> then, what an invincible march of Democracy to triumph over every
> enemy—over the English king, over the American Indian, over the un-
> civilized Mexican, over the American champions of slavery betraying
> American freedom, over everything, to the very day of the history
> lesson.
> (34)

Freedom and democracy: these were the ideals of the American civil
religion, a youthful faith whose expansiveness and celebration of individual initiative seemed to offset the unyielding restrictiveness, dutifulness,

and deference to elders that the boy perceived in his father's religion. In effect, Kallen's allegiance gradually shifted from one chosen people to another. Not surprisingly, Spinoza was a catalyst in this metamorphosis, for in his last year of high school Kallen happened upon his father's German edition of Spinoza's *Theological-Political Treatise:* "It set me free. . . . His image, his thought, and his story became the point of no return in the ongoing alienation from my father and the ancestral religion. I identified with Spinoza" (Klingenstein, *Academy* 36). With this identification, Kallen rejected both his father *and* his father's religion in favor of secular knowledge and a de-theologized politics. His nascent Americanism and the liberating example of Spinoza helped the immigrant boy overcome the authority of old-world Judaism: "In the Oversoul of Emerson . . . and in the God of Spinoza . . . , I found weapons with which to confound the Jehovah of my father and his rule" (Schmidt, "Zionism" 35).

Turning his back on Judaism and his father's rule, Kallen embarked upon an academic career. He went first to Harvard University, studying philosophy with George Santayana and William James and American literature with Barrett Wendell. After he graduated in 1903, he spent two years as an instructor in English at Princeton University, where he was denied reappointment when it was learned that he was Jewish. Following this unsettling experience, Kallen eagerly returned to Harvard for graduate work, writing his doctoral dissertation under James's direction. So impressed was James with his student that at his death he left the unfinished manuscript for his book *Some Problems in Philosophy* for Kallen to complete. At Harvard, Kallen was employed as a lecturer and an assistant to James, Santayana, and Josiah Royce. In 1907, while still a graduate student, he received a fellowship for study in Europe, which took him to Oxford to work under the pragmatist F. C. S. Schiller and to Paris to attend lectures by Henri-Louis Bergson. After receiving his degree in 1908, Kallen spent the next couple of years lecturing at Harvard and at Clark University (where he met Sigmund Freud). Then, in 1911, he took a position at the University of Wisconsin, but resigned in 1918 over issues of academic freedom. In 1919 he was invited to join the founding faculty of the New School for Social Research in New York City, which included Thorstein Veblen and John Dewey; he remained there until he retired (Konvitz 17–18).

While Kallen was a graduate student at Harvard, he participated in the founding of the Menorah Society, contributing its motto, "for the study and promotion of Hebraic culture and ideals." In a retrospective article on "The Promise of the Menorah Idea" (1962), Kallen explains why the term *Hebraic* was used: "The reason lay . . . in the English tradition of comparing and contrasting Hebraism with Hellenism. Further, there was a certain anxiety lest 'Jewish' or 'Judaic' should imply a disproportionate concern with Judaist creeds and codes, instead of concern with a comprehensive humanism which would take in every aspect of the Jewish heritage, not the religious alone" (13). This anxiety about appearing "too Jewish" was not only directed toward a religious/secular divide among the Jewish students; it also reflected pressures from without. The Harvard authorities, for instance, gave the Menorah Society a hearty welcome that showed more than a little sense of relief, since the group promised to help alleviate some of the "symptoms" of Jewish particularism. Kallen reports that "President Eliot welcomed the Society as being one more expression of the Harvard endeavor 'to search for truth in freedom,' and as marking the end of the self-isolation of the Jewish student body. He urged his Jewish listeners to fight the ghetto's handicaps of inferior physique, to rid themselves of a peculiar nervousness—Richard Cabot of the Harvard Medical School had classified it as 'Hebraic debility'—and to do something about the new trends toward criminal behavior then becoming noticeable in New York."[13] Apparently, the Harvard authorities had as great an interest in the success of this group as the students had in cultivating the goodwill of their professors and administrators. (It would be easy to identify analogies between this instance of providing both support and control for a group of socially dangerous students and the forms of coercive tolerance now applied to the campus life of African-American students.) To show their support for the Menorah Society and to subtly provide it with direction, President Eliot and many other prominent professors addressed the group: "At different times—I name only those I knew personally—Barrett Wendell, George Santayana, David Gordon Lyon, George Foot Moore, discussed one or another aspect of 'Hebraic culture and ideals' at Menorah gatherings" (14).

One of these professors in particular exercised a remarkable sway over the intellectual and social life of Horace Kallen. Barrett Wendell, a Boston Brahmin possessing Tory views and an impeccable New England pedigree, was a pioneer in the study of American literature and a lifelong influence upon this liberal Jewish immigrant. In Wendell's books, according to his biographer, "he constantly spoke of Americans of 'the better sort,' meaning those upon whom the advantages of breeding and education had bestowed a position of social superiority" (Howe 6); Wendell was also "fond of using the word 'gentleman,' and prepared to accept equally the privileges and the responsibilities implied in the term" (6). This classconsciousness was as much in evidence in Wendell's lifelong friendship with the conservative senator Henry Cabot Lodge as it was in his insistence that Kallen, too, accept his own privileges and responsibilities. As a man secure in his awareness of class privilege and responsibility (that is, possessed of *noblesse oblige*), Wendell incited Kallen's own self-acceptance. When Kallen had entered college, he was aware, he says, "that my Jewish difference, even if it was only a seeming difference, yet could and did cripple my strivings for a life and a living," and so he had resolved to "look and act and talk like the model of my choice." In other words, as he puts it, "I could 'pass.' What then was the point of not-passing, of suffering the lameness that not-passing entailed?" (Kallen, "Promise" 10).

With his heightened awareness of class and "racial" differences, Wendell was not fooled by Kallen's performance. Rather than publicly expose his student as an impostor, however, Wendell sought to make Kallen accept his Jewish "difference" and to regard it as a virtue, based upon the fact that it had played, in Wendell's opinion, a significant part in the formation of the American character. In a course on the literary history of America, Wendell persisted in confronting Kallen, until he broke through the latter's cosmopolitan mien. As Kallen reports it, "He showed how the Old Testament had affected the Puritan mind, traced the role of the Hebraic tradition in the development of the American character. I wrote a paper challenging that entire position. . . . [H]e went over that essay with me, paragraph by paragraph, and somehow I began to see the whole thing in a different perspective and everything that I had been shutting out . . . turned back" (Schmidt, "Zionism" 38). Years later, in 1916, Kallen fictionalized this "conversion" (Kallen, *Judaism* 66) through the medium of a character named Simon, one of whose friends tells the story:

> His "Americanism" had, he discovered, unconscious origins and roots. Its beginnings were nourished by a tradition that he despised, because belonging to it had hurt him. . . . At first he wouldn't endure the notion that Americanism owed anything to the Hebraic tradition; he used to spend long hours elaborating dialectic to prove it wasn't so. . . . The professor knew his history, you see. He told him that he was really a coward and a sham, passing as something that he really wasn't. He told him that he was disgracing a great tradition. He told him the meaning of *noblesse oblige* for Jews. Simon was dumbfounded. He had had no idea that he might be cutting so poor a figure in the eyes of others.
> (Kallen, *Judaism* 64–65)

Again, the term *noblesse oblige* makes a striking appearance—although it is impossible to know if it was actually used by Wendell in 1902 or if, in 1916, Kallen was employing a term taken from Dubnow or a term made newly prominent in the 1915 statement of intent of the *Menorah Journal*. Setting aside the provenance of specific terms, I suspect that this fictional-

ized treatment, twice distanced by being presented as the experience of
one fictional character told by another, gives a fairly accurate account of
the dramatic turn by which Hebraism became for Kallen a privileged form
of Americanism.

As the instigator of this conversion, Wendell attacked Kallen with an
unbeatable one-two punch: first he shamed the Jewish student by dis-
robing him of his masquerade, and then he offered the naked foreigner a
way of regaining his dignity by cloaking his circumcised difference in the
robes of the Americanism he worshipped. This climactic attack proved to
be the central moment in Kallen's intellectual development. In one stroke,
Wendell seemingly resolved Kallen's guilt and self-hatred by converting
them into patriotism and nationalism. Wendell's intervention made it
possible for Kallen to imagine the early American puritans as Zionists *avant
la lettre:* "For the democracy of America had its first articulate voicing in
the Pilgrim Fathers and the Puritans of New England. These men and
women, devoted to the literature of the Old Testament, and upheld by
the ancestral memories of the Jews, were moved to undertake their great
American adventure by the ideal of nationality" (Kallen, "Nationality"
81). When comparing Puritans to Zionists, however, Kallen had to ac-
knowledge that the Puritan effort "to realize their national genius in their
own individual way" meant becoming not more Jewish but more English;
as he admits, "Their English manners, English speech, English history, and
English loyalty were, in fact, more important to them than their Hebrew
Bible" (81). Ultimately, though, Kallen wants to see Jewish and English
nationality as equivalents, and so he ascribes both of them to the Puritans:
"Hebraism and English nationality—these are the spiritual background of
the American commonwealth" (82).[14]

Here is where the double binds in Kallen's life experience can be seen
most clearly to influence his ways of thinking. On the one hand, he tries
to unite "Hebraism and English nationality" as the core values of the
American character, while on the other he invents cultural pluralism as a
means of fighting off the assimilation of Jewish ethnicity to an Anglo-
Saxon ideal. There is no question that Kallen wants to have it both ways:
he wishes to preserve a Jewish "difference" while refashioning Jewish culture in an American image. In the first declaration of cultural pluralism,
articulated in his essay "Democracy Versus the Melting-Pot" (1915), Kallen finds his synthesis of Hebraism and Americanism under attack by nativism. Against the alarm expressed at the effects of unlimited immigration
by a revived Ku Klux Klan and by racist writers such as E. A. Ross and
Madison Grant, Kallen argues that cultural diversity represents not a liabil-
ity but a strength in American culture. He fears that the popular symbol of

the melting pot denies the specific contribution of Hebraism to American nationalism, that it plays into the hands of his antagonists by implicitly authorizing the effacement of ethnic differences and by enforcing assimilation to an Anglo-Saxon ideal. In place of the melting pot, a term that was invented, ironically, by the Anglo-Jewish writer Israel Zangwill, Kallen offers a countersymbol, the orchestra, to evoke the notion of ethnic groups as separate instruments contributing to the overall symphony of American culture: "As in an orchestra every type of instrument has its specific *timbre* and *tonality,* founded in its substance and form; as every type has its appropriate theme and melody in the whole symphony, so in society; each ethnic group may be the natural instrument, its temper and culture may be its theme and melody and the harmony and dissonances and discords of them all may make the symphony of civilization" (Kallen, *Culture* 124–25).[15]

Some American Jewish writers, such as Henry Roth and Grace Paley, have incorporated cultural pluralism directly into their works. In "The Rail," the last chapter of *Call It Sleep* (1934), Roth stages exactly the sort of "symphony" of ethnic voices that Kallen imagines. As David, the young Jewish protagonist, proceeds to toss a milk dipper on a rail for a near-fatal electric shock, Roth weaves together twenty pages of voices representing all of the ethnic groups vying for position in the first decades of the twentieth century. At the climactic moment, when the incandescent shock blasts through David, the people whose voices we've been hearing are startled and express their consternation, each in his or her own accent:

> "W'at?
>> "W'ut?
>>> "Va-at?
>>>> "Gaw blimey!
>>> "W'atsa da ma'?" . . .
>>> "Hey!"
> "Jesus!"
> "Give a look! Id's rain—"
>>> "Shawt soicit, Mack—"
>>> "Mary, w'at's goin'—"
>>>> "Schloimee, a blitz like—"
>>>> "Hey mate!"

(419–20)

In the midcentury stories of Grace Paley's *Enormous Changes at the Last Minute* (1974), women with Italian, Irish, Jewish, WASP, Hispanic, and African-American backgrounds encounter one another over issues pertaining to child-rearing and politics. Sometimes these women create momentary utopian spaces in which their clearly articulated differences achieve a harmony of mutual acknowledgment. Paley's loving portrayal of ethnic differences and accommodations delicately fulfills Kallen's faith that "the harmony and dissonances and discords of them all may make the symphony of civilization."

From the perspective of American Jewish intellectuals of his own generation, Kallen's conflation of Hebraism and Americanism functioned as, in the words of Susanne Klingenstein, an "ingenious reconciliation of two heretofore mutually exclusive affiliations" (*Academy* 51). This sort of unstable synthesis was crucial in empowering American Jews to mitigate both the effects of anti-Semitism and its offspring, self-hatred—that is, to begin to accept themselves as Jews and find acceptance as Americans. As Klingenstein points out, Kallen showed how an American Jew could take a decisive step beyond the earlier formulation of Y. L. Gordon: "be a man abroad, a Jew at home." Rabbi Mordecai Kaplan, founder of that quintessentially American form of Judaism, Reconstructionism, characterized Kallen this way: "I have always regarded you as the foremost creative American Jewish thinker who demonstrates by actual example that it is possible to live with distinction synchronously in two civilizations" (Schmidt, "Kallen" 76). Although angles of attack exist through which Kallen's philosophy dissolves into a pile of logical inconsistencies, sending the philosopher into an ideological pratfall, this vulnerability may not be so surprising in an influential ideologue of the condition of betweenness.[16] Kallen's restless repositioning of the concept of Hebraism illustrates dramatically the tensions at work in Jewish intellectuals' endeavors, during the teens and twenties, to open a space for themselves within a resistant American culture.

Unlike the Jewish fiction writers, the Objectivists did not make cultural pluralism an explicit theme of their writing, but the example of Horace Kallen is pertinent to a discussion of the conflation of Hebraism and Americanism in their work. In Reznikoff's case, this fusion takes place especially in his historical writings (both poetry and prose). In the prose *Testimony,* for instance, published like *Call It Sleep* in 1934 and dedicated to Louis Zukofsky, he selects for narration episodes from American law cases that often express cultural conflicts. Through scenes pertaining to Southern slavery, marine commerce, and rural violence in the East and West, he portrays wandering, exile, and arbitrary persecution—ills that characterize much of Jewish history—as suffered by Americans of the lower classes.[17] Filled as it is with obsessive depictions of accidental and premeditated violence, the American text of *Testimony* (in each of its several forms)

forms a direct precursor to Reznikoff's last book of poems, *Holocaust*. For Reznikoff, Kallen, and many other American Jews, the vast and unruly tapestry of American social experience provides a fluid plane upon which to project Jewish concerns, thereby making these concerns American ones (and vice versa).

Nowhere has this conflation of Hebraism and Americanism been more fruitful or more influential than in Hollywood, where Jewish studio heads, producers, directors, and writers have created a mythic American history that encodes values conducive to the acceptance of Jews—values such as admiring outsiders, rooting for underdogs, condemning persecution, and rewarding individual initiative over class privilege.[18] In 1938 and 1939, Reznikoff worked in Hollywood, developing ideas for screenplays with his old friend, the producer Albert Lewin (1894–1967), but he could not make its values his own.[19] As his letters and poems from that period demonstrate, Reznikoff was decidedly uncomfortable in the West Coast myth-making factory. His "Autobiography: Hollywood" contains twenty-seven short poems that comment ironically upon the unreal world, constructed mainly by Jewish immigrants, that was peopled by the "stars" upon whom the disempowered projected their fantasies:

> *Rainy Season*
> It has been raining for three days.
> The faces of the giants
> on the bill-boards
> still smile,
> but the gilt has been washed from the sky:
> we see the iron world.
> (*CP* 2.41)

Reznikoff splashes cold water upon the illusions created by Hollywood and advertising, exposing the implacable, manufactured apparatus behind the enticing images. In another poem in the series, he comments upon the mythical aspect of the movies by portraying one of the "starlets":

> The Greeks would have made a myth about you, my fine girl,
> and said a god, because of this indifference,
> because you walk away quickly, turning
> your beautiful head with its sleek black hair away,
> changed you into the starling that flies with angry cries
> from branch to branch
> after the indifferent passer-by.
> (2.42)

Like Athena in the poem "Hellenist," this "Greek" apparition displays her scorn for the Jewish onlooker. In this case, though, the "passer-by" fantasizes his revenge in the form of a metamorphosis in which the starlet becomes a starling, her earlier indifference repaid by that of the scorned passer-by.

For Reznikoff, there is a correct Jewish way to conduct oneself within the "Greek" mythical world of Hollywood. This Jewish way, though, has nothing to do with the conspicuous style of "success" achieved by his mentor Lewin or by Lewin's mentor Irving Thalberg. In an exquisitely ironic poem, Reznikoff presents his own negative triumph in Hollywood:

> The flies are
> flying about
> and about
> the middle of the room—
> jerkily
> in geometrical figures:
> what are they trying to prove—
> my guardian angels?
>
> I have said good morning to the man at the door,
> good morning to the man polishing the stairs.
> Seated in my arm-chair,
> on a cushion,
> I, the shepherd, stare at my flock—
> ten flies.
> I came penniless
> and found only a few,
> never bothered my head about them,
> did not pay them,
> neither gave them to eat or to drink
> nor even spoke to them,
> and, look!
> I shall cross the Jordan with at least twelve flies,
> maybe, twelve times twelve:
> how unworthy am I
> of all this generosity!
>
> I have become poor, it seems:
> my flies are gone—except one

flying jerkily
about the room.
You do not buzz, my fly:
deep in thought, no doubt.
That is well.
I, too, am learning how to be silent,
and have learnt long ago how to be alone.
(2.43–44)

In Reznikoff's Hollywood, the most important tasks of the day consist of acknowledging the invisible people, "the man at the door" and "the man polishing the stairs," who have been rendered as insignificant as flies by the aristocracy of glamour that rules their world. Although Reznikoff is plainly aware of his own insignificant status (he complains in the poem preceding this one of a director who "managed to give me only his fingers / when we were introduced" [2.43]), he reserves a more profoundly ironical role for himself in this poem—that of the Jewish patriarch whose "flock" consists only of flies.[20] The ironical effect is heightened by the mock-biblical diction of phrases like "neither gave them to eat or to drink." In keeping with the greatest American poem about flies, Emily Dickinson's "I heard a Fly buzz—when I died," Reznikoff subdues the comic mood in the last stanza. In Dickinson's poem, the portentous moment of death is disturbed by the buzz of a fly, which "interposed . . . Between the light—and me" (Dickinson 112), so that a living vibration seems to counteract briefly the process of slipping into death. Reznikoff inverts the conflict between the buzzing fly and the dying speaker of Dickinson's poem by rendering the fly silent and discovering a kinship between fly and human. In this way, he underscores his own utter insignificance as well as the compensatory virtues arising from it: knowing how to be silent and how to be alone. Although these virtues are born of necessity, they are virtues just the same; they could have been included in the litany of treasures in "A Compassionate People," for these virtues, too, have been learned through long years of Jewish misfortune. Like Kallen, Reznikoff finds ways to unite Hebraism and Americanism, but rather than taking the high road of promulgating a philosophy of cultural pluralism, Reznikoff shares the low road of silence and loneliness with "the man at the door" and "the man polishing the stairs."

FOUR

SINCERITY AND OBJECTIVISM

"THE JEWISH SPIRIT IN
MODERN AMERICAN POETRY"

In the twenties, aspiring poets found extremely few models of modern
Jewish poetry in English—particularly if, like Oppen and Zukofsky, they
valued "sincerity" over nostalgia, sentimentality, or moral uplift. The pau-
city of strong poets is evident, for instance, in a 1921 article for the *Menorah
Journal,* "The Jewish Spirit in Modern American Poetry," written by poet,
critic, and anthologist Louis Untermeyer. A look at two of the poets he
treats and the terms in which he discusses their work will give us a fair
sense of where Reznikoff stood in relation to other Jewish modernists in
America. In keeping with the identity politics of the time, Untermeyer
professes an interest in detecting the "racial characteristics" (121) in contemporary American Jewish poets; he does so primarily by loosely corre-
lating their work with particular biblical qualities. The poets accorded
this attention include James Oppenheim, Alter Brody, Lola Ridge (non-
Jewish author of *The Ghetto and Other Poems* [1918]), Maxwell Bodenheim, Babette Deutsch, Florence Kiper Frank, Untermeyer, and his wife,
Jean Starr Untermeyer. The poet whom Untermeyer values highest,
James Oppenheim (1882–1932), could hardly provide more of a contrast
to Reznikoff's plain style.[1] Oppenheim grew up in New York City, attended Columbia University from 1901 to 1903, and then became a social worker, a muckraking novelist, an early popularizer of psychoanalysis,
and a founding editor of the important, though short-lived, review *The
Seven Arts.* Speaking of his poetry, Untermeyer claims that Oppenheim's

"literary ancestry can be found in the psalms of David, the denunciations of Jeremiah, the confident fervors of Isaiah." In addition to that distant ancestry, Walt Whitman and Sigmund Freud provide more direct influences. Untermeyer sums up his sketch of Oppenheim by saying that "his books read like the work of a challenging minor prophet with (and here is Oppenheim's response to modernity) a flair for analysis" (122). Oppenheim's effusive, didactic style can be seen in "Let Nothing Bind You," a poem from his most acclaimed book, *Songs for the New Age* (1914):

> Let nothing bind you:
> If it is Duty, away with it.
> If it is Law, disobey it.
> If it is Opinion, go against it . . .
>
> There is only one Divinity: Yourself.
> Only one God: You . . .
>
> Beware that you worship no false idols:
> Take no crust of manners or whimsical desires,
> No surface-lusts and frailties,
> For the real You hidden down beneath:
> But dig . . .
> Dig with shovel of will and engine of love and passion,
> When the lonely day drags toward the lonelier night,
> When betrayal and malice trip you and throw you on yourself,
> Dig down to Self, and set God free . . .
>
> Bethink yourself!
> God is the Life surging forward creatively,
> The swimmer in space whipping up a foam of stars:
> Clear your little channel for him . . .
> He is you . . .
>
> Then, shall a law be greater than God,
> Shall an opinion shrink him,
> A duty stay him?
>
> Forth! Let nothing bind you!
> (Oppenheim 5–6 [ellipses in the original])

With its "prophetic" voice and Whitmanian bluster, this poem reads like an uncanny precursor to Allen Ginsberg. In fact, one erotico/mystical line, "The swimmer in space whipping up a foam of stars," sounds as if

Ginsberg could have written it. What Oppenheim lacks, though, is Ginsberg's "nakedness," the self-deflating glimpses of loneliness, desire, and anguish that earn a reader's sympathy as a counterpoint to the vatic pronouncements. Placed in the context of today's popular culture, Oppenheim's poetry can't help but produce a shudder of recognition, for myriad "Songs for the New Age" crowd the book racks. The iconoclasm, the hortatory tone, the self-aggrandizement, the effusive rhetoric of pop psychology and pop mysticism are unmistakable. If this represents the blend of Judaism and modernism appropriate to the "New Age" (the teens and twenties)—a blend in which the only noticeably Jewish element is the command to "worship no false idols"—then Reznikoff and the other Objectivists would emphatically reject it. The rhetorical animus against "duty" and "law" in Oppenheim's poem has little real force because it empties out the tension inherent in the conflict between Judaism and modernism, a tension Reznikoff assiduously maintains in verses like the following:

> A hundred generations, yes, a hundred and twenty-five,
> had the strength each day
> not to eat this and that (unclean!)
> not to say this and that,
> not to do this and that (unjust!),
> and with all this and all that
> to go about
> as men and Jews
> among their enemies
> (these are the Pharisees you mocked at, Jesus).
> Whatever my grandfathers did or said
> for all of their brief lives
> still was theirs,
> as all of its drops at a moment make the fountain
> and all of its leaves a palm.
> Each word they spoke and every thought
> was heard, each step and every gesture seen,
> by God;
> their past was still the present and the present
> a dread future's.
> But I am private as an animal.
> (*CP* 2.25)

In this stanza from a longer poem celebrating the faith, sanctity, tenacity, solidarity, and self-acceptance of traditional Jews, Reznikoff marks a dramatic turnaround with his concluding line. By looking at himself as if from the perspective of a traditional Jew, he enhances the tension between tradition and modernity. Where tradition provides an all-encompassing wholeness that unites the observant Jew with the entire Jewish community (past, present, and future) and with God, the modern Jew, by contrast, forfeits both this vast communal solidarity and his status as a righteous human being. In the next stanza, Reznikoff elaborates upon this self-accusatory view by confessing, "I have left the highway like a dog / to run into every alley." This sort of self-examination, which takes into account not only the heady freedom of modernism but also the historical layers that undergird and create conflict within a modern American Jew, seems infinitely more compelling than the facile freedom and rebellion urged upon the reader of Oppenheim's poem.

Nonetheless, like Ginsberg forty years later, Oppenheim cut an imposing literary figure from the teens to the thirties. To some extent this can be explained by his energetic pursuit of a variety of activities beyond poetry. The Library of Congress lists twenty-one books by James Oppenheim, many of them novels or collections of short stories of social protest, and several of them early treatments of psychologists such as Freud and Jung. His stories were regarded highly enough to be included in *The Best Short Stories* of 1920 and 1922. He was a fixture of Greenwich Village and close to the influential Jewish critics Waldo Frank and Paul Rosenfeld, with whom he founded *Seven Arts,* and he edited a posthumous volume by his friend Randolph Bourne. Oppenheim thought of himself primarily as a poet, though, and Untermeyer enthusiastically endorsed his ambitions—not only in the *Menorah Journal* article but also in a critical book, *The New Era in American Poetry* (1919). For Untermeyer, Oppenheim represents the major recipient of the Whitman legacy: no one else has carried Whitman's "vision or his philosophy to its natural social (and even psychical) conclusion. Only one poet has attempted it thoroughly. And James Oppenheim, starting from the Whitman foundation, has reared his own imposing and native structure" (42). Of the Jewish spirit in Oppenheim's poetry, Untermeyer exults, "Here one sees no placid, intangible Jehovah, but a God working among men; the toiling Infinite, the Deity in overalls" (51). Untermeyer's high estimate of Oppenheim's stature was shared widely enough that in 1934, a year after Oppenheim died, he still provided the available yardstick against which Charles Reznikoff would be measured. Writing on Reznikoff's Objectivist Press book, *In Memoriam: 1933,* for the *Saturday Review,* William Rose Benét proclaims of Reznikoff, "He seems to me the best of the definitely Jewish poets writing today, since the death of James Oppenheim" (571).

In his *Menorah Journal* article and in his book, Untermeyer lauds another Jewish poet who has more affinities with Reznikoff. A nearly exact contemporary of Reznikoff's, Alter Brody (1895–1981) was born in Russia and came to New York when he was eight. Contrasting Brody with Oppenheim, Untermeyer states, "Brody does not use the Biblical-Whitmanian sonority dear to Oppenheim; he employs the condensed *vers libre* of the Imagists varied with a kind of heightened prose" ("Jewish Spirit" 125). Unlike the boisterous exhortations of Oppenheim, Brody's writing sounds a keynote of lamentation, conveying a sense of wreckage and loss without the solace of explanation or belief. Although he published poetry, plays, and abundant journalism in major magazines and anthologies, Brody collected his work in only two books, both fairly early: *A Family Album and Other Poems* (1918) and *Lamentations: Four Folk-Plays of the American Jew* (1928). Brody's plays, which often contrast Jewish life in New York City to the life left behind in Russia, gained wide performance by Yiddish theater groups; in keeping with the tone of lamentation, they embody feelings of distress, disappointment, anger, bitterness, and mourning. One of his most frequently cited poems makes explicit his central thematic concerns:

Lamentations

In a dingy kitchen
Facing a Ghetto backyard
An old woman is chanting Jeremiah's Lamentations,
Quaveringly,
Out of a Hebrew Bible.

The gaslight flares and falls. . . .

This night,
Two thousand years ago,
Jerusalem fell and the Temple was burned.
Tonight
This white-haired Jewess
Sits in her kitchen and chants—by the banks of the Hudson—
The Lament of the Prophet.

The gaslight flares and falls. . . .

Nearby,
Locked in her room,
Her daughter lies on a bed convulsively sobbing.

Her face is dug in the pillows;
Her shoulders heave with her sobs—
The bits of a photograph lie on the dresser. . . .
(*Family Album* 36 [ellipses in the original])

Of this poem Untermeyer observes, "In spite of his objective attitude, suffering and seclusion find a new voice in his lines" ("Jewish Spirit" 125). This statement could just as aptly describe Reznikoff's accomplishment, although Reznikoff (whose first book also appeared in 1918) portrays "suffering and seclusion" even more strikingly through an "objective attitude." In "Lamentations" Brody, like Reznikoff, ties the contemporary American Jew to a biblical past ("chanting Jeremiah's Lamentations"), even to the point of locating the old woman "by the banks of the Hudson"—a less elegant allusion to the psalm than Reznikoff's trademark, "By the Waters of Manhattan." Likewise, the presentational force that Brody achieves by juxtaposing the pious, lamenting mother to the sobbing daughter, disappointed in love, finds employment in many poems by Reznikoff, but with greater tension and compression. Consider, for example, the following from *Poems 1920:*

She sat by the window opening into the airshaft,
and looked across the parapet
at the new moon.

She would have taken the hairpins out of her carefully coiled hair,
and thrown herself on the bed in tears;
but he was coming and her mouth had to be pinned into a smile.
If he would have her, she would marry whatever he was.

A knock. She lit the gas and opened the door.
Her aunt and the man—skin loose under his eyes, the face slashed
    with wrinkles.
"Come in," she said as gently as she could and smiled.
(*CP* I.32)

In this poem, the juxtaposition takes the form not of a stationary tableau, as in Brody's poem, but of an active encounter of the girl with her aunt and her "intended." The compression and the detail of Reznikoff's poem make it much more striking than Brody's, capturing succinctly the girl's desperate resolution in phrases such as "she would marry whatever he was." This poem in particular elicited admiring comments from Allen Ginsberg, during a class he devoted to Reznikoff's poetry at the Naropa Institute:

that is one of the great narrative poems of the 20th century . . . a complete
lifetime, a complete moral lifetime, complete emotional growth indicated. . . . a complete presentation of an economic, social, living situation: 'sat by the window opening into the air shaft' . . . family situation:
'her aunt and the man' . . . and ultimately psychological, love situation,
loneliness situation: 'Come in, she said as gently as she could and smiled.'
Sounds like some sort of saint!

(*MP* 140 [ellipses in the original])

Having denigrated Ginsberg by comparing his work with Oppenheim's,
I must also point out his love for Reznikoff, whom he wished to install
in his own poetic pantheon as an honorary Jewish precursor, occupying
a place similar to that of William Carlos Williams. Ginsberg began reading
Reznikoff in the sixties; in the "Reznikoff" section of a poem called
"After Whitman & Reznikoff" (1980), he displays what he has learned:

Lower East Side

That round faced woman, she owns the street with her three big
   dogs,
screeches at me, waddling with her shopping bag across Avenue B
Grabbing my crotch, "Why don't you talk to me?"
baring her teeth in a smile, voice loud like a taxi horn,
"Big Jerk . . . you think you're famous?"—reminds me of my
   mother.

(Ginsberg, *Poems* 732)

Although the persona in this poem is unmistakably Allen Ginsberg's, he
borrows from Reznikoff the device of presenting an epiphany through a
chance encounter on the street with a social outcast. Like Reznikoff, too,
Ginsberg only receives the epiphany because of his openness to a figure
whom others shun. The sense of humor in this poem is broader than
Reznikoff's, but the two poets share a humorous delight in moments
of ironic self-deflation—a delight that seems characteristically Jewish.

Returning to the comparison of Reznikoff and Brody as American Jewish poets, we can begin to account for some of their differences by speci-
fying the literary models for their respective methods of juxtaposition:
Carl Sandburg and Edgar Lee Masters, for whom juxtaposition is largely
a form of dramatic irony, figure prominently for Brody, while Reznikoff
finds his juxtapositional model in the jump cuts of Imagism. Anthony Rudolf helps to differentiate Brody from Reznikoff further by delineating
the backgrounds of Brody's poetry: "His poems, consciously or uncon-
sciously, draw on three traditions: the European city 'mood' poem of
the 'nineties deriving ultimately from Baudelaire (a mood found also in

the early Eliot), the native American poetry of Sandburg, Masters and others, and the proletarian Yiddish poets of New York of the early part of the century" (112). Although Reznikoff also knew these three traditions, he did not look to any of them as a decisive influence. Finally, and from an altogether different angle, the poets can be compared through the visceral sense they share of an American Jewish life that takes place against a Russian backdrop. In Brody's case, this backdrop hovers closer than the family tales of life in Russia rehearsed by Reznikoff, for Brody spent his first eight years in a Russian town. Dedicated "To Russia," *A Family Album,* published a year after the Russian Revolution, bears witness to the extent to which the country of his birth still occupies Brody's thoughts.

By aligning their work with that of the prevailing American poets of their time, Jewish poets such as Oppenheim and Brody gained the benefit of immediate recognition by critics and other readers of poetry. As Harold Bloom does much later, Untermeyer points out the logical affiliation of a Jewish poet with a Whitmanian tradition that draws so strongly from biblical prophecy and psalmody. Reznikoff, on the other hand, pursued a more solitary, less recognizable path by adapting the literary experiments of Imagism to his explorations of Jewish history and of the contemporary urban world. This more radical mix of Judaism and modernism proved more difficult for even a Jewish critic to see, as is illustrated by the fact that although Brody receives abundant attention from Untermeyer—not only in *The New Era in American Poetry* (1919) and in his *Menorah Journal* article of August 1921, but also in his *American Poetry since 1900* (1923)— Brody's contemporary Reznikoff remains absent from Untermeyer's early accounts of modern poetry.[2] It took a poet-critic with the acuity of Louis Zukofsky to see that Reznikoff's adaptation of Imagist experiments to his own sociological and historical purposes offered "an objective" for young Jewish poets to focus upon. In the *Menorah Journal* and beyond—in Yiddish, in English, and in European languages—many new Jewish poets were available as potential models for young Americans like Zukofsky and Oppen. Yet only Reznikoff's severely disciplined exploration of much of the unstable territory between Judaism and modernism finally proved persuasive.

"WE HAD A SPEECH, OUR CHILDREN HAVE EVOLVED A JARGON."

Having placed Reznikoff within the ranks of American Jewish poets of the twenties, we are finally ready to tell an enhanced story of the founding of the Objectivist movement. A salient moment to begin a new history of Objectivism would be in 1929, when a precocious, twenty-five-year-old Jewish poet was casting about for an entrée to the *Menorah Journal*. Initially, this poet sent in a review of Max Brod's recently translated novel, *Three Loves;* next, he offered a sample translation from Yiddish of the beginning of Sholem Asch's new novel, *Die Mutter;* finally, he was working on a major essay on a Menorah poet, "Charles Reznikoff: Sincerity and Objectification," which he planned to submit to the journal. The work of the young poet did not make a favorable impression, however, upon Elliot Cohen, the *Menorah Journal*'s managing editor. In conversation with Cohen, Reznikoff heard his opinion: "Elliot told me that Zukofsky could not write, that he had done a poor piece of translation" (*Selected Letters* 78). After duly receiving a rejection notice, Louis Zukofsky, the precocious poet in question, complained in a letter to Ezra Pound:

> The Menorah just sent me a printed rejection slip with the beginning of Asch's Die Mutter which I had not submitted to them, but merely left as an example [of] the kind of translation I could do from the Yiddish. Which is all balm to my righteous see: I'd hate to be wrong about my notice of these people in A-4. I've always avoided them, wished to avoid them, and things seem to be turning out the way I wanted them to: since my seeing the Sanhedrin a few weeks ago was only a temporary fall to the plea of "thoughtful" heads.
> (Ahearn, *Pound/Zukofsky* 32)

Given the difficulty he was experiencing both in earning a living and in finding outlets for his work, Zukofsky was understandably bitter that the *Menorah Journal* would not engage a bright, young Jewish writer to produce a review, translate from Yiddish, or write an essay about one of the journal's featured authors. The slight to his skill in translating from Yiddish, his native language, must have been particularly galling. In *"A"*-4, Zukofsky had already staged a rebellion of the lively, modern "jargon" of Yiddish (as exemplified in his own translations from the Yiddish poet Yehoash [Solomon Bloomgarden]) against a stultifying and hieratic Hebrew, whose symbolic value was espoused by the *Menorah* writers. After an opening passage describing lights along the river, *"A"*-4 shifts abruptly into a voice Zukofsky attributes, in the letter above, to the *Menorah* circle:

> Wherever we put our hats is our home
> Our aged heads are our homes,
> Eyes wink to their own phosphorescence,
> No feast lights of Venice or The Last Supper light
> Our beards' familiars; His

Stars of Deuteronomy are with us,

Always with us,

We had a Speech, our children have evolved a jargon.

. . . .

Deafen us, God, deafen us to their music,

Our own children have passed over to the ostracized,

They assail us—

           'Religious, snarling monsters'—

And have mouthed a jargon:

(*"A"* 12–13)[3]

Zukofsky records a generational battle in which he describes the Hebraist *Menorah* circle as righteous graybeards sitting in judgment upon a more modern group of Yiddish writers: "We had a Speech," the "aged heads" complain, "our children have evolved a jargon." The "children," on the other hand, vilify their elders as "religious, snarling monsters," and Zukofsky himself sarcastically dubs the *Menorah* editors "the Sanhedrin" (the ancient assembly of elders) in his letter to Pound. In *"A"*-4 the elders are portrayed as nearly cursing the new poetry ("Deafen us, God, deafen us to their music") and as admitting that they themselves are so antiquated that "[e]ven the Death has gone out of us—we are void" (*"A"* 13)— which presumably accounts for the deliquescence of the light in their eyes into a ghostly "phosphorescence."

In a version of *"A"*-4 printed in *An "Objectivists" Anthology* (1932), Zukofsky notes with exasperation that he had already been "published" in the *Menorah Journal.* He quotes verbatim the portion of a sentence devoted to him by his Columbia University professor, Mark Van Doren, in an article for the journal entitled "Jewish Students I Have Known" (June 1927): "I shall skip a pale and subtle poet who was not in fact lazy, but the memory of whose painfully inarticulate soul forbids me to use him for any purpose however respectful . . ." (Van Doren 267). It's hard to imagine Zukofsky as ever having been "painfully inarticulate," since he presents himself to the world and in private letters as aggressively articulate— but perhaps the verbal aggression is a form of compensation. Zukofsky makes his own sarcastic comment on Van Doren's portrait after he quotes it in his poem: "(in a journal,— / Associations: we had a menorah, and / It is, indeed, an honor to be circumcised)" (*"Objectivists" Anthology* 126). The savagery with which Zukofsky condemns the *Menorah Journal* testifies to the strength of his desire to be taken seriously by it. Why is he so bitter? Probably because the journal represents the only space in which he might maintain a connection with the Jewish world while pursuing his career as modern writer: no other venue in English would foster such a combination. Moreover, his rejection by the journal occurs at a critical juncture, when he is, in effect, choosing between the examples of Pound and of Reznikoff. To follow Reznikoff's example would entail a Jewish identification and an entrance into the *Menorah* circle; to follow Pound's would mean forming a group of avant-garde poets and collectively storming the little magazines. When, over the course of several months and several publishing schemes, Zukofsky transfers his hopes for the essay on Reznikoff from the *Menorah Journal* to *Poetry,* his own horizon as a writer alters correspondingly. In the midst of this shift, at a time when Zukofsky is actively negotiating between Reznikoff and Pound, "Objectivism," as Zukofsky defines it, emerges.[4]

On November 22, 1929, while engaged in writing his essay on Reznikoff for the *Menorah Journal,* Zukofsky attempts to elicit Pound's interest by sending him a large packet of Reznikoff material: three plays, *Rashi, Coral,* and *Meriwether Lewis;* the biblical reworkings in "Editing and Glosses" (*CP* 1.77–103) and another batch of poems selected from *Five Groups of Verse* (1927); and Reznikoff's mother's memoir, published soon thereafter in *By the Waters of Manhattan* (1930) (Ahearn, *Pound/Zukofsky* 27). Pound's response from Rapallo, Italy, shows more enthusiasm than a facile view of his anti-Semitism might lead one to expect: "The Reznikof [*sic*] prose very good as far as I've got at breakfast. . . . Capital in idea that next wave of literature is jewish (obviously) Bloom casting shadow before, prophetic Jim. [Joyce] etc. also lack of prose in German due to all idiomatic energy being drawn off into yiddish" (26). Thinking, no doubt, of figures such as Zukofsky, Reznikoff, and Carl Rakosi (whom he had also published in *The Exile*), Pound senses a new avant-garde in the making, spearheaded by Jewish writers. In the midst of applauding this endeavor, Pound's discomfort with the notion of a Jewish avant-garde shows itself in his circumscribing the "next wave" within hierarchies of writing he himself has constructed: he moves quickly to credit Joyce with the prescience to represent, with his character Leopold Bloom, the modern urban everyman as a Jew. Characteristically, too, Pound seeks a sociolinguistic cause for the rise of Jewish literature, attributing it to the vernacular liveliness of Yiddish, which flourishes, supposedly, at the expense of a moribund German. This is a somewhat flippant remark, but by implying that some of the power of modern Jewish writing derives from the intonation, syntax, phraseology, and heteroglossia of Yiddish, Pound rehearses an argument now being made by critics for a variety of Jewish writers.[5] As we will see shortly, Pound's remark provides a key to understanding Zukofsky's poetry, in particular.

In his reply to Pound, stressing Reznikoff's poverty and asceticism, Zukofsky expresses anguish about "the life of the poet" as portrayed by Reznikoff's example.[6] To Pound's reasonable query about whether Reznikoff, as owner of a printing press, could not become the publisher of a group of young poets, Zukofsky answers:

> Dear E: Re—Reznikoff: Yah—the blighter has a press, but lord knows in what forsaken town upstate. . . . Besides, the fellow has to spend the years remaining to him, past 35, in a law office, working on definitions. What with this, his own work, and his daily consummation of Bible, Homer and Dante, why shd he sink in 200 or 300 dollars on ginks like myself—. It's enough he has to *give* his own works away. . . . More anon—as soon as my article on him for the Menorah Jl. is completed. If "they" take it. Do I luf my peepul? The only good Jew I know is my father: a coincidence.
>
> (27)

Identifying with Reznikoff, Zukofsky is disturbed by both the working conditions and the neglect suffered by the older poet. In the version of his article written for the *Menorah Journal,* for instance, Zukofsky begins his second paragraph with a lament that Reznikoff's writing has not been printed by any influential publishers or magazine editors (a slight exaggeration). In the aforementioned correspondence to Pound, having already heard that the *Menorah Journal* was not interested in his review of Max Brod's *Three Loves,* Zukofsky has begun to fear that his long article on Reznikoff will also be rejected, and so he lashes out at the journal with a sarcastic rhetorical question, uttered in the sort of Yiddish accent that Pound was fond of imitating: "Do I luf my peepul?"

Zukofsky's ambivalence toward Jewishness—compounded of pride and self-hatred, of affection for his father and disdain for his father's religion—finds further expression in this letter to Pound. He next asks permission to quote, in a footnote to his Reznikoff essay, Pound's pronouncement that the "next wave of literature is jewish." Zukofsky professes to be grateful that Pound has made the statement because "it wouldn't have been the likes of an antisemite like myself to disseminate suzh malinformation: however, with your kosher label on it . . . I hope you don't feel the Jews are roping you in" (27–28; ellipsis in original). In order to mask his eagerness for securing Pound's imprimatur on the Jewish poets, Zukofsky casts himself as the anti-Semite and Pound as a rabbi who ensures that items of food are kosher. At another level, though, this marvelously ironic turnabout may testify to a realistic understanding on Zukofsky's part that, in the present anti-Semitic climate, only someone like

Pound, who has little sympathy for Judaism, might be capable of claiming major stature for Jewish writing.

Throughout their early correspondence, Pound and Zukofsky perform a contorted dance around the issue of anti-Semitism, twirling Jewish stereotypes back and forth. Their interchange on this subject reaches a kind of climax in Pound's scurrilous ditty, "Der Yiddisher Charleston Band" (published eventually by Zukofsky in *An "Objectivists" Anthology* [1932]), in which Pound dons a Yiddish accent to sing about an unholy Jazz-Age alliance between mercenary Jews and African queens:

> Gentle Jheezus sleek and wild
> Found disciples tall an' hairy
> Flirting with his red hot Mary,
>> Now hot momma Magdalene
> Is doing front page fer the screen
>>> Mit der yittischer Charleston Pband
>> Mit
> deryiddischercharles
>>> tonband
>
>
>> ole king Bolo's big black queen
> Whose bum was big as a soup tureen
>> Has lef' the congo
>>>> and is now seen
>> Mit der *etc.*
>
>
>> Red hot Mary of Magdala
>> Had nine jews an a Roman fellow
> Nah she'z gotta chob much swellah
>> Mit der yiddisher Charleston Band.
>>> mit der YIDDISHER
>>>> Charleston BAND.
>
>
>> Calvin Coolidg dh' pvwezident
>> He vudn't go but dh' family vwent,
>>> Vuddunt giff notding but his name vass lent
>
>>> For deh yidtischer Charleston pband.
>
> (44–45)[7]

Pound's entire "genealogy of demons" (the phrase from *The Cantos* that Robert Casillo uses to title his study of Pound's anti-Semitism) makes an appearance in this song, which features anti-Semitism as the umbrella under which a collection of anti-Christian, racist, and misogynist views are gathered. Recognizing the defamatory nature of his song, Pound tells Zukofsky he doubts whether it "wd. git by" Harriet Monroe's printer and into *Poetry,* but he claims a reluctance to see it in print primarily because it "JUST *has to be sung* and I aint never had patience to write down the beeyeauteeful muuziK" (Ahearn, "Ezra Pound" 173). He ends this letter insisting, "Must positively NOT be released till we can get Pathe disc, like our old friend Mr. Choice. Somebody OUGHT to sing it to the Americanacademy o fart an latters. The YOUNG mustn't be shocked" (174). It's hard to tell how serious Pound is about the merits of his ditty, since he seems to be speaking tongue in cheek. One would be tempted to categorize "Der Yiddisher Charleston Band" as merely an egregious example of the anti-Semitic joking between Pound and Zukofsky, but this is not so easy to do given the song's later appearance—with Pound's blessing—in Zukofsky's anthology. What I find even more astonishing, though, than Zukofsky's publishing the song in an anthology of Jews and leftists in 1932, is the fact that Pound was still singing it, still captivated by its humor, sixteen years later, *after* World War II! According to Charles Olson, reporting on a conversation he had with a Dr. Kavka, a Jewish psychiatrist treating Pound at St. Elizabeth's, "Pound had also performed for K what he calls his YIDDISH CHARLESTON, composed originally for Louis Zukofsky. K says it is something! and regrets he didn't get a recording. A dance which Pound does, with gesture, movement, words" (Olson 66).[8]

All of this flirting with Yiddish accents and Jewish stereotypes between a Jewish poet and his anti-Semitic mentor can become quite dizzying. It is difficult to see how to compartmentalize feelings such as self-hatred, envy, and pride with regard to Jewishness—in the case of either actor in this bizarre vaudevillian correspondence. And ultimately, I don't think it would be fruitful to isolate individual feelings or assign them to only one of these two figures, for Zukofsky and Pound are equally trapped (each in his own way) in the dilemma of betweenness that vexes Jewish intellectuals, and to both of them Yiddish is a central feature of this dilemma. From his side, Pound chants back in a Yiddish accent to the Jewish Objectivists; while from his side, Zukofsky translates a poem by Yehoash in *"A"*-4 that sounds like a Poundian imitation of a Japanese original:

"Rain blows, light, on quiet water
    I watch the rings spread and travel
Shimaunu-San, Samurai,
        When will you come home?—
            Shimaunu-San, my clear star."
(13)

This is the first of four stanzas that Zukofsky translates from the Yiddish, and it is prompted by the previously quoted lament of the Hebraic elders, who implore God to deafen them to the music of the younger poets, written in "jargon." In other words, the jargon (Yiddish) that Zukofsky flings back into the faces of his elders at the *Menorah Journal* consists of an imitation-Japanese poem in the mode of Pound's *Cathay* (1915). Emphasizing this point, Zukofsky follows the attribution ("—*Yehoash*") of his four quoted stanzas with the lines "Song's kinship, / The roots we strike" (14).

Zukofsky recognizes the need to choose between linguistic taproots: Hebrew or Yiddish. He strikes the root bearing the greatest kinship to the songs that inspire him, for the vernacular tradition of Yiddish allows him to connect with the Asian sources of Pound's poetry and, thus, with Pound himself. He selects Yiddish over Hebrew because, unlike Reznikoff and the *Menorah* writers, he no longer seeks a way to become American while remaining Jewish; instead, Zukofsky looks toward the lively, cosmopolitan, secular, politically engaged culture of Yiddish. Yiddish matters terribly to Zukofsky, not just as a first language in which he communicates with his family, but also because, through its porosity with respect to other languages, it has managed to imbibe the major innovations in modern Russian, English, and French poetry. By embracing Yiddish, Zukofsky can make himself a "natural" heir to the most advanced trends in modernism. In fact, if we can regard Zukofsky as a Yiddish poet writing in English, then a number of the hallmarks of his writing come into focus with a startling clarity.[9]

The Yiddish that Zukofsky spoke and read was itself a multilingual language, composed primarily of German, Hebrew, and Slavic features, with borrowings from many other languages as well. In order to facilitate daily communication among its speakers, Yiddish achieved a kind of fusion of its constituent languages. On the other hand, as Benjamin Harshav explains,

> Yiddish always was an open language. . . . For Yiddish was, almost by definition, a language used by multilingual speakers. They were always aware of the component languages of their speech: they lived among those languages and recognized their imprint. It is precisely because the

very problem of fusion was at the center of Yiddish language consciousness and the components did not really fully melt [sic], that openness
and overstepping the boundaries into another language were a viable
option. It is the most typical habit of Yiddish conversation—by simple
and learned people alike—to borrow expressions from beyond the language border and to shift for a while from Yiddish proper to pieces of
discourse in other languages and back.
(*Meaning* 28)

What is both fascinating about Yiddish and striking about Zukofsky's poetry is the constant invitation to multilinguistic play. In Zukofsky's verse,
as in typical Yiddish utterance, "purity of diction" would be a hopelessly
banal ideal, for Yiddish revels in the signifying possibilities of the many
ranges of diction available. A Yiddish speaker remains aware of multiple
registers, borrowed but not wholly assimilated from a variety of languages,
and consciously selects an expression from among these various registers
for a specific effect. A speaker can, for instance, play a "Germanism" off
against a "Hebraism" or an "Americanism," thus adding a witty metalinguistic significance to the utterance. Because of the openness of Yiddish—first to Hebrew, then to the many other languages among which
Yiddish speakers found themselves—there exists, above the linguistic
structure of Yiddish, what Harshav calls a "semiotics" of the language, in
which the historical resonances of the various component languages and
their expressions speak to one another.

In much of his poetry, Zukofsky writes as an aggressively "unidiomatic"
speaker of English, choosing words and expressions from the widest
possible registers of the language (and using many non-English words as
well). In a sense, Zukofsky, like his contemporary Henry Roth, turns English into a kind of Yiddish, a language that resists fusion of its elements
and maintains their separateness. By partially prying apart the many languages and historical phenomena that have gone into the formation of
English, Zukofsky opens up the language to new signifying possibilities.
This metalinguistic activity has been one of the main elements in his work
that both captivates and, to a certain extent, authorizes many of the later
Language poets. In opening up English in this way, Zukofsky engages
in what Walter Benjamin thinks of as the most profound task of the
translator: Benjamin insists that the true purpose of a translation is not to
convey the "sense" of a text from one language to another, but rather to
have a more formative impact upon the target language by incorporating
into it "the original's mode of signification" (78). Zukofsky makes a
lifework of this translative activity, carrying the metalinguistic mode
of signification from Yiddish into English poetry. Working as a kind of

translative poet, he unites the opposing intentions that Benjamin assigns to the poet and the translator: "The intention of the poet is spontaneous, primary, graphic; that of the translator is derivative, ultimate, ideational" (76–77). Where Hebrew signifies to Reznikoff a lost patrimony whose recovery is central to his poetic project, Yiddish works for Zukofsky as a kind of "secret language" that marks his difference not only from the *Menorah* writers but also from other modern American poets writing in English.[10]

Although "sincerity" acts as a master term for Zukofsky, it really applies to the poetic half of Benjamin's dichotomy; Zukofsky's poetry goes beyond the criterion of sincerity by encompassing both halves. Like other Yiddish poets, Zukofsky is highly attuned to forms of multilinguistic play, such as irony, parody, mimicry, and aural and visual punning. Among a list of traits that define the Yiddish intellectual, we can find many that apply to Zukofsky: "alertness, adaptability (what Woody Allen in *Zelig* called 'the Chameleon Phenomenon'), irony (developed by people with a pluricultural perspective or those whose language thrived on the margin of several languages), and swift shifting from one attitude to another" (Harshav, *Meaning* 135). "The Chameleon Phenomenon," for instance, comes into play in Zukofsky's manifold impersonations of English and European poetry, in which he combines an exquisite formal perfection with what we think of now as a "postmodern" sense of weightlessness. Even the bizarre fact that Yiddish is a language formed on a Germanic base but written in Hebrew characters finds an analogy in the uncanny linguistic doubling of Zukofsky's translations of Catullus—in which he attempts to write an English translation that *sounds like* the Latin original. The doubling quality of such Yiddish mental habits finds its complement in "a deep-seated penchant for theorizing and abstracting," which Harshav ascribes to "the fact that Jews were newcomers to the languages they mastered and learned them not in the dialects of local and concrete speech but in the idealized form of intellectual and literary discourse." Like a Jewish violin virtuoso (which his son Paul became), Zukofsky plays every register of the English language, creating poems with astoundingly hybrid diction. As an outsider, he enacts a defensive/aggressive stance toward English, wishing to master it in its entirety, but doing so only by an incomparably virtuosic mimicry. Although he eschews the Hebraism of the Menorah movement, Zukofsky's defensive/aggressive posture—his attempt to "out-English" the most cultivated native speakers—corresponds, ironically, to the way that *noblesse oblige* functioned for Dubnow and the founders of the Menorah movement.

"WITH SPECIAL REFERENCE TO THE WORK
OF CHARLES REZNIKOFF"

Zukofsky's "deep-seated penchant for theorizing and abstracting" is nowhere more apparent than in his essay on Reznikoff; after he saw a draft
of it, Reznikoff himself characterized it as "a kind of Ph.D. study of my
work" (*Selected Letters* 91). The essay began life as an article intended for
the *Menorah Journal,* "Charles Reznikoff: Sincerity and Objectification"
(1930, unpublished), was printed in the "Objectivist" issue of *Poetry* as
"Sincerity and Objectification: With Special Reference to the Work of
Charles Reznikoff" (1931), and resides in *Prepositions,* Zukofsky's collected essays, as a page and a half of "An Objective" (1967)—without
reference to Reznikoff. In the first version, Zukofsky seeks to account for
the entire career of an important *Menorah* contributor, discussing at length
not only his poetry but also his plays and prose and commenting upon
how his works have been received. Starting out with a list of Reznikoff's
books in print, Zukofsky quickly turns to consider his relative obscurity:

> That no influential American publisher or magazine editor has ever
> printed Reznikoff's work might supposedly be "explained away" by "of
> regional interest." Yet even a cursory glance thru Reznikoff's volumes
> should affect one's awareness with the retention that this author has
> written not only of Genesis, Rashi, Uriel Acosta and Jehudah Halevi,
> but of Nat Turner, Meriwether Lewis, Chatterton, Farquhar and
> Aphrodite Urania.
> (UCSD 400.0.1)

Using the phrase "of regional interest" as code for "narrowly Jewish,"
Zukofsky defends Reznikoff against charges of "clannishness" (such as
might be leveled at authors perceived as "ethnic") by showing that his
subjects extend beyond Jewish history to American and English history
and to Greek mythology. By invoking the rhetoric of ethnic exclusion,
this passage also serves to explain to *Menorah* readers that Reznikoff's poor
circulation outside of Jewish venues stems from "racial" prejudice rather
than from inherent limitations in his work. Zukofsky's next move is to
turn the tables on ignorant editors and readers by claiming that the dearth
of recognition has been detrimental primarily not to Reznikoff but to
"certain people interested in craftsmanship," who "have missed access to
this work" (UCSD 400.0.1). To clinch the point about his subject's craftsmanship and formal invention as strongly as he can, Zukofsky speaks of
the lines of Reznikoff's poem, "Wringing, wringing his pierced hands"
(*CP* 1.16), as "containing in their elements the atmosphere of Eliot's *Waste
Land* and *Hollow Men.*"[11] Singling out the line "Smooth and white with

loss of leaves and bark," Zukofsky notes that it appeared in 1918, prior to
Eliot's *Poems* (1920); he claims, therefore, that it anticipates Eliot's innovations (*Poetry* 272). Since terms such as "smooth," "white," and "loss"
describe both concrete reality and emotional mood, Zukofsky may be
reasoning that they exemplify what Eliot called in 1919 "the objective
correlative" (Eliot, "Hamlet" 48). In addition, Zukofsky may be comparing the irregular but carefully balanced meter of the line—in other
words, "with loss of" acts as a fulcrum between "smooth and white" and
"leaves and bark"—with the carefully balanced irregularities of Eliot's
verse.

The claim that Reznikoff anticipates Eliot forms the opening of the
second version of Zukofsky's essay, as it appears in the "Objectivists"
issue of *Poetry*. In this version, which differs from the first only by virtue
of deletions (primarily of discussions of Reznikoff's drama and prose),
Reznikoff's verse constitutes the prime example of the kind of poetry
Zukofsky advocates as "Objectivist." Quoting a three-line poem of Reznikoff's,

> Showing a torn sleeve, with stiff and shaking fingers the old man
> Pulls off a bit of baked apple, shiny with sugar,
> Eating with reverence food, the great comforter.

Zukofsky contends that this short poem suggests "entire aspects of
thought: economics, beliefs, literary analytics, etc. The entire matter involves the process of active literary omission and a discussion finding its
way in the acceptance of two criteria: sincerity and objectification" (*Poetry*
273). In other words, from this three-line poem we can move in two
directions: outward, to unpack economic views, moral beliefs, and esthetic criteria; and inward, toward an understanding of excision as a compositional technique in the service of "sincerity" and "objectification."
These arguments for this short poem, like the earlier insistence that a specific poem (and especially one line) of Reznikoff's anticipates the development of Eliot's poetry, are large ones to make for such diminutive speci-
mens. This speaks of a habit of thought that Zukofsky shares with
Reznikoff and Oppen, and for which Pound provides a model: the notion
that in the smallest details one finds structures of the greatest significance.
Of all these poets, Zukofsky carries this habit of thinking—which we
might, particularly in his case, designate as midrashic or kabbalistic—to
the greatest extreme. This faith in the endless significance of minute details
finds application not only in Zukofsky's mode of argument in the essay
but also in his building an entire epic upon the letter *A*.

Such midrashic thinking shatters the discursive surface of the text, or
the socially expressive aspect of language, penetrating to material ele-

ments that can refract a new interpretive light. When writing in this way, a poet will practice, as Reznikoff does, "active literary omission," cutting away discursive words and phrases in order to draw the reader's attention to the radiant minimal elements that await midrashic expansion. This compositional method turns everything written into an "objective," that is, an object of intense focus (272). The Jewish language magic of Objectivist poetry has been passed on as a major legacy to poets (many of whom are not Jewish) who take their bearings from Objectivism, such as Charles Olson, Robert Duncan, Robert Creeley, Denise Levertov, Charles Tomlinson, David Meltzer, Jerome Rothenberg, Susan Howe, John Taggart, Michael Palmer, Lyn Hejinian, Michael Davidson, Ron Silliman, Ted Pearson, Charles Bernstein, and Barbara Einzig. In some ways, one could argue that this objectifying method defines the term *objectification* more exactly than Zukofsky's own definition of a "rested totality" (273–74), which seems to mean something like a well-formed object, a rather universal criterion for poetry. Zukofsky does employ the notion of objectification as pertaining to a potentially multilingual objective, though, when he says that "each word in itself is an arrangement, it may be said that each word possesses objectification to a powerful degree" (274).

If objectification opens the poem up to multiple linguistic registers, then what about "sincerity," which would seem to imply a unitary personality that would be inimical to the kind of poetry Zukofsky values? Rather than a sign of personal authenticity, Zukofsky enlists sincerity as the moral aspect of representation, which involves an implicit avowal of the factual nature of what is said and also the conviction that the language used can adequately evoke the experience represented. In the first draft of his essay, Zukofsky states, "Sincerity in writing is the representation of having heard, considered and seen and the certain avowal which follows that 'this is so'" (UCSD 400.0.1). Although it vouches for an attentive representation of the world, sincerity, too, partakes of what we have been calling "objectification" because both the perception and the thought about what is perceived must participate in the magnifying process: "Writing occurs which is the detail, not mirage, of seeing, of thinking with the things as they exist, and of directing them along a line of melody" (*Poetry* 273). "Mirage" refers to the quality Zukofsky has earlier disparaged as the "*symboliste* semi-allegorical gleam"; the Objectivist poem, by contrast, would do the following: focus upon the actual "details" of perception that can be opened up interpretively, think about a variety of relations among "things" in the world, and arrange a representation of those things in a "melodic" form (i.e., by constructing an artful arrangement of phonemes and pauses). Ostensibly, Zukofsky sees "sincerity" and "objectification" in a relation between part and whole: he posits objectification as "the arrangement, into one apprehended unit, of minor units of sincerity—in other words, the resolving of words and their ideation into structure" (274). Although he tries to limit the connotations of "sincerity" to the realm of the technical, the term begs to be read from other directions too. Shortly, for example, we will look at "sincerity" as a term in the moral equations of Lionel Trilling. In addition, Jerome Rothenberg wondered aloud in conversation (San Diego, December 30, 1994) whether what Zukofsky really meant by "sincerity" was that Reznikoff remained committed to Judaism while he (Zukofsky) was more evasive.

In the two longer versions of the essay, Zukofsky next illustrates his primary terms with three examples from Reznikoff's poetry, explicated in detail, and then makes a list of poems by other poets that qualify as attaining objectification. The rest of the essay, in these versions, consists nearly exclusively of a reading of Reznikoff's poetry, which Zukofsky praises as "almost constant examples of sincerity." In passages like the following, Zukofsky characterizes Reznikoff's poetry as a virtual template for Objectivist writing:

> There is to be noted in Reznikoff's lines the isolation of each noun so that in itself it is an image, the grouping of nouns so that they partake of the quality of things being together without violence to their individual intact natures. The simple sensory adjectives are as necessary as the nouns. If Reznikoff has written elsewhere of the "imperious dawn," the single abstract adjective occurs without the pang of reverie. The metaphor, as in all good writing, has been presented with conciseness in a word.
> (*Poetry* 278)

Although Reznikoff's example was unquestionably primary when Zukofsky was formulating his Objectivist theories, he later chose, probably in the interests of concision and generalization, to eliminate Reznikoff completely from the rigorous definitions he condensed into "An Objective" (1967). The new essay combines drastically compressed versions of his three essays on Objectivism: "Program: 'Objectivists' 1931," "Sincerity and Objectification," and "'Recencies' in Poetry," devoting less than two pages to the second essay. At this late date, after the "rediscovery" of Objectivism in the sixties, Zukofsky presents his ideas as standing alone, without the support of an elder example—although in many ways his succinct statements in "An Objective" hark back to Pound's Imagist manifesto, "A Retrospect" (1918). When Hugh Kenner looks at "Sincerity and Objectification," he does so from the perspective of Zukofsky's final revision. After discussing a couple of Zukofsky's interpretations of Reznikoff poems, Kenner claims, "Despite the attribution of two brief examples, no effort was underway to empedestal Reznikoff, who was dropped from later reprintings of the essay" (167). This willful misreading of the essay, deflating the reputation of Reznikoff, corresponds with Kenner's general opinion of Objectivism as a diminutive movement, played out wholly in the shadow of the great modernists. Interestingly, Kenner characterizes "objectification" as "puritan in its formulations as in its exemplars"; like Arnold, he seems to see puritanism as a form of Hebraism (168).

At the time of composing the essay as a critical article for the *Menorah Journal,* however, Zukofsky eagerly showed it to Reznikoff, who was quite flattered. In a letter to Marie Syrkin, Reznikoff discusses his reaction to the essay and his sense of its prospects for publication:

> Sunday night I met Zukowski—as I wrote you I would—and read his essay on me called "Objectivity and Sincerity"—about 25 pages (including quotations). Well, I am sure The Menorah will not take it; for on Saturday Elliot told me that Zukowski could not write, that he had done a poor piece of translation, etc. Zukowski can write; and although I do not react to parts, to other parts I am—to say the least—attentive. In his essay on me he interpreted some things in a way new to me: for instance, in the thing to Athena, he showed the resemblance of the verse to the classic hexameter; in one about old men on the stoops, he saw the lines of the steps of the stoops, the wrinkled faces etc. in a design of which I had only seen part. I told him so. However, I am sure The Menorah will not care for any of his work—and they will undoubtedly take Trilling instead.
> (UCSD 9.25.3, *Selected Letters* 78–79; spelling as per typescript)

Reznikoff responds appreciatively to having his poetry read "objectively" by Zukofsky, recognizing the gains to be made from Zukofsky's attention to detail. Notwithstanding his defense of Zukofsky's ability as a writer, Reznikoff knows that Elliot Cohen, the *Menorah Journal*'s editor, will not accept the dense, difficult essay. Instead, Zukofsky's former Columbia University classmate, Lionel Trilling, then writing fiction and reviews for the journal, would be given the assignment to review Reznikoff's work: Trilling's review of Reznikoff's novel *By the Waters of Manhattan,* entitled "Genuine Writing," appeared in October of 1930.

Although Zukofsky's article on Reznikoff was published in *Poetry* rather than in the *Menorah Journal,* the journal left its imprint upon the essay and upon the selection of poetry assembled by Zukofsky—as a letter to the editor of *Poetry* makes clear.[12] With no apparent need to explain his references, the poet Horace Gregory writes of the February 1931 issue:

I believe the issue is a landmark, an important historical event in the writing of American poetry. It is, however, a Left Bank issue with offices on lower Fifth Avenue, New York, where the *Menorah Journal* appears whenever it can raise enough money to ship copy to the printer. There is a curious strain of Jewish nationalism, disguised as a Greek chorus, reciting its refrain throughout the poems. As a middle-westerner of pioneer American stock, with a touch of Edgar Lee Masters in my make-up, I feel a bit lonely, particularly in New York.
(Gregory, "Correspondence" 51–52)

To Gregory it was patently obvious that Objectivism evolved from the *Menorah Journal:* in what other venue could one find so many Jewish and leftist poets? His complaint that "there is a curious strain of Jewish nationalism, disguised as a Greek chorus," brings up once again the prominent Jewish dilemma of negotiating between Hebraism and Hellenism—although in this case the model for Hellenism would be Ezra Pound rather than Matthew Arnold. With wistful humor, Gregory finds these Jewish matters limiting to "a middle-westerner of pioneer American stock, with a touch of Edgar Lee Masters in [his] make-up," but he is especially concerned about the danger presented by the model for the new poetry. He complains that "Mr. Zukofsky has placed Charles Reznikoff, a man of minor abilities, at the top of his scale and then proceeded downward" (52).[13]

Although he later revised upward his own evaluation of Reznikoff, Gregory is attentive enough to locate in Reznikoff's writing, in particular, a tension between the Greek and the Jewish; as a representative Objectivist, Reznikoff can be seen working hard to apply a "Greek" surface to poems having a Jewish import. Stylistically, the Hellenic strain comes to Reznikoff most directly from the Imagist work of Ezra Pound and H.D., much of which is modeled explicitly upon classical verse. For instance, Reznikoff's one-line entry in the Imagist brevity sweepstakes, "Aphrodite Vrania" ("The ceaseless weaving of the uneven water" [*CP* 1.36]), can stand ably alongside H.D.'s famous "Oread":

Whirl up, sea—
whirl your pointed pines,
splash your great pines
on our rocks,
hurl your green over us,
cover us with your pools of fir.
(H.D. 55)

Zukofsky praises Reznikoff's intricately sounded representation of churning desire in "Aphrodite Vrania" as a notable example of sincerity, "each word" in it "possessing remarkable energy as an image of water as action" (*Poetry* 275); the effect of sincerity in this poem thus depends upon "the veracity of the particular craft" (275). At another level of technique, Reznikoff follows the example of H.D. by superimposing an alien image upon the moving water; where H.D. effects a cinematic dissolve between the similar patterns created by pines and by waves, Reznikoff, in distinction, makes a more literary connection between the Grecian craft of weaving and the fluctuating water—as though he would kabbalistically encode the entire *Odyssey* through the phrases "ceaseless weaving" (Penelope) and "uneven water" (Odysseus).

Moreover, Reznikoff's stylistic affinity to Greek poetry goes beyond his debt to Ezra Pound and H.D., for he had a profound preoccupation with the simple, rustic forms found in the Greek anthology and in post-Poundian translations of certain Chinese and Japanese poetry.[14] This "Greek" style, whose hallmark Nietzsche identified as a "profound superficiality" (38), also informs Reznikoff's approach to Hebrew, particularly the Hebrew Scriptures. His biblical translations in "Editing and Glosses" (*CP* 1.77–103), for instance, seek to overcome the chiaroscuro quality that Erich Auerbach has famously noted in the Hebrew Bible by presenting the episodes he translates in the bright foreground of historical attention. In *Mimesis,* Auerbach maintains that "the literary representation of reality in European culture" has a long history of navigating between the Greek and the Hebrew styles. Using Homer as his model, Auerbach lists the following qualities of Greek style: "fully externalized description, uniform illumination, uninterrupted connection, free expression, all events in the foreground, displaying unmistakable meanings, few elements of historical development and of psychological perspective." Biblical style, by contrast, contains "certain parts brought into high relief, others left obscure, abruptness, suggestive influence of the unexpressed, 'background' quality, multiplicity of meanings, universal-historical claims, development of the concept of the historically becoming, and preoccupation with the problematic" (23). In a unique fashion, Reznikoff blends the two styles Auerbach delineates not only by foregrounding and illuminating uniformly the particular elements of his poems and not making universal-historical claims, but also by interrupting connections among the elements in his poems, preoccupying himself with the problematic, and inviting a multiplicity of meanings.

In Reznikoff's synthesis, both the Greek and the Hebrew agree about the value not only of brevity and immediacy, but also of simple diction and of ordinary experience. Milton Hindus labels the style based on these criteria "a Doric music," using a term that Reznikoff himself employed:

Reznikoff's taste was for music of a particular kind—he called it (beautifully enough) "a Doric music." The original meaning of the word Doric implied something unrefined, rustic, even uncouth. In English, it was, less than two centuries ago, an epithet of disdain. When critics spoke of the "Doric dialect" of the Lake Poets, they did not mean to flatter Wordsworth. But to Reznikoff, who credits Wordsworth even more than Whitman with the introduction into high poetic style of "the language of common speech," Doric was an adjective with attractive associations. The word, of course, is also a term in architecture. It is the name of the oldest and simplest of Greek orders, a column of which was adopted in a modified form by the Romans. In printing, Doric is an old kind of type face, impressive in its simplicity of design. The various senses all point to an austere beauty.
(*Reznikoff* 58)

Reznikoff's "Doric music" accounts for much, though by no means all, of what Zukofsky means by "sincerity" as a quality of Objectivism. Although knowing how to value this quality, Zukofsky had little use for a Doric music in his own poetry, basing his adherence to "sincerity" not primarily on virtues such as honesty, straightforwardness, or genuineness, but on the rigor of his often baroque technique. Ultimately, a "Jewish" language is central to the program of both writers and to their different kinds of sincerity; the disparity in their styles can be linked to the wildly different characters of the respective linguistic taproots each had chosen. Or to put it another way: where Reznikoff seeks to find a synthesis of the Hebrew and the Greek, Zukofsky works to make English accommodate Yiddish.

In the first two poems of *Jerusalem the Golden* (Objectivist Press, 1934), which Reznikoff was writing while Zukofsky composed his essay, Reznikoff stages a direct confrontation between Hebraism and Hellenism that incorporates the dichotomy into the heart of Objectivist practice.[15] The initial poem we have considered in chapter 1; it addresses the Hebrew language as fashioned by poets:

> The Hebrew of your poets, Zion,
> is like oil upon a burn,
> cool as oil;
> after work,
> the smell in the street at night
> of the hedge in flower.
> Like Solomon,
> I have married and married the speech of strangers;
> none are like you, Shulamite.
> (*CP* 1.107)

By celebrating the return to Hebrew from a foreign tongue, this poem recognizes implicitly the dichotomy between Hebraism and Hellenism. From the perspective of Jewish history, "Hellenism" has been a general term for the temptation to look outside Judaism, beginning during the Hellenistic Era itself. Marrying "the speech of strangers" represents a yielding to this temptation by entering into a world outside that sanctified by Jewish law. Hoping that the return to Hebrew will promote healing and the satisfaction of desire, Reznikoff signals a rueful rejection of this temptation and a renewal of Hebraic allegiance. The next poem, however, which we looked at briefly in the introduction, seems to offer the diametrically opposed position, for the speaker celebrates the learning not of Hebrew but of Greek:

> *Hellenist*
>
> As I, barbarian, at last, although slowly, could read Greek,
> at "blue-eyed Athena"
> I greeted her picture that had long been on the wall:
> the head slightly bent forward under the heavy helmet,
> as if to listen; the beautiful lips slightly scornful.
> (*CP* 1.107)

Exchanging her traditional gray eyes for blue, Athena poses as the ultimate *shiksa,* whose language a Jewish "barbarian" might learn but whose favor he could never earn. In chapter 1, we observed how the erotic component of Hebrew emerges in the previous poem; in "Hellenist," on the other hand, Greek bears the erotic charge. Although the tone of the poem is largely self-deprecatory, there also may be an undertone of slight horror at the image of Athena: as if for the first time, the speaker seems to notice the militaristic style of this portrait of the "blue-eyed" goddess with "heavy helmet."

This poem functions significantly as the initial example of objectification in Zukofsky's essay for *Poetry.* Commenting upon its formal qualities, he draws attention to

> the purposeful crudity of the first line as against the quantitative (not necessarily classic) hexameter measures of the others, the use of words of two syllables (*greeted, picture, slightly,* etc.) with suitable variations of words of four and three (*barbarian, beautiful*); the majority of the words accented on the first syllable, all resolve into a structure (which incidentally translates the Hellenic) to which the mind does not wish to add; nor does it, any more than when it contemplates a definite object by itself.
> (275–76)

In addition to noting the "Doric music" of the first line, Zukofsky dubs the careful, self-sufficient structuration of this poem "objectification," which he views as a "Hellenic" virtue. By aligning structure with Hellen-ism, Zukofsky follows in the footsteps of Horace Kallen, who wrote in 1908 about the contrasting "essences" of Hellenism and Hebraism: "that essence was for the Greek, structure, harmony, order immutable, eternal; for the Hebrew, flux, mutation, imminence, disorder" (*Judaism* 9). If the structure of this poem is "Hellenic," then the "Hebraic" quality must re-side in the mutations that occur: as the (Jewish) barbarian transforms into a reader of Greek, the goddess Athena hovers between being a desirable beauty and a scornful admonisher of Jewish presumptions. For a Jewish poet with an eastern European background, learning to write in the mod-ernist style of Pound and Eliot was akin to "reading Greek." Whether the "slightly scornful" Greek lips were those of a beautiful goddess or of fellow poets like Horace Gregory (who felt, after all, "a bit lonely" in Jewish company, "particularly in New York"), the Hellenic "picture . . . had long been on the wall" of Western culture and unavoidably confronted poets such as Reznikoff and the other Jewish Objectivists.

With his avid apprenticeship to Pound, Zukofsky espoused Hellenic stylistic values too; more surreptitiously, though, he introduced into his poetry translations from Hebrew and Yiddish, biblical allusions, and issues of Jewish ethnicity. These broadly "Hebraic" elements are especially no-ticeable in "Poem beginning 'The'" and in *"A"*-12, which memorializes his father. Beyond their use of specific Hebraic elements, both Reznikoff and Zukofsky looked to the *Menorah Journal* as an arena for their negotia-tions between Hebraism and Hellenism, but it functioned differently for each of them. Although he had conflicts with editors over specific texts, Reznikoff found the journal to be largely an encouraging and reassuring institution, which gave him the space he needed to develop his own unique synthesis of the Jewish and the American. For Zukofsky, however, who was a full generation younger than the *Menorah* founders, the journal was a frustrating, patriarchal institution; it accounted for a significant por-tion of the horizon in which his poetry and the Objectivist movement emerged, and yet it was unreceptive to his (Yiddish-inflected) stylistic and theoretical breakthroughs.

"EACH WORD UNDERSTOOD AND IN ITS RIGHT PLACE"

Reznikoff's sincerity also caught the eye of Lionel Trilling (1905–75), who, as Reznikoff had inferred from his discussion with *Menorah Journal* editor Elliot Cohen, was chosen over Louis Zukofsky to treat Reznikoff's writing. "Genuine Writing" begins by praising *By the Waters of Manhattan* as "remarkable and original in American literature." In particular, the novel possesses a "prose style that, without any of the postures of the 'stylist,' is of the greatest delicacy and distinction. But more importantly," insists Trilling, "by virtue of this prose style, he has written the first story of the Jewish immigrant that is not false" (*MP* 371). Like Zukofsky, Trilling finds a genuineness or sincerity in the correspondence between Reznikoff's plain style and his painstakingly observed subject matter. Also like Zukofsky, Trilling finds a distant model for Reznikoff's style; rather than pointing to Greek hexameters, though, Trilling shows how Reznikoff has employed "the dry, casual prose-tempo of the Icelandic sagas" (372) for his novel. Comparing a passage from a saga with one from Reznikoff's novel, Trilling persuasively demonstrates their affinities, commenting that

> [t]he choice of style was a happy one. The off-hand simplicity of the sagas is well fitted for the trivial family events of which they are so full, and this same tone, used for tragic events or for incidents of courage and prowess, gives to the more momentous matter a stoic, ironic understatement that is deeply effective. In using this style Mr. Reznikoff not only achieves for his simple domestic story this same effect of understated tragedy but by a legitimate connotation he evokes the heroism of the sagas as an aura for his Jewish chronicle.
> (373)

This is an astute observation about Reznikoff's style and its effect, and it could be applied to much of his writing, especially to *Testimony* (in both prose and verse versions), which likewise strives for the "effect of understated tragedy" in its sagas of the violent lives of ordinary people. Further on in his review, Trilling underscores the purity and lack of pretension in Reznikoff's writing: "Certainly it is not great prose in the sense that it is exciting or compelling. It makes no pretensions to this. Perhaps it is merely such prose as we should expect at the least from every writer—each word understood and in its right place; each word saying exactly what it should say and not forced beyond its meaning" (374). That last sentence must have pleased Reznikoff immensely, for it seems to name the full extent of his literary and moral intentions. For both Reznikoff and Trilling, a sincere style is a moral style, capable of rendering human truth: "In short, style forms its writer's morality. . . . The charm of Mr. Reznikoff's book lies in his avoidance of . . . falsification. His book has true words, hence truth—solid, raw, sociological truth" (376).

Trilling's own preoccupation with sincerity was a lifelong matter; it came to the fore in his 1970 Charles Eliot Norton lectures at Harvard, which were published as *Sincerity and Authenticity* (1972). A major Jewish intellectual—whose first book was devoted to Matthew Arnold—Trilling was another figure poised between Hebraism and Hellenism.[16] In contrast to the figure Zukofsky cut as a "painfully inarticulate soul" in Mark Van Doren's pantheon of "Jewish Students I Have Known," Trilling gave the impression of being a *flâneur* with a streak of "fastidiousness": "What he will eventually do, if he does it at all, will be lovely, for it will be the fruit of a pure intelligence slowly ripened in not too fierce a sun" (Van Doren 268). Van Doren seems to have had no inkling that Trilling was capable of becoming the Jackie Robinson of Jewish intellectuals through his successful battle for tenure at Columbia years later. During and after college, though, Trilling considered himself mainly a writer of fiction and published his first work in the *Menorah Journal,* where he was included in Elliot Cohen's stable of young, irreverent writers. In all, he contributed four short stories, eighteen book reviews, a personal essay, an essay in literary history, and two translations from French (Grumet, "Apprenticeship" 153). Initially, both Trilling and Zukofsky won teaching positions at the liberal University of Wisconsin, but while Trilling pursued a career of international renown at Columbia, Zukofsky was relegated to teaching in high schools and eventually secured tenure at Brooklyn Polytechnic Institute. Such intriguing parallels between Trilling and Zukofsky highlight the widely divergent paths that two brilliant young Jewish writers could take from a similar starting point. Beyond their many differences, though, a kind of occult connection persists through their mutual allegiance to the term *sincerity* and in their application of it as a criterion for praising Reznikoff's work.

By the time of Trilling's late *Sincerity and Authenticity,* the term had acquired a wealth of connotations for him, drawn from literary works of the last few centuries that he especially valued. Primarily, Trilling thought of sincerity as being who you say you are; thus, he conceived of it as a central strand in the moral fabric that holds together a bourgeois society. This notion of sincerity contains a politically conservative flavor that differs substantially from the sort of sincerity that George Oppen attributed to Reznikoff—a sincerity that holds society together through a mutual recognition of common humanity. Although both Oppen and Trilling were strongly impressed with the lack of pretension in Reznikoff's "plain" style, Oppen values Reznikoff's sincerity from a more populist vantage point: "The small and common words that build Reznikoff's tremendous poems will be with me, I think, in my last moments: these common words, the common scenes that build a universe" ("On Charles Reznikoff" 7). Trilling's notion of sincerity implies taking responsibility for oneself; Oppen's notion implies taking responsibility for being with others.

Reznikoff's invocation of a common world through simple language had a profound effect upon Oppen. As an aspiring, nineteen-year-old poet (fourteen years younger than Reznikoff), Oppen and his wife, Mary, met Zukofsky and then Reznikoff soon after they arrived in New York City in the late twenties. As he did for Zukofsky, Reznikoff provided for the Oppens a model of the poet's life and work—as conducted in an urban setting. In gratitude for the initiation he provided them, the Oppens referred to Reznikoff as their most valuable teacher for the remainder of their lives:

> GO: I really think we learned almost everything from Reznikoff. Certainly we learned to understand that city. We called on Reznikoff—
> I'm not sure that it was by his suggestion—we called on him regularly once a week. . . . So we had little trouble understanding each other. We watched him, we listened to him, we read his poetry, we just sat there and looked at him.
>
> MO: We also walked with him.
>
> GO: We walked.
>
> MO: Charles worked at the American Law Book Company down on the Brooklyn side of the Manhattan Bridge and after work in the evening sometimes we would meet Charles and walk with him across Manhattan Bridge the full length of Manhattan, stopping at his favorite restaurants. Here to have blueberry muffins, another place to have some other specialty that he knew about. And so we reached his home up in the Bronx; it was a *long* walk. Charles did this every morning to get to work and every evening to get home, and when he didn't walk with us he wrote as he went along. This was how he had time to himself and this was how he wrote his poetry.
> ("Memorial" 30–31)

In letters and interviews George Oppen states repeatedly that he was inspired by Reznikoff's engagements with language, with poetic form, with Jewishness, and with a populous urban world. For instance, when asked point blank, "Among your contemporaries, which poets had a particular influence upon your work?" Oppen answers, "First, and with a box drawn around it, Charles Reznikoff. . . . [T]o me, Reznikoff is *the* poet among the moderns" ("Interview" 14). To the question of whether Jewishness played a great part in any of Reznikoff's writing, Oppen responds, "I would say all of it, but it wasn't a patriotism, it was a fact and a depth of feeling of his own depth" ("Memorial" 35), indicating again his admiration for Reznikoff's "sincerity" with regard to Jewish identity.

Summing up his "criticism" of Reznikoff in a letter, Oppen recounts a climactic moment during World War II:

> I was with ((tho perhaps not very useful to)) the US infantry in France during the Second World War, and in the final days of that war found myself trapped in a fox-hole, slightly injured, and with no apparent means of escape, certainly no possibility until night-fall. I waited, I think, some ten hours, and during those hours Wyatt's little poem—"they flee from me . . . ," and poem after poem of Rezi's ran thru my mind over and over, these poems seemed to fill all the space around me and I wept and wept. This may not be literary criticism, or perhaps, on the other hand, it is.
>
> (*Selected Letters* 338)

Oppen's testimonial to the existential impact of Reznikoff's poetry seems to speak again to the complex notion of "sincerity" we have been considering. If we think of sincerity as an outcome of a direct approach to both form and content in a poem, then surely Reznikoff is a master of this approach. Stylistically, he achieves sincerity by writing with an "artful plainness," employing a carefully constructed plain style that subtly elevates a reader by its simplicity, groundedness, lack of pretension, and respect for the "materials" of the poem. As we have seen, Milton Hindus borrows Reznikoff's own term, "a Doric music," to describe this style, and he comments upon Reznikoff's affinity with William Wordsworth. This plain style also has a long American ancestry, beginning with the Puritan translators of *The Bay Psalm Book* (1640) and persisting into the present with a New England poet such as Robert Creeley.

With Oppen's claims for the ethical impact of Reznikoff's plain style in view, it makes sense to return to Harold Bloom's objections to that style. In the introduction, we discussed Bloom's disappointment with Reznikoff's choice as a Jewish poet to follow the Imagists rather than to adopt the prophetic style favored by English Romanticism. According to Bloom, the use of a plain style diminishes Reznikoff's ability to have a moral impact upon his readers, since it eschews the power of prophetic sublimity. It seems to me that what Reznikoff's plain style forfeits in poetic decorum—that is, by turning away from the matching of high style to sublime content—it gains through a pointed and challenging directness that moves a reader not by rhetorical power but by implicating one directly in the ethical encounters it depicts.

In a poem that we first explored in chapter 2, we can see Reznikoff crafting his own response to issues raised by practitioners of the Romantic sublime. We could imagine the following poem as a direct reply to Bloom's objections:[17]

As I was wandering with my unhappy thoughts,
I looked and saw
that I had come to a sunny place
familiar and yet strange.
"Where am I?" I asked a stranger. "Paradise."
"Can this be Paradise?" I asked surprised,
for there were motor-cars and factories.
"It is," he answered. "This is the sun that shone on Adam once;
the very wind that blew upon him, too."
(*CP* 2.75)

This poem contains many allusions to English Romantic poetry. The first line, for instance, can be read as a variation on Wordsworth's "I wandered lonely as a cloud" (Gill 303–4). In Wordsworth's famous poem about a field of daffodils, the wandering seems to be a natural activity ("as a cloud") outside the realm of social concerns ("lonely"). The Edenic scene that presents itself, composed of "waves" of daffodils, produces a feeling of joy in the speaker that returns to him in moments of solitary contemplation. Reznikoff's speaker, a "wandering" Jew, does not begin his experience "lonely as a cloud," but rather is preoccupied with "unhappy thoughts." Even more ironically, his Eden proves to be not a natural paradise evocative of bliss but a cityscape composed of cars and factories. Similarly, he does not store up this joyful experience, like Wordsworth does, for later contemplation, but speaks of it in the present tense. In other words, Reznikoff's poem does not celebrate "emotion recollected in tranquility," but rather the shock of discovering Eden hidden within the sordid details of daily life.

In his awareness of the need to find paradise within the urban wasteland, Reznikoff also comes close to the poetry of William Blake. In "London," from *Songs of Experience,* Blake laments the plight of the people he sees while wandering through the city:

I wander thro' each charter'd street,
Near where the charter'd Thames does flow.
And mark in every face I meet
Marks of weakness, marks of woe.
(Erdman 26)

When Reznikoff later wanders with his "unhappy thoughts" through New York City, he, too, may be lamenting the social conditions he observes; like Blake before him, Reznikoff remains acutely aware of the often immitigable distress caused by urban life. In the rousing preface to

the prophetic book *Milton,* written ten years after "London," Blake seeks
to redeem the fallen landscape of industrial England by imagining that
Jesus walked upon it and that paradise can still be discovered there by a
new vision:

And did those feet in ancient time,
Walk upon Englands mountains green:
And was the holy Lamb of God,
On Englands pleasant pastures seen!

And did the Countenance Divine,
Shine forth upon our clouded hills?
And was Jerusalem builded here,
Among these dark Satanic Mills?

Bring me my Bow of burning gold:
Bring me my Arrows of desire:
Bring me my Spear: O clouds unfold!
Bring me my Chariot of fire!

I will not cease from Mental Fight,
Nor shall my Sword sleep in my hand:
Till we have built Jerusalem,
In Englands green & pleasant Land.
(Erdman 95–96)

Looking like a direct precursor of Reznikoff's poem, this poem of
Blake's provides a model that will help us to make clear how Reznikoff
chooses to differ stylistically from the Romantic sublime. Both poets look
for a glimpse of paradise amid a profane urban world, portrayed by Reznikoff as a realm of "motor-cars and factories" and condemned by Blake for
its "dark Satanic Mills." In place of Blake's apocalyptic determination to
wage mental and sexual warfare for the sake of resacralizing the blighted
landscape, however, Reznikoff depicts the surprised witness to a revelation that paradise already inheres in whatever landscape we come upon
in daily life. The difference in tone is striking. Blake's third stanza, in
particular, reaches up for the sublime, signaling the immense bodily/
emotional/spiritual effort needed to overturn a mercantile and industrial
worldview. Reznikoff's tone of bemused surprise, on the other hand,
makes it seem that a new perception of reality is available to anyone willing
to shift perspective in any present moment. Although Blake's vision seems
more encompassing, more political and social than Reznikoff's, the sub-

lime rhetoric seems to draw attention ultimately to the heroic posture of the poet. Conversely, Reznikoff's vision, although it seems more personal than Blake's, succeeds in broadcasting widely to common readers one person's extraordinary perception by virtue of the plain style in which it is couched. Distrusting the rhetorical power of the Romantic sublime, Reznikoff makes equally stringent demands upon his readers by the feint of a rigorous simplicity.

In order to place Reznikoff's poetic accomplishments in the brightest possible light, the present study has taken off in a variety of directions; it was led by the notion that through uncovering the dilemmas that contribute to points of tension in a text, we gain the ability to say something valuable about what the text accomplishes. To remind us of some of what we have learned by doing this, I would like to offer a schematic overview of the Jewish dilemmas and responses to them treated in each chapter. In chapter 1, we considered the myriad ways in which Reznikoff placed himself between Hebrew and English. For Reznikoff, the dilemma of languages seems to ground itself in the negative space of the burnt book; out of this space arises the remarkable openness to others that characterizes his writing. Chapter 2 broadened the scope to explore ways in which Reznikoff and the *Menorah Journal* found themselves between the two stools of Judaism and modernity. Behind this dilemma lurks the historical condition of the Marrano, which is exemplified by Uriel DaCosta and Baruch Spinoza. One creative response offered to both forms of betweenness is the philosophy of immanence, invented by Spinoza and applied by Reznikoff, Zukofsky, and Oppen as a materialist and diasporic ideology. In chapter 3, we looked at two dilemmas, observing Reznikoff and the *Menorah Journal* negotiating between Hebraism and Hellenism and then watching Reznikoff and Kallen make their ways between Hebraism and Americanism. These dilemmas spawned vigorous research into Jewish history, for the purposes of displaying alternative Jewish identities and promoting the concepts of Jewish humanism and cultural pluralism. In chapter 4, we have considered how Zukofsky's position between Reznikoff and Pound was responsible for the birth of Objectivism. We have also seen how Reznikoff's plain style represents a blending of elements of Hebraism and Hellenism, which eschews the Romantic sublime that Bloom attributes to a stricter Hebraism (Bloom 249).

Throughout this study, the Jewish dilemmas faced by the Objectivists and other American intellectuals have appeared as forms of betweenness. As a "Land of In-Between," the Menorah movement and the resulting journal first brought the Jewish dilemmas out into a public space where they could be examined and initial solutions offered. Adopting a defensive posture in the journal, some writers mimicked the tones of European high culture, asserting that Jews ought to belong in such company; other Menorah thinkers offered genuinely new approaches, such as cultural pluralism and the historical reconception of the Jewish past, which gave rise to a perspectivist humanism. Drawing sustenance from the Menorah enterprise and inspiration from the reinsertion of Jewish culture into world history, Reznikoff, Zukofsky, and Oppen crafted a new poetry in which Jewish betweenness was at the heart of the dilemmas of urban modernity. For many Jewish poets (and many non-Jews as well) who began writing after World War II, the Objectivists became an indispensable foundation for building an avant-garde American poetry of international stature. Since the high modernist poets such as Pound, Eliot, Stevens, Moore, and H.D. have little to say about how to live in the multiethnic urban setting that characterizes most of the twentieth-century world, the task of articulating in poetry the ethics of such a world—and the forms appropriate to represent this ethics—fell to the Objectivists (including Niedecker and Williams). The resulting poetry represents a new arena in which language, society, and the individual can interanimate one another, and its accomplishment reverberates through much of the American poetry written in the second half of the twentieth century. One among a company of Jewish intellectual pioneers in modern Western culture, Charles Reznikoff lifted up his menorah in an inimitable, if ironic, greeting to the steely-eyed goddess of wisdom. The light struck by this encounter radiates still.

TRILLING AND GINSBERG

This book began by noting that the Objectivists deserve to occupy a much more prominent place on the map of Jewish poetry in America—a map that has, in many ways, been oriented around the gargantuan figure of Allen Ginsberg. Having made a case for the merits and importance of these earlier poets, I would like to look anew at Ginsberg himself, in order to see how the Jewish dilemmas undergone by a prior generation might have affected him. As I mentioned earlier, Ginsberg had great respect and affection for Reznikoff's poetry, but it was not a formative influence upon him. His father, the poet Louis Ginsberg (1895–1976), was a contemporary of Reznikoff's and published poems in the *Menorah Journal,* so that his son was certainly aware of the periodical and of the Jewish issues we have been considering. The most intense interaction with this earlier generation for which we have documentation, however, took place between Ginsberg and Lionel Trilling, and it is some of the Jewish nuances of this relationship that I would like to consider.

As we discussed in chapter 2, the philosophy of immanence, first promulgated by Spinoza, forms a central feature of Objectivist poetry. Building upon this feature of Objectivism, later American Jewish writers have found themselves involved in further dilemmas, corresponding to two of the major legacies of Spinoza's philosophy of immanence—a mystical legacy and a skeptical legacy. On the mystical side, Spinoza holds that God is coextensive with nature and thus is manifest everywhere, but there is also a demythologizing strain to Spinoza that can be seen in his critique of religion and of religious institutions. In European Jewish history during the eighteenth and nineteenth centuries, a roughly corresponding conflict between mystical and rational approaches to Judaism was played out in

the dramatic struggle between the populist Hasidic movement and its normative and intellectual opponents, the Mitnagdim, both of whom, moreover, believed in God's immanence.[1] In American Jewish culture after
World War II, these two strains reappear in symbolic guise and thus form
the basis for new Jewish dilemmas. Mystical and demythologizing impulses are rampant in Jewish-American literature of the second half of the
twentieth century. I will use the Hasidic/Mitnagdic dichotomy as a lens
for viewing the tensions between Allen Ginsberg and Lionel Trilling, but
I could just as easily employ it as a basis for reading the relationships of
specific poets following Ginsberg, such as Jerome Rothenberg (Hasid)
and David Antin (Mitnaged).

In 1943, the year Allen Ginsberg entered Columbia University, one of
his professors, Lionel Trilling, published in *Partisan Review* a story, "Of
This Time, of That Place," in which an English professor struggles with
strong sentiments of warmth and aversion toward his student—a seemingly mad, Romantically inspired poet. What is most remarkable about
the story is the exquisite balance in the narrator's ambivalence toward his
student, whose unorthodox brilliance he wishes to encourage and whose
rhapsodic mysticism he wishes to condemn as insane. That the student,
Tertan, is Jewish, comes out in subtle, but nonetheless convincing, ways:
"His face . . . was confusing, for it was made up of florid curves, the nose
arched in the bone and voluted in the nostril, the mouth loose and soft
and rather moist. Yet the face was so thin and narrow as to seem the very
type of asceticism" (*OTT* 82). This "racialized" description features the
stereotypes of the prominent Jewish nose and the weak and sentimental
Jewish mouth, combined with the thin facial structure ascribed to the Jewish intellectual. Also pronounced in Joseph Howe's portrait of his student
is an image of unhealthy poverty associated with the ghetto: "Howe noted
that his suit was worn thin, his shirt almost unclean. He became aware,
even, of a vague and musty odor of garments worn too long in unaired
rooms" (83).

Many people have considered Ginsberg the model for the bohemian
poet in Trilling's story (Klingenstein, *Jews* 186), but its early publication
date would seem to make such a direct identification unlikely. The fictional encounter between the young writer and his simultaneously encouraging and disapproving teacher offers a perfect model, though, for an
understanding of Ginsberg's relationship to Trilling and of the relationship
each has to the Jewish background that they share. As Jews in flight from
Judaism, Ginsberg and Trilling transpose different, but, in fact, well-worn
Jewish attitudes into their routes of escape: Ginsberg adopts an "Hasidic"
path away from Judaism, while Trilling pursues a "Mitnagdic" retreat.
In the eighteenth century, when Hasidism first arose in Poland and the

Ukraine, its ecstatic prayer communities were vehemently denounced by more legalistic and rationalistic Jews, called Mitnagdim (which means "opponents"). Just as the complex social world of eighteenth- and nineteenth-century Jewish Europe found expression in the bitter opposition of these two groups, so the American Jewish intellectual community of the fifties finds its hopes and fears represented in the tension between the mad, ecstatic, earthy Ginsberg and the rational, moralistic, refined Trilling—a tension that continues in American Jewish culture during the sixties and on into the present. Discussing Trilling in a history of Jews in the academy, Susanne Klingenstein sees this tension in precisely the terms I am offering: "What the Mitnagdim feared in the Hasidim . . . was precisely what Trilling criticized in the neo-romantic culture of the sixties" (*Jews* 158). These complementary Jewish positions form the symbolic basis for a kind of family romance involving Ginsberg, Trilling, and his wife, Diana.

As the first Jewish professor of English to fight his way into the Ivy League, Trilling's presence at Columbia held great significance for Ginsberg, for whom he was not only a reassuring Jewish mentor but also a stern father figure. Trilling had traded his early identification with Jewishness in the *Menorah Journal* for a career as genteel intellectual, modeling his thought and demeanor directly upon Matthew Arnold—whose ideas loomed so large for the *Menorah* intellectuals. He must have found Ginsberg's enactment of the stereotypes of Jewish pushiness, exhibitionism, sexual perversity, and madness a vision of his own worst nightmare. But Trilling did not distance himself from his student; instead, he acted as confidant and mentor and also intervened on Ginsberg's behalf in two major crises, both of which revolved around the poet's "mental health." The first took place in Ginsberg's senior year at Columbia, when the dean of students, who came to check on a cleaning woman's allegations that Ginsberg had traced obscene graffiti on a dirty window, found him in bed with Jack Kerouac. Homosexuality was such a taboo subject that the dean focused his outrage upon the graffiti. As Diana Trilling tells the story:

> [T]he words were too shocking for the Dean of Students to speak, so he had written them on a piece of paper which he pushed across the desk to my husband: "Fuck the Jews." Even the part of Lionel that wanted to laugh couldn't; it was too hard for the Dean to have to transmit this message to a Jewish professor—this was still in the forties when being a Jew in the university was not yet what it is today. "But he's a Jew himself," said the Dean. "Can you understand his writing a thing like that?" Yes, Lionel could understand; but he couldn't explain it to the Dean. ("Other Night" 57–58)

As Jews in the academy, Ginsberg and Trilling shared an unspoken kinship. Beyond this, as Jews in retreat from Judaism, both had adopted a
complex insider/outsider stance, in which Jewishness was an object of
scorn from which to distance oneself and also the most intimate part of
one's identity. Ginsberg's childhood identification with being a Jew was
complete, but most of his public statements about Jews and Judaism were
negative.[2] In a notebook, Trilling describes the intense and inescapable
awareness of being Jewish in terms that apply to both of them: "Being a
Jew is like walking in the wind or swimming: you are touched at all points
and conscious everywhere" (Klingenstein, *Jews* 157). For these two figures, such an acute awareness was a source at once of pride, anguish, and
not a little confusion. Trilling's reflection has a certain affinity with Emerson's famous depiction of the "transparent eyeball," but where Emerson's
vision is wholly transcendent ("the currents of the Universal Being circu-
late through me; I am part or particle of God" [Emerson 189]), Trilling's
image invokes an acute corporeal awareness. Such a vision of extreme
sensitivity—both to the texture of the world and to the haunting gaze
of anti-Semitism—provides an inner locus where Ginsberg and Trilling
meet. This palpable and encompassing sense of Jewishness may have contributed to Ginsberg's alternating fits of consciousness-expansion and
paranoia and to the fear of madness in Trilling's stories like "Of This Time,
of That Place" and in critical works like *Sincerity and Authenticity,* which
contains a scathing attack on the sixties youth culture spawned by Ginsberg and the Beats.

As a result of the incident at Columbia, Ginsberg was suspended for a
year and ordered to seek psychiatric treatment. Later, a second, more serious crisis occurred, and Trilling's intervention in it probably had a greater
impact as well. In 1949, after he had graduated, Ginsberg was arrested
while riding in a car full of stolen goods. On the basis of testimony by the
Trillings, Mark Van Doren, and several others, Ginsberg was committed
to a mental hospital rather than sent to prison. Like the character Howe
in his 1943 story, Trilling felt that his "mad" student was seriously out of
touch with reality and had to be brought back in line. Ironically, it was
during his stay at the Psychiatric Institute that Ginsberg met Carl Solomon, to whom he later dedicated "Howl"—the poem in which his rebellion against "reality" received definitive expression. Throughout this entire decade from 1945 to 1955, Trilling's fondness for and active support
of the young Ginsberg alternates with feelings of revulsion and attempts
at stern admonition.

In 1956, before *Howl and Other Poems* was published, Ginsberg sent
Trilling a copy of the manuscript, with the request "Let me know what
you think of them. I can't really imagine what your reaction should

be, and I'm interested" (*Howl* fac. 155). In addition, Ginsberg sought
to inform Trilling about the new poetry scene, extolling the merits of
Charles Olson, Black Mountain College, and "several good unknown
Zen poets" (156) and including a general evaluation of contemporary poetry:

> I think what is coming is a romantic period (strangely tho everybody
> thinks that by being hard-up and classical they are going to make it like
> Eliot which is silly). Eliot & Pound are like Dryden & Pope. What gives
> now is much more personal—how could there be now anything but a
> reassertion of naked personal subjective truth—eternally real? Perhaps
> Whitman will be seen to have set the example and been bypassed for
> half a century.
> (156)

Trilling's response could not have been more disparaging:

> Dear Allen,
>   I'm afraid I have to tell you that I don't like the poems at all. I hesitate
> before saying that they seem to me quite dull, for to say of a work which
> undertakes to be shocking that it is dull is, I am aware, a well known
> and all too easy device. But perhaps you will believe that I am being
> sincere when I say that they are dull. They are not like Whitman—they
> are all prose, all rhetoric, without any music. . . . As for the doctrinal
> element of the poems, apart from the fact that I of course reject it, it
> seems to me that I heard it very long ago and that you give it to me in
> all its orthodoxy, with nothing new added.
>
>   Sincerely yours,
>   Lionel Trilling
> (156)

These letters contain several issues worth remarking upon. In the first
place, how could Ginsberg pretend not to know what Trilling's reaction
would be? "Howl" and its accompanying poems dramatize profoundly
antisocial emotions and actions that Trilling would feel compelled to condemn unequivocally; in addition, "Howl" celebrates the very pitfalls of
homosexuality and insanity from which Trilling had tried desperately to
save Ginsberg. There may have been anger and remorse in Trilling's tone
as well, for he had felt a responsibility toward the poet that he did not
know how to discharge. Remembering how Ginsberg had come to Lionel as a student with tales like those recounted in "Howl," Diana says
that her advice to her husband was, "'He wants you to forbid him to
behave like that. He wants you to take him out of it, or why does he
choose people like you and Mark Van Doren to tell these stories to?' To

which I received always the same answer: 'I'm not his father,' a response that of course allowed no argument" ("Other Night" 60–61). Why did this truism allow no argument? Although it was meant to place a boundary around Trilling's responsibility for Ginsberg, it was, in fact, emotionally inaccurate, for their relationship was nothing if not that of a father and son.

Another intriguing feature of the Ginsberg-Trilling correspondence is Ginsberg's prophecy of the coming romantic period in poetry, which would supersede the neoclassicism of Eliot and Pound. Writing to a man who believes that "subjectivism" is a central feature of the moral disease of our time, Ginsberg blithely asks, "How could there be now anything but a reassertion of naked personal subjective truth—eternally real?" It's not surprising, then, that Trilling harps upon the "dullness" of Ginsberg's poems, as though he were Pope writing a new book of The Dunciad, and that he rejects the "doctrinal element" of the poems as representing an ancient, pernicious "orthodoxy." His use of "doctrinal element" and "orthodoxy" seems a particularly cruel attempt to deflate Ginsberg's enthusiastic espousal of a new vision and a new community. We could also hear this as a reproach by a modern refuser of Jewish Orthodoxy leveled at an Hasidic enthusiast—for who has become more orthodox and doctrinaire, ironically, than the Hasidim? Taking this criticism a step further, it is possible to imagine Trilling, if he had lived longer, leveling the same reproach against Ginsberg the Tibetan Buddhist. There may be another source for Trilling's accusation of orthodoxy, audible in the passage "it seems to me that I heard it very long ago and that you give it to me in all its orthodoxy, with nothing new added." I suspect that the time "very long ago" when Trilling heard such a doctrine was during the thirties, when revolutionary feelings ran high and gave rise to all sorts of countercultural orthodoxies.

Diana Trilling offers some support for this suspicion in "The Other Night at Columbia: A Report from the Academy," which she wrote for Partisan Review following Ginsberg's triumphant return to Columbia to read his poetry in 1959. The article is remarkable for its Jamesian sentences (full of qualifications, reversals, and conditional and subjunctive verbs), for its wild swings between condescension and appreciation, and for its portrayal of Diana herself as a kind of Jamesian female innocent—through whose sometimes mute awareness we glimpse a titanic struggle. A regular contributor to Partisan Review, Diana disingenuously sets the scene by presenting herself as a "wife from the English department" who goes to view the latest phenomenon: "The 'Beats' were to read their poetry at Columbia on Thursday evening and on the spur of the moment three wives from the English department had decided to go to hear them" (56). We later find out that, as Diana already knew, the English department itself was boycotting the reading, with the exception of Fred Dupee, whose job was to introduce the poets and thus to contain their outrageousness through the exercise of academic decorum. In reality, then, Diana has come to the reading as a maternal mediator between official Columbia and its rebellious children—Ginsberg in particular. In a strangely qualified statement, she sets forth an interesting analysis of Ginsberg's motive for arranging the reading: "I suppose I have no right to say now, and on such early and little evidence, that Ginsberg had always desperately wanted to be respectable, or respected, like his instructors at Columbia, it is so likely that this is a hindsight which suits my needs. It struck me, though, that this was the most unmistakable and touching message from platform to audience the other night, and as I received it, I felt I had known something like it all along" (60).

From within the cloud of circular reasoning, Diana seems to have named one of the magnetic poles of Ginsberg's nature—his desperate desire for respectability. There is a similar, though opposite, observation to be made about her husband's deep but seldom acknowledged desire to write fiction. Believing that "the artist derives his powers from . . . a species of insanity," Lionel opted instead for social adjustment; comparing himself to Jewish writers like Mailer, Bellow, and Malamud, he confesses, "I defeated myself long ago when I rejected the way of chutzpah and mishagass in favor of reason and diffidence" (Klingenstein, *Jews* 186–87). We could say, then, that Lionel's wish to possess the mad, creative abandon of the true artist, repressed in favor of seeking unimpeachable respectability, mirrors the way Ginsberg uses his exhibitionist and confrontational behavior to mask a powerful longing "to be respectable, or respected, like his instructors at Columbia." The link between the Trillings and Ginsberg becomes even stronger when Diana looks back to the thirties to explain her misgivings about even her most positive responses to Beat poetry. Speaking of poems like Ginsberg's "Ignu" and Corso's "Marriage," Diana finds that their "chief virtue . . . was their 'racial-minority' funniness, their 'depressed-classes' funniness of a kind which has never had so sure and live a place as it did in the thirties, the embittered fond funniness which has to do with one's own impossible origins" ("Other Night" 61). These poems were funny, she admits, but they would have been even funnier and had more bite had they been delivered at a time when ethnic Americans were still outsiders, rather than the "Americans-like-everyone-else" they have become. Speaking of her own "impossible origins," she notes, "The Jew in particular is a loss to literature and life—I mean the Jew out of which was bred the Jewish intellectual of the thirties. For a few short years in the thirties, as not before or since, the Jew was at his funniest, shrewdest best" (62). The most salient quality of the thirties for Diana— the quality that differentiates it most strongly from the fifties—was the sense of community among intellectuals:

> [T]here was never a less lonely time for intellectuals than the Depression, or a less depressed time. . . . Actually, it was a time of generally weak intellection—or so it seems to me now—but of very strong feeling. Everyone judged everyone else; it was a time of incessant cruel moral judgment. . . . In the thirties one's clinical vocabulary was limited to two words, escapism and subjectivism, and both of them applied only to other people's wrong political choices.
> (62–63)

As Diana presents it, the thirties was a time when the Hasidic and Mit-nagdic impulses actually joined together, so that a kind of intellectual strictness married a kind of mad humor and abandon. Such a vision of the thirties as compounded of an exhilarating sense of community and noisy doctrinal disputes is likely being invoked by Lionel when he dismisses the "doctrinal element" of "Howl" as something he had heard "very long ago." When Ginsberg writes enthusiastically of "a reassertion of naked personal subjective truth," Trilling might be thinking to himself, "Oy! subjectivism again?" In this way, Trilling can be linked once more to Objectivism, for he understood, as did the poets, that among Jewish radicals "subjectivism" denoted a misunderstanding of what Zukofsky called "the direction of historic and contemporary particulars" (*Poetry* 268). This gives us a new, political way to hear the term *Objectivism:* if marxist analysis were seen as "scientific" and thus as objective, then an "objectivist" poet would understand the economic underpinnings of "historic and contemporary particulars" in a way that a "subjectivist" (i.e., politically benighted) poet never could. As Diana seems to be saying in her article, without an objectivist brake against his runaway subjectivism, Ginsberg would never develop a sincere relationship to his historical moment. Unlike her husband, though, she feels the necessity of actively acknowledging a filial bond between her generation and the Beats: "But they have their connection with us who were young in the thirties, their intimate political connection, which we deny at risk of missing what it is that makes the 'Beat' phenomenon something to think about" ("Other Night" 63).

Diana is willing to go further even in claiming a connection between the Trillings and the Beats. During the Columbia reading, when Ginsberg read from his new poem to his mother, "Kaddish," Diana was fascinated to know that Louis Ginsberg was in the audience and that the younger Ginsberg wept for that reason while he read the poem. She tries to speculate about what the elder Ginsberg felt, but professes ignorance: "I have no way of knowing what Ginsberg's father felt the other night about his son being up there on the stage at Columbia (it rather obsesses me)" (70). She gives vent to her obsession in an imaginative misreading of Ginsberg's poem, "The Lion for Real":

> Clearly, I am no judge of his poem "Lion in the Room," which he announced was dedicated to Lionel Trilling; I heard it through too much sympathy, and also self-consciousness. The poem was addressed as well as dedicated to Lionel; it was about a lion in the room with the poet, a lion who was hungry but refused to eat him; I heard it as a passionate love-poem; I really can't say whether it was a good or bad poem, but I was much moved by it, in some part unaccountably. (70–71)

Not only did Diana mishear the title of the poem, but she created an intriguingly deviant interpretation, decoding the poem through the lens of family romance. By most critical accounts, "The Lion for Real" is a straightforward allegory of the difficulties Ginsberg was having in remaining faithful to his 1948 visionary experience, in which he heard William Blake recite from *Songs of Innocence and Experience*. The "lion in my living room" (*CP* 174) would then symbolize the powerful vision; the vicissitudes of the trapped lion result from the poet's confusion about how to nurture it. According to his biographer, Barry Miles, "Ginsberg's ironic dedication to Trilling referred to the line 'a lion myself starved by Professor Kandisky, dying in a lion's flophouse circus'" (259). Instead of hearing the hostility or disappointment in that particular line, Diana seems to have taken "lion" to refer to "Lionel"—thus producing a completely different reading, which makes her husband central to the poem. In her reading, "The Lion for Real" records an oedipal struggle in which the son comes to love rather than to kill the overbearing father; as mediating mother, Diana can effect a rapprochement between lionized poet and leonine critic.

After the Columbia reading, standing close by the poet, Diana resists an impulse to overhear his conversation with his father and to join that conversation herself: "In some part of me, I wanted to speak to Ginsberg, tell him I had liked the poem he had written to my husband, but I didn't dare: I couldn't be sure that Ginsberg wouldn't take my meaning wrong" ("Other Night" 73). I assume that she was concerned that the Hasidic poet might consider her maternal intimacy and approval something more than an imaginative connection: he might regard it as a literal invitation to rejoin her Mitnaged "family." When she returns home, to find in progress a meeting "of the pleasant professional sort," though, she reveals to the eight professors gathered there that she had been moved by the evening's reading. "I'm ashamed of you," W. H. Auden chides her, as if to extinguish completely the warmth the evening had generated in her. On her way out of the room, though, she says to her husband, "Allen Ginsberg read a lovely poem to you, Lionel. I liked it very much" (73–74). Nothing more is spoken aloud, but Diana ends her "report" by confirming an unspoken, and in some ways unspeakable, connection between "Ginsberg" and "Trilling," a connection implicit in what she has just said to Lionel: "I'm certain that Ginsberg's old teacher knew what I was saying, and why I was impelled to say it" (74). Without saying so, by an imaginative and subterranean route, Diana, as mediating mother, had momentarily resynthesized the opposing impulses of what we might think of as the Jewish First Family of the postwar era.

CHRONOLOGY

1887 Ezekiel Wolvovsky, Reznikoff's maternal grandfather, dies in Russia; his Hebrew poetry is burned by his wife.

1894 August 30, Charles Reznikoff born to Sarah Yetta Wolvovsky Reznikoff and Nathan Reznikoff in the "Jewish Ghetto" of Brownsville, Brooklyn, New York.

1899 Marie Syrkin, daughter of Nachman Syrkin (founder of Labor Zionism), born in Switzerland.

1910 Graduates from high school.

1910–11 Freshman in the School of Journalism at University of Missouri.

1912–15 New York University Law School, LL.B., graduates second in his class and admitted to bar in 1916.

1918 *Rhythms,* self-published. Joins the ROTC at Columbia, prepares to fight in Europe. War ends.

1919 *Rhythms II,* self-published.

1920 *Poems,* published by Samuel Roth, New York.

1921 *Uriel Accosta: A Play & a Fourth Group of Verse,* self-published.

1922 *Chatterton, the Black Death, and Meriwether Lewis* (plays), self-published.

1923 *Coral and Captive Israel* (plays), self-published.

1924 Begins to publish in the *Menorah Journal.* First four pieces to appear are plays.

1927 *Nine Plays* and *Five Groups of Verse,* both self-published.

1928 Goes to work for *Corpus Juris* writing legal definitions.

1929 *By the Waters of Manhattan: An Annual,* self-published.

1930 Marries Marie Syrkin. His novel *By the Waters of Manhattan,* one of the earliest paperbacks, published by Charles Boni. Introduction by Louis Untermeyer. Enthusiastic reviews, including one by Lionel Trilling. Reznikoff receives $1000.

1931 The "Objectivist" issue of *Poetry* appears in February, introduced by Louis Zukofsky's "Sincerity and Objectification: With Special Reference to the Work of Charles Reznikoff."

1932 An *"Objectivists" Anthology,* edited by Louis Zukofsky and including work by Reznikoff, published by TO, Publishers, France.

1933   Marie's first visit to Palestine.

1934   Publishes *Jerusalem the Golden, Testimony* (introduction by Kenneth Burke), and *In Memoriam: 1933,* all with the Objectivist Press. *In Memoriam: 1933* was first published, in its entirety, in the *Menorah Journal* 22.2 (1934).

1936   *Separate Way* published by the Objectivist Press. *Early History of a Sewing Machine Operator* (with Nathan Reznikoff), self-published.

1937   His mother, Sarah Yetta Reznikoff, dies February 12.

1938-39   Goes to Hollywood as assistant to producer Albert Lewin, an old friend. Lives in Santa Monica, where Marie visits him during the two summers.

1941   *Going To and Fro and Walking Up and Down,* self-published.

1942   *Jewish Frontier* publishes first American account of Holocaust in Europe, introduced by Marie.

1944   His novel *The Lionhearted: A Story about the Jews in Medieval England* published by the Jewish Publication Society. His poem "A Compassionate People" leads off the thirtieth anniversary issue of the *Menorah Journal.*

1950   Marie appointed professor of English literature at Brandeis University and moves to Boston. Charles stays in New York. *The Jews of Charleston: A History of an American Jewish Community* (with Uriah Engelman) published by the Jewish Publication Society.

1951   Translation of Emil Bernard Cohn, *Stories and Fantasies from the Jewish Past,* published by Jewish Publication Society.

1956   Translation of Israel Joseph Benjamin, *Three Years in America, 1859–1862,* published by Jewish Publication Society.

1957   Edits *Louis Marshall: Champion of Liberty; Selected Papers and Addresses,* published by Jewish Publication Society.

1959   *Inscriptions: 1944–1956,* self-published.

1961   "Rediscovered" by Milton Hindus in the January 16 issue of *The New Leader.*

1962   *By the Waters of Manhattan: Selected Verse* published by New Directions and San Francisco Review (edited by June Oppen Degnan). Introduction by C. P. Snow.

1963   *Family Chronicle* (with Sarah and Nathan Reznikoff), self-published. 1971 Introduction to British edition by Harry Golden.

1965   *Testimony: The United States 1885–1890: Recitative* published by New Directions.

1966   Marie retires from Brandeis and returns to live with Charles in New York.

1968   *Testimony: The United States (1891–1900): Recitative,* self-published.

1969   *By the Well of Living and Seeing and The Fifth Book of the Maccabees,* self-published.

1974 Reading at San Francisco State College, March 21; introduced by George Oppen. *By the Well of Living & Seeing: New and Selected Poems 1918–1973* published by Black Sparrow Press. Introduction by Seamus Cooney.

1975 *Holocaust* published by Black Sparrow Press.

1976 Dies in Manhattan January 22.

1976-77 *Complete Poems* published by Black Sparrow Press in two volumes. Edited by Seamus Cooney.

1977 *The Manner "Music"* published by Black Sparrow Press. Introduction by Robert Creeley.

1978-79 *Testimony: The United States (1885–1915): Recitative* published by Black Sparrow Press in two volumes.

1988 Marie dies February 1.

NOTES

In citing works in the text and notes, short titles have been used. Works frequently cited have been identified by the following abbreviations:

CP1, CP2 Reznikoff, Charles. *Poems 1918–1975: The Complete Poems of Charles Reznikoff.* Ed. Seamus Cooney. 2 vols. Santa Barbara: Black Sparrow, 1976–77.

MP Hindus, Milton, ed. *Charles Reznikoff: Man and Poet.* Orono: National Poetry Foundation, 1984.

OTT Trilling, Lionel. *Of This Time, of That Place and Other Stories.* New York: Harcourt, 1979.

UCSD Charles Reznikoff Papers. MSS 9. Mandeville Special Collections Library, U of California, San Diego. Abbreviation is followed by numbers representing collection, box, and folder.

1. Strangely, given Kenner's lasting advocacy for at least some of the writers he discusses in *A Homemade World*—Zukofsky in particular—the book reads like an exercise in wishing away several generations of American writers, portraying those who did not expatriate and join the international wing of modernism—such as William Carlos Williams and Wallace Stevens—as Lilliputians among the Gullivers such as Pound and Eliot.

2. It is important to mention two other non-Jewish participants in the Objectivist movement, whose poetic careers were intertwined significantly with those of one or more of the Jewish Objectivists: Basil Bunting (1900–85) and Lorine Niedecker (1903–70). It would take an entire chapter to discuss the various critical attempts at defining Objectivism. A short list of useful efforts at definition include Altieri; DuPlessis, in Oppen, *Letters* vii–x; Fredman 87–89; Heller; McAllister; Palmer; Quartermain (1–20); Sharp, "'Objectivists'"; Silliman; and Williams 264–65. In addition, a case could be made that L. S. Dembo, in the interviews he conducted with Oppen, Rakosi, Reznikoff, and Zukofsky in 1968 (Dembo and Pondrom 172–232), had a hand in reviving the term *Objectivism* as important for literary history. A new volume of essays edited by DuPlessis and Quartermain, *The Objectivist Nexus: Essays in Cultural Poetics,* was published too late for consideration in the present study. This volume reprints essays I have cited by Altieri, Bernstein, and Franciosi.

3. See Jenkins for a discussion of the centrality of ethics to the entire "objectivist strain" in twentieth-century American poetry.

4. There is no biography of Reznikoff. Biographical materials can be found in his *Letters* and interviews (*MP* 97–136 and Rovner); in Milton Hindus's introductions to the *Letters* (5–16) and the *Man and Poet* volume (*MP* 15–33); in Hindus's short essay, "Charles Reznikoff," and his longer monograph, *Reznikoff;* in Marie Syrkin's memoir (*MP* 37–67); and in Franciosi, "Story."

5. For information about and analysis of the *Menorah Journal,* see Alter, "Epitaph"; Grumet, "Menorah Idea"; Harap; Hurwitz and Sharfman; Joselit, "Without Ghettoism"; Strauss; and Wald.

6. Mumford did not discover his own Jewish background until the late 1930s.

7. The following is a complete list of Reznikoff items in the *Menorah Journal:*

- "Captive Israel." 10.1 (1924): 38–45.
- "The Black Death." 10.4 (1924): 381–85.
- "Abram in Egypt." 10.5 (1924): 514–15.
- "Uriel Acosta." 11.1 (1925): 35–42.
- "Apocrypha." 14.2 (1928): 163–87.
- "Hebrew." 14.5 (1928): 434.
- "By the Waters of Manhattan." 16.4 (1929): 346–47.
- "Nudnik." 17.2 (1929): 184–87.
- "Salesmen." 17.3 (1929): 279–80.
- "A Dialogue: Padua 1727." 18.3 (1930): 220.
- "By the Waters of Manhattan: 1930." 18.5 (1930): 417–21.
- "Passage-At-Arms." 19.1 (1930): 63–66.
- "In the Country." 19.2 (1930): 185–88.
- "Meetings and Partings, Friends and Strangers." 20.1 (1932): 75–79.
- *In Memoriam: 1933.* 22.2 (1934): 103–33.
- "Land of Refuge." 24.1 (1936): 30–32.
- "A Group of Verse." 24.2 (1936): 116–18.
- "A Short History of Israel." 28.1 (1940): 9–16.
- "A Story for a Dramatist." 28.3 (1940): 269–78.
- "The King's Jews: A Historical Novel." 29.3 (1941): 312–28.
- "Scenes and Characters from the American Epic: I. Jews Enter Georgia." 31.2 (1943): 125–36.
- "Scenes and Characters from the American Epic: II. Secretary of War Judas." 31.3 (1943): 263–72.
- "A Compassionate People." 32.1 (1944): 1–4.
- "Pharisee: From a Historical Novel." 32.2 (1944): 203–15.
- "Scenes and Characters from the American Epic: III. Gold-Rush Days (1849)." 33.2 (1945): 153–61.
- "Scenes and Characters from the American Epic: IV. Bleeding Kansas (1856)." 35.1 (1947): 42–56.
- "Scenes and Characters from the American Epic: V. The Search for the Indian Scout." 36.2 (1948): 216–28.
- "By the Waters of Manhattan, 1948." 37.1 (1949): 71–74.
- Lionel Trilling, "Genuine Writing," rev. of *By the Waters of Manhattan,* by Charles Reznikoff. 19.1 (1930): 88–92.
- Libby Benedict, "History Alight." rev. of *The Lionhearted,* by Charles Reznikoff. 33.1 (1945): 101–103.

8. See Perloff, "Pound/Stevens: Whose Era?" (*Dance* 1–32), for an illuminating discussion of the opposing positions on modern poetry taken by Kenner and Bloom.

9. Zukofsky had noted the same quality of "adjacency" many years earlier, drawing attention to "the grouping of nouns" in Reznikoff's poetry "so that they partake of the quality of things being together without violence to their individual intact natures" (*Poetry* 278).

CHAPTER ONE

1. Even when critics treat Reznikoff as both Objectivist and Jewish poet, they usually separate the two aspects and often argue that Reznikoff is more successful at embodying one of these identities than the other. In a careful account of what he describes as conflicts between Objectivism and Judaism in Reznikoff's writing, Robert Alter ("Charles Reznikoff"), for example, sees Reznikoff's Objectivist writing as much more convincing than his Jewish writing, except when the poet registers his own sense of exile from traditional Judaism. Welcome exceptions to the critical tendency to separate these two sides of Reznikoff can be found in Hindus, *Reznikoff*; Cohen-Cheminet; Syverson; and Auster.

2. *Reznik* is a translation into Russian of *shokhet,* the kosher slaughterer.

3. Reznikoff's father, Nathan, also seemed to have some discomfort about his name, for he starts off his autobiographical narrative, *Early History of a Sewing-Machine Operator,* with the sentence, "I should have been named after my father's father" (*Family Chronicle* 101). In fact, he did receive this name, but only after a miraculous intervention. According to the family legend, shortly before Nathan's birth his mother's grandfather died, leaving her the most precious of legacies for her first-born son, "the phylacteries [small leather boxes containing biblical texts, worn by Jewish men during morning prayer] for which Jacob the Scribe had written the passages from the Torah. Jacob had been the most pious of scribes: whenever he had to write the name of the Lord he would immerse himself in a ritual bath, and so his phylacteries cost fifty roubles in days when common phylacteries could be had for a rouble" (101–2). Everyone agreed that "for such an inheritance, . . . I should be named Nehemiah, after my mother's grandfather" (102). But when he was born, the baby refused to nurse and the mother fell into a fever. A puppy was found to suck the milk, after which the baby was induced to nurse. When she awoke, the mother told of a dream in which a stranger came to her bed and reassured her that the child would suck. When she described the stranger, her mother-in-law identified him: "That was not a stranger, my child: that was your father-in-law, may he rest in peace! He surely begged the Lord for your life" (103). And so, overcoming the grandfather who provided a holy text, the father-in-law won out in the naming contest and was allowed to give his own name, Nathan, to the baby. In this case, the fluency of the mother's milk was more important than the fluency of prayers offered while wearing the holy phylacteries. The conflict between

Hebrew prayers and motherly intimacy recurs in Reznikoff's life, as we shall see later in this chapter.

4. See Omer-Sherman for a more extended discussion of the urban stranger in Reznikoff's poetry.

5. The temptation to view Reznikoff as a tragic figure is countered by his own summation of his life, as remembered by his wife: "'You know, I never made money but I have done everything that I most wanted to do.' I have always been glad to remember that on the day he did not know would be his last he spoke with such deep satisfaction of his eighty years" (*MP* 65).

6. See Boyarin ("Placing Reading") for a fascinating discussion of the socio-cultural distinctions between Jewish reading practices, as they developed in biblical and rabbinic times, and European reading practices, invented in the Middle Ages. In Judaism, "reading" has always been a public activity with the force of a religious speech-act. Beginning with Augustine and culminating in writers such as Dante and Chaucer, European reading has striven to become private, taking place archetypally in the monk's cell or the lover's bedroom. The differences in the two types of schooling available to Reznikoff replicate these ethnographically diverse forms of reading.

7. My thanks to Mary Burgess for drawing my attention to the mediating function of *between* in this stanza, and to Vincent Sherry for commenting upon the rhythmic and syntactic stress the word receives.

8. In a fascinating account of the sociological and ideological dimensions of the "miraculous" revival of Hebrew as the base language of the State of Israel, Harshav sketches out the nearly impossible process by which Hebrew was reinvented as a living language *(Language)*. This reinvention of Hebrew in the last century is a purely secular phenomenon—one aspect of the secular, nationalist, and cosmopolitan trends of modernity.

9. I want to thank Alexander Gelley for pointing out to me that Benjamin's "quasi-kabbalistic" perspective depended not only upon his conversations with Gershom Scholem but also upon his knowledge of the German Romantics—which accounts in turn for his speaking generally of "sacred writings" and "Scriptures" rather than explicitly invoking Torah. As Robert Alter puts it, "Benjamin's theory of language is Hebrew as conceived by the Kabbalah transposed into a universalized metaphysical abstraction" (*Necessary Angels* 46). For Benjamin, as for Reznikoff, Hebrew remains a kind of buried language whose acquisition is intensely desired but ever deferred.

10. See also Wyman 48–49.

11. In her autobiography, *The Promised Land* (1912), Mary Antin speaks of Hebrew as a similarly palpable language: "I loved the sound of the words, the full, dense, solid sound of them" (quoted in Wirth-Nesher, "Language As Homeland" 214).

12. For a recent anthropological account of "the savage in Judaism," see Eilberg-Schwartz.

13. For a discussion of the gender dynamics of Yiddish and Hebrew, see N. Seidman.

14. Thanks to Rachel Blau DuPlessis for pointing out the conjunction of blessing and kissing.

15. In a note to the author, Henry Weinfield speculates that Reznikoff borrowed the name Jude from Thomas Hardy's protagonist in *Jude the Obscure,* who is himself a *poète manqué.* "Jude" is also the German word for "Jew."

16. This characterization of Hebrew is written from the imagined point of view of Reznikoff. In fact, at the time of Reznikoff's grandfather's death, Russian Jewish writers like Ahad Ha-Am and H. N. Bialik were composing a new secular literature in Hebrew, which came to undergird the modern revival of Hebrew in Israel (see Harshav, *Language*).

17. This stanza was excised by Reznikoff when he printed it in his New Directions book of selected poems, *By the Waters of Manhattan.* Was its equation of fire with poetic creation too hard to bear in 1962?

18. Interestingly, the burnt book as a symbolic actor in the turbulent social life of America also figures in Reznikoff's prose version of *Testimony* (1934). In one of the first pieces, a murderer receives a prophetic dream, in which a burning Bible appears as a sign of divine judgment: "When Jim was put in jail he dreamed a dream, and then he knew he would be hanged. He dreamed that his two hands were tied together, and were on fire; there was a book hung before them—it had a leather cover just like the one they swore him on at the trial— the book caught fire and all the leaves were burning" (7).

19. For a thorough discussion of the issues involved in testimony, particularly Holocaust testimony, see Felman and Laub.

20. Sidra Ezrahi comments that *Holocaust,* Reznikoff's last book, varies from *Testimony* by foregrounding the legal framework with slightly more intensity. This is because we are more aware of the contextual pressure of the Nuremberg and Eichmann trials than we would be of the legal setting for the turn-of-the-century American material Reznikoff uses in *Testimony.* In both of his books, however, the emphasis remains on lifting the testimony out of its legal context, for what matters to the poet is that the recounting of events has occurred under conditions that press for maximum veracity. As Ezrahi admits, "whatever irony is brought to bear on the notion that the legal procedure can contain or avenge the horrors of genocide must be read into the text" (37). Michael Davidson sees the legal framework of *Testimony* not as a source of irony but rather as providing a principle for organizing Reznikoff's documentary history of America (*Ghostly Demarcations* 149–70). Like Kathryn Shevelow, Davidson also gives a careful account of the procedures Reznikoff used to cull, compose, and edit the poems of *Testimony.*

CHAPTER TWO

1. Once the cliché of falling between two stools emerges from an analysis of the theme of the double bind in Reznikoff's and Alter's work, it's hard to stop noticing it in the literature on this period in Jewish history. In a five-

volume history, *The Jewish People in America,* for instance, the New York Intellectuals, many of whom began their careers in the *Menorah Journal,* are described as follows: "Writers like Philip Rahv, William Phillips, Lionel and Diana Trilling, Meyer Shapiro, Clement Greenberg, Elliot Cohen, Paul
Goodman, Harold Rosenberg, Sidney Hook, and Lionel Abel were part of a
cohort that had fallen between two chairs, neither belonging to the Jewish culture of their parents nor feeling fully part of American culture" (Feingold 79).
In Milton Hindus's *Charles Reznikoff,* we learn that in Reznikoff's negotiations
between Judaism and Americanism, "He is not among those writers who have
striven to suppress one or another of these motivations and have sometimes succeeded only in falling between two stools" (23). Finally, Jonathan Boyarin
drew my attention to the title of Werner Fuld's biography of Walter Benjamin:
Walter Benjamin: Zwischen den Stuhlen.

2. For a more thorough analysis of how the Marx Brothers negotiate betweenness, see Winokur 125–78.

3. Sharp ("*Nine Plays*") provides a general discussion of Reznikoff's plays.

4. Stanley Burnshaw, American Jewish poet and critic (b. 1906), wrote
a work entitled *The Refusers: An Epic of the Jews* (1981), which he calls
"A trilogy of novels based on three heroic lives," those of Moses, Uriel
Da Costa, and Burnshaw's father, each of whom made resistance a central
virtue.

5. Sharp quotes from "An Introductory Note to *Genesis.*" In June 1925,
after Reznikoff's four plays were published in the *Menorah Journal,* he unsuc-
cessfully submitted a fifth play, *Genesis,* along with the introductory note. "His
cover letter described and justified his plans for writing a series of plays beginning with *Genesis* to tell 'the story of the Jews from their beginning until the
present'" ("*Nine Plays*" 272).

6. In *Marrano as Metaphor,* Elaine Marks adapts Yovel's discussion of the
Marrano character of modern Jewish culture to a reading of the Jewish presence in French literature.

7. In the chapter "Dismantling 'Mantis,'" Davidson gives a subtle reading of
the interplay of Marx and Spinoza in Zukofsky's poetry (116–134). See also
Marsh, Ahearn (100–115), and Quartermain (70–89).

8. Reznikoff wrote this statement in a letter to the *Menorah Journal*'s managing editor, Elliot Cohen, on December 1, 1929—evidently in answer to a request for an endorsement of the chronically underfunded magazine.

9. Although in many ways Nietzsche and Spinoza are polar opposites, Yovel
draws attention to Nietzsche's professed love for Spinoza and even contends
that they "offer two rival options within the same radical conception, that of
total immanence. Both declare the 'death' of the transcendent God, and see life
within immanence as all there is" (Yovel 2.106).

10. DuPlessis examines Oppen's pregnant silence from many directions in
"'The familiar / becomes extreme.'"

11. These lines are a direct quotation from Hawthorne's *House of the Seven
Gables,* as Taggart points out (59).

CHAPTER THREE

1. Dubnow's importance as a historian arises from his pioneering use of anthropological and sociological rather than theological terms to study Jewish history. His stature is reflected in the fact that his ten-volume history of the Jews, published during the 1920s, remains a standard work. "Together with the histories by Heinrich Graetz and Salo Wittmayer Baron it belongs to an extremely rare, and by now probably extinct, genre: the attempt to encompass single-handedly the whole of Jewish history within one massive and conceptually unified work of high scholarship" (Frankel 2).

2. Also recognizing that Paul must be considered a significant Jewish thinker, Daniel Boyarin discusses the ways in which he transgresses the diasporic model of Jewish identity in *A Radical Jew: Paul and the Politics of Identity.* Scholars no longer believe that Paul wrote the Epistle to the Hebrews.

3. Joselit is quoting Henry Seidel Canby in the last sentence.

4. Robert Franciosi notes that "[o]n May 8, 1934 Reznikoff sent a lengthy manuscript under the title 'If I forget you, Jerusalem: In Memoriam, 1933' to Harriet Monroe. . . . As Reznikoff explained to Monroe, he had written the poem as a response to the 'Nazi triumph' in 1933" ("Story" 196–97). Monroe's rejection must have come quickly, for on July 11, Henry Hurwitz, publisher of the *Menorah Journal,* wrote of the poem in glowing terms, thanking Reznikoff for the honor of publishing it (Hurwitz Collection).

5. In the *Saturday Review,* William Rose Benét also identifies *In Memoriam: 1933* as a "racial" book: "Charles Reznikoff is another free-versifier whose work I have already mentioned as distinguished. His 'In Memoriam: 1933' is published by The Objectivist Press at 10 West 36th Street, this city, and is strongly racial. He seems to me the best of the definitely Jewish poets writing today, since the death of James Oppenheim. This poem of his, which might be subtitled 'a short history of the Jews,' appeared originally in The Menorah Journal. It has both dignity and power, sonorous language and brilliant atmosphere, and it is well condensed" (571).

6. Thanks to John Felstiner for pointing out the literal meaning of the Hebrew word *ivri.*

7. Louis Harap speaks of the journal's success in maintaining "simultaneous residence in both the Jewish and the larger American communities": "At the end of its first decade, an editorial statement in the February, 1925 issue articulated the aims of the magazine. Without false modesty or exaggeration the magazine could assert that it had become the foremost Jewish publication in English and 'now holds a position in the front rank of American magazines'" (52).

8. Arnold wrote to his mother regarding Lady de Rothschild, with whom he had a "long and intimate relationship" (Ragussis 221): "What women these Jewesses are! with a *force* which seems triple that of the women of our Western and Northern races" (220). The sexual politics of Arnold's conception of Hebraism deserves further study. For a recent discussion of Arnold's use of the dichotomy of Hebraism and Hellenism, see Stone.

9. The essays edited by Hohendahl and Gilman provide a useful treatment of Heine's conflicted identity and of its legacy for European and American writers.

10. For a biography of Marvin Lowenthal, see Klingenstein, "Lowenthal."

11. The Jewish ability to survive as a "nation" during the long years of dispersion has been noted, for instance, by the contemporary Tibetan Buddhists, who foresee a similar fate for themselves. In a fascinating book about Jewish identity, *The Jew in the Lotus,* Rodger Kamenetz chronicles the meeting of a group of Jewish rabbis and scholars with the Dalai Lama and his followers in Dharamsala, India, in 1990. The explicit topic of the meeting was how to survive a diaspora, but many other compelling issues also arose for Jews and Buddhists alike. In the course of an extremely rich and illuminating interchange, the primary advice the Jews had for the Tibetans was to transform their Buddhism from a temple-based to a family-based religion, as the rabbis had done after the fall of Jerusalem in 70 C.E. Equally interesting to the Tibetans was the admission by a number of the rabbis that their sense of vocation had been awakened at Jewish summer camps. On the basis of this testimony, the Dalai Lama sent several of his lamas to visit Jewish camps in upstate New York.

12. In 1968 a rabbinical student at Hebrew Union College in Cincinnati employed the poem as a liturgical prayer. To make it symmetrical, he suggested a responsive for the end of the poem, which Reznikoff amended to read:

> Blessed are You, God of the Universe,
> Who has kept Israel alive to this day
> and the scrolls of the Law to be read and studied, praised and obeyed.
> (UCSD 9.2.30)

When Reznikoff used the poem to open *Inscriptions: 1944–1956* (1959), he eliminated the title and the dedication to the *Menorah Journal.*

13. Sander Gilman has written extensively on the medicalization of racism. See especially *The Jew's Body* and *The Case of Sigmund Freud.* On the issue of Jewish crime in New York, see Joselit, *Our Gang.*

14. Werner Sollors presents a cogent summary of the development of Kallen's ethnicization as an interplay of Hebraism and Americanism:

> Kallen's activities in the Menorah Society and as a self-styled Zionist permitted him to have it two ways, "to retain," or, perhaps more accurately, to reinvent, "his Jewish identity and to become, thereby, a better American." Americanization and ethnicization went hand in hand as Kallen developed a modern ethnic identity that continued to remain at odds with his father's traditional faith. Kallen's transformation can be seen in the context of what Herbert Gans has termed "symbolic ethnicity" which goes along with assimilation: Kallen absorbed concepts from the surrounding culture (the American idea), but gave it an ethnic name (the Jewish idea). Kallen's own life story illustrates Higham's generalization that pluralism "has unconsciously relied on the assimilative process which it seemed to repudiate."
> (265)

15. Howard Sachar notes that "[t]he metaphor of the orchestra, in fact, was originated not by Kallen, or even William James, but by Judah Magnes, in a 1911 sermon delivered at Temple Emanu-El in irate criticism of Israel Zangwill's [1908] play The Melting Pot" (426–27). Kallen joined prominent Zionists such as Magnes and Solomon Schechter in his condemnation of the melting pot as a goal for American culture. A major thrust of Zionism in America has been against assimilation and for the preservation of ethnic identity—a trend that received a powerful boost when the State of Israel was formed in 1948.

For a full treatment of the various meanings of the symbol of the melting pot and of its confrontations with the doctrine of cultural pluralism, see Gleason. Ratner provides a useful summary of the antecedents to cultural pluralism and of its changing meanings during Kallen's career.

16. See Sollors and Michaels for discussions of some of the contradictions in Kallen's liberal philosophy of cultural pluralism.

17. See Davidson (149–70) for an extended discussion of the prose *Testimony*.

18. Gabler gives an informative history of Jews in Hollywood.

19. See Felleman for information about Albert Lewin's work in Hollywood.

20. In an interview, Reznikoff comments upon his role as "shepherd" in this poem (*MP* 99–100).

CHAPTER FOUR

1. Coincidentally, Oppen and Oppenheim actually share the same original last name, Oppenheimer. A third American Jewish poet, Joel Oppenheimer (1930–88), joins them. For a brief biography of Oppenheim, see the reprinted version of his *The Nine-Tenths* (n.p.).

2. Presumably, Reznikoff would have come to Untermeyer's notice in 1924, when he began publishing in the *Menorah Journal*. By 1930 Untermeyer was writing the introduction to Reznikoff's novel *By the Waters of Manhattan*, but at no point in the introduction does he mention that Reznikoff is a poet. Untermeyer does notice Reznikoff's "sincerity," however: the introduction begins, "It is a long time since I have read a story so obviously sincere" (7).

3. In an otherwise very informative article on Zukofsky's relationship to Yiddish, Harold Schimmel imagines Zukofsky to be the one lauding "Speech" and condemning "jargon," unaware of the bitterness with which Zukofsky set up that opposition. By not reading correctly the valences Zukofsky assigns to Hebrew and Yiddish, Barry Ahearn, too, misses the opposition between languages in *"A"*-4 (Ahearn, *Zukofsky's "A"* 51–52).

The competition between Yiddish and Hebrew was particularly intense in the early twentieth century, especially during the twenties. Each language had its passionate advocates, its linguistic codifiers, and its own stable of remarkable writers; through heated debates and adamant resolutions at international conventions, each also claimed the right to become *the* national language of the

Jews. At the time Zukofsky was writing, there was no way to know which language had the upper hand: "in the 1920s, it was impossible to predict that, in the competition between the two languages, Hebrew, with its base in a tiny community in Palestine, would survive and become a full-fledged state language while Yiddish, a 'World Language,' with its mass newspapers and millions of readers, would disappear" (Harshav, *Meaning* 87–88).

4. Perelman (176–81) offers a good summary of the Pound/Zukofsky relationship.

5. See, for instance, Wirth-Nesher's excellent essay on Henry Roth's *Call It Sleep* or Damon on David Antin and Lenny Bruce.

6. Robert Franciosi ("Reading Reznikoff") contends that the most important lesson Zukofsky learned from Reznikoff was how to suffer neglect. Without question, Reznikoff's example of dignity and persistence in the face of neglect influenced Zukofsky, Oppen, and many subsequent poets. Of course, Reznikoff also offered a positive example to the other Objectivists, as Franciosi himself shows in discussing Oppen's meditations upon Reznikoff's line "a girder, still itself among the rubbish" (*CP* 1.121). Hugh Seidman, a student of Zukofsky's at the Polytechnic Institute of Brooklyn from 1958–61, affirms that Reznikoff continued to figure in Zukofsky's highly exclusive poetic pantheon. On one occasion, Seidman recalls, "Louis confided that 'Rezzy' was one of the few poets that had ever taught him anything" (100).

7. The version of this song in *An "Objectivists" Anthology* ends with some notes by Pound to Zukofsky and a variant on the final stanza. The image of "ole king Bolo's big black queen" was borrowed by Pound from T. S. Eliot, who sprinkles verses about this character throughout his early correspondence (*Letters*).

8. The references to "Kavka" and "K" evoke a modern writer who was hypersensitive to the operation of anti-Semitic stereotypes in modern culture. One wonders what sort of creature Kafka, who generally used animals and insects to embody the pernicious qualities of such stereotypes, would have enlisted to portray the mad poet engaged in his Yiddish Charleston.

9. For a detailed description of the Yiddish poetry written by Zukofsky's contemporaries, see Benjamin Harshav's "American Yiddish Poetry and Its Background" (B. and B. Harshav 3–62). Harshav's essay and the "Documents of Introspectivism" (773–804) provide the basis for Norman Finkelstein's suggestive article on Zukofsky and Yiddish poetry.

10. On the "secret language of the Jews," see Gilman, *Jewish Self-Hatred*.

11. Weinfield, too, sees this as a poem in the Symbolist mode, which would account for its kinship with the poetry of Eliot. Calling the poem "a point of origin from which the work will emerge and against which it will turn" (225), Weinfield makes a case for it as a central expression of Reznikoff's Jewish dilemmas.

12. For other helpful attempts to widen our view of the context for the emergence of Objectivism, see Perloff ("Barbed-Wire"), who chronicles a questioning of modernist forms of representation; Homberger, who places Objectivism in the context of the contemporaneous marxist movement; and von

Hallberg, who sees the poetic movement as an outgrowth of Alfred North Whitehead's objectivist philosophy.

13. By 1934, when he reviewed Reznikoff's *Jerusalem the Golden* for *The American Mercury,* Gregory had considerably revised his opinion. Reviewing Reznikoff's text alongside five other books of poetry, including William Carlos Williams's *Collected Poems* and George Oppen's *Discrete Series,* Gregory characterizes Reznikoff as a "post-imagist" who follows but "is no mere imitator of Williams." Commending Reznikoff's originality and his success in "the infusion of adult emotion with the personal memories of a past that can never be regained," Gregory ends by claiming, "Of all the poets in the present collection Reznikoff is the most scrupulous craftsman" (383).

14. In a letter to Reznikoff (November 23, 1959), Lorine Niedecker invokes Chinese and Japanese models for Objectivist poetry: "Reading *Inscriptions: 1944–1956* I often feel a kinship between us in the short poem. And if you are my brother-in-poetry then we have Chinese and Japanese brothers. But I have a great deal of practicing to do—of quiet insight—before I can enter such a good family." Niedecker also finds a kinship in their shared attention to the ordinary and the intractable: "Hard to write and then get it printed. I try to along with scrubbing floors in a hospital. Every now and again, tho, there's a chink where a poem comes thru. Altogether life is not really too hard— I gather this is what you say too" (UCSD 9.4.1; quoted in Franciosi, "Reading Reznikoff" 394).

15. For a careful reading of this sequence and of the "groups" of poems in *Jerusalem the Golden,* see Hatlen. In addition, Hatlen's claim that "Objectivism was born at the juncture between Jewish immigrant culture and Modernism" (147–48) reinforces the central contention of the present chapter.

16. A number of significant discussions of Trilling as a figure of betweenness exist: see, especially, Grumet, "Menorah"; Grumet, "Apprenticeship"; Krupnick; O'Hara 29–66; Shechner, *Conversion* 134–45; Shechner, *Revolution* 71–90; and Diana Trilling, "Lionel Trilling."

17. Thanks to Henry Weinfield for discussing with me Reznikoff's relations to Romanticism.

AFTERWORD

1. See Nadler, who demonstrates that the Mitnagdim held a similar doctrine of immanence to that of the Hasidim, so that "the dispute between Hasidism and Mithnagdism was *not* rooted in the issue of divine immanence . . . , but rather in radically differing assessments of human spiritual capacities" (20).

2. An instance of Ginsberg's identification with being Jewish: "At the end of the weekly *Eddie Cantor Show,* the comedian sang, 'I love to spend this hour with you, as friend to friend. I'm sorry it's through.' Allen recalled later: 'It was a really sad Jewish moment that was the high point of the week, I guess because he was Jewish and a national comedian, and everybody in the family identified with him'" (Miles 19).

WORKS CITED

Abrams, M. H. *Natural Supernaturalism*. New York: Norton, 1971.

Adorno, Theodor. *Notes to Literature*. Ed. Rolf Tiedemann. Trans. Shierry Weber Nicholsen. Vol. 1. New York: Columbia UP, 1991.

Ahearn, Barry. *Zukofsky's "A": An Introduction*. Berkeley: U of California P, 1983.

⸻, ed. "Ezra Pound & Louis Zukofsky: Letters, 1928–1930." *Montemora* 8 (1981): 149–83.

⸻, ed. *Pound/Zukofsky: Selected Letters of Ezra Pound and Louis Zukofsky*. New York: New Directions, 1987.

Alter, Robert. "Charles Reznikoff: Between Present and Past." *Defenses of the Imagination: Jewish Writers and Modern Historical Crisis*. By Alter. Philadelphia: Jewish Publication Soc., 1977. 119–35.

⸻. "Epitaph for a Jewish Magazine: Notes on the 'Menorah Journal.'" *Commentary* 39.5 (1965): 51–55.

⸻. *Necessary Angels: Tradition and Modernity in Kafka, Benjamin, and Scholem*. Cambridge: Harvard UP, 1991.

Altieri, Charles. *Enlarging the Temple: New Directions in American Poetry during the 1960s*. Lewisburg: Bucknell UP, 1979.

⸻. "The Objectivist Tradition." *Chicago Review* 30.3 (1979): 5–22.

Arnold, Matthew. *Culture and Anarchy*. Ed. Samuel Lipman. New Haven: Yale UP, 1994.

Asch, Sholem. *Die Mutter*. Berlin: Paul Zsolnay, 1929.

Auerbach, Erich. *Mimesis: The Representation of Reality in Western Literature*. 1946. Trans. Willard R. Trask. Princeton: Princeton UP, 1953.

Auster, Paul. "The Decisive Moment." *MP* 151–65.

Baron, Salo W. "Ghetto and Emancipation." Schwarz 50–63.

Benét, William Rose. Rev. of *In Memoriam: 1933*, by Reznikoff. *Saturday Review of Literature* 11 (23 March 1935): 571.

Benjamin, Walter. "The Task of the Translator." *Illuminations*. Ed. Hannah Arendt. Trans. Harry Zohn. New York: Harcourt, 1968. 69–82.

Bernstein, Charles. *My Way: Speeches and Reviews*. Chicago: U of Chicago P, 1999.

Bernstein, Michael André. "Foregone Conclusions: Narrating the Fate of Austro-German Jewry." *Modernism/Modernity* 1.1 (1994): 57–79.

Bhabha, Homi. *The Location of Culture*. New York: Routledge, 1994.

Biale, David, Michael Galchinsky, and Susannah Heschel, eds. *Insider/Outsider: American Jews and Multiculturalism*. Berkeley: U of California P, 1998.

Bloom, Harold. "The Sorrows of American Jewish Poetry." *Figures of Capable Imagination*. By Bloom. New York: Seabury, 1976. 247–62.

Boyarin, Daniel. "Placing Reading: Ancient Israel and Medieval Europe." *The Ethnography of Reading*. Ed. Jonathan Boyarin. Berkeley: U of California P, 1993. 10–37.

———. *A Radical Jew: Paul and the Politics of Identity*. Berkeley: U of California P, 1994.

Boyarin, Daniel, and Jonathan Boyarin. "Diaspora: Generation and the Ground of Jewish Identity." *Identities*. Ed. Kwame Anthony Appiah and Henry Louis Gates. Chicago: U of Chicago P, 1995. 305–37.

Brody, Alter. *A Family Album and Other Poems*. New York: Huebsch, 1918.

———. *Lamentations: Four Folk-Plays of the American Jew*. New York: Coward, 1928.

Burnshaw, Stanley. *The Refusers: An Epic of the Jews*. New York: Horizon, 1981.

Carroll, Joseph. *The Cultural Theory of Matthew Arnold*. Berkeley: U of California P, 1982.

Casillo, Robert. *The Genealogy of Demons: Anti-Semitism, Fascism, and the Myths of Ezra Pound*. Evanston: Northwestern UP, 1988.

"Clod." *The American Heritage Dictionary of the English Language*. 1969 ed.

Cohen-Cheminet, Geneviève. "'L'Entretien Infini': Modernité Poétique et Tradition Appropriée dans L'Oeuvre de Charles Reznikoff." Diss. Université de Clermont-Ferrand, 1996.

Cohn, Jim. "A Conversation with Carl Rakosi." *Carl Rakosi: Man and Poet*. Ed. Michael Heller. Orono: National Poetry Foundation., 1993. 43–51.

Damon, Maria. "Talking Yiddish at the Boundaries." *Cultural Studies* 5.1 (1991): 14–29.

Davidson, Michael. *Ghostlier Demarcations: Modern Poetry and the Material Word*. Berkeley: U of California P, 1997.

DeLaura, David. *Hebrew and Hellene in Victorian England: Newman, Arnold, and Pater*. Austin: U of Texas P, 1969.

Dembo, L. S. "Objectivist or Jew: Charles Reznikoff in the Diaspora." *MP* 187–97.

Dembo, L. S., and Cyrena Pondrom. *The Contemporary Writer: Interviews with Sixteen Novelists and Poets*. Madison: U of Wisconsin P, 1972.

Deutscher, Isaac. *The Non-Jewish Jew and Other Essays*. London: Oxford UP, 1968.

Dickinson, Emily. *Final Harvest: Emily Dickinson's Poems*. Ed. Thomas H. Johnson. Boston: Little, Brown, 1961.

The Dictionary of Cliches. New York: Facts on File, 1985.

Dobrzynski, Judith H. "Representing America in a Language of Her Own." *New York Times* 30 May 1999, sec. 2: 1, 30.

H.D. *Collected Poems: 1912–1944*. Ed. Louis Martz. New York: New Directions, 1983.

Dubnow, S. M. *Jewish History: An Essay in the Philosophy of History.* 1893. Trans. Henrietta Szold. Philadelphia: Jewish Publication Soc., 1903.

DuPlessis, Rachel Blau. "'The familiar / becomes extreme': George Oppen and Silence." *North Dakota Quarterly* 55.4 (Fall 1987): 18–36.

———. "Objectivist Poets and Political Vision: A Study of Oppen and Pound. *George Oppen: Man and Poet.* Ed. Burton Hatlen. Orono: National Poetry Foundation., 1981. 123–48.

Du Plessis, Rachel Blau, and Peter Quartermain, eds. *The Objectivist Nexus: Essays in Cultural Poetics.* Tuscaloosa: U of Alabama P, 1999.

Eilberg-Schwartz, Howard. *The Savage in Judaism: An Anthropology of Israelite Religion and Ancient Judaism.* Bloomington: Indiana UP, 1990.

Eliot, T. S. "Hamlet." *Selected Prose of T. S. Eliot.* Ed. Frank Kermode. New York: Harcourt, 1975. 45–49.

———. *The Letters of T. S. Eliot.* Ed. Valerie Eliot. Vol. 1: 1898–1922. San Diego: Harcourt, 1988.

Emerson, Ralph Waldo. *Selected Writings of Ralph Waldo Emerson.* Ed. William Gilman. New York: New American Library, 1965.

Englebert, Michael, and Michael West. "George and Mary Oppen: An Interview." *American Poetry Review* 14.4 (1985): 11–14.

Erdman, David, ed. *The Complete Poetry and Prose of William Blake.* Rev. ed. Berkeley: U of California P, 1982.

Ezrahi, Sidra DeKoven. *By Words Alone: The Holocaust in Literature.* Chicago: U of Chicago P, 1980.

Feingold, Henry L. *A Time for Searching: Entering the Mainstream 1920–1945.* Baltimore: Johns Hopkins UP, 1992. Vol. 4 of *The Jewish People in America.* 5 vols. 1992.

Felleman, Susan. *Botticelli in Hollywood: The Films of Albert Lewin.* New York: Twayne, 1997.

Felman, Shoshana, and Dori Laub. *Testimony: Crises of Witnessing in Literature, Psychoanalysis, and History.* New York: Routledge, 1992.

Felstiner, John. *Paul Celan: Poet, Survivor, Jew.* New Haven: Yale UP, 1995.

Finkelstein, Norman. "Jewish-American Modernism and the Problem of Identity: With Special Reference to the Work of Louis Zukofsky." Scroggins 65–79.

Franciosi, Robert. "Reading Reznikoff: Zukofsky and Oppen." *North Dakota Quarterly* 55.4 (Fall 1987): 383–95.

———. "A Story of Vocation: The Poetic Achievement of Charles Reznikoff." Diss. U of Iowa, 1985.

Frankel, Jonathan. "S. M. Dubnov: Historian and Ideologist." *The Life and Work of S. M. Dubnov: Diaspora Nationalism and Jewish History.* By Sophie Dubnov Erlich. Trans. Judith Vowles. Bloomington: Indiana UP, 1991. 1–33.

Fredman, Stephen. *Poet's Prose: The Crisis in American Verse.* 2nd ed. Cambridge, Eng.: Cambridge UP, 1990.

Fuld, Werner. *Walter Benjamin: Zwischen den Stuhlen.* Munich: Hanser, 1979.

Funkenstein, Amos. *Perceptions of Jewish History.* Berkeley: U of California P, 1993.

Gabler, Neal. *An Empire of Their Own: How the Jews Invented Hollywood*. New York: Crown, 1988.

Gill, Stephen, ed. *William Wordsworth*. The Oxford Authors. Oxford: Oxford UP, 1984.

Gilman, Sander. *The Case of Sigmund Freud: Medicine and Identity at the Fin de Siècle*. Baltimore: Johns Hopkins UP, 1993.

———. *Franz Kafka, the Jewish Patient*. New York: Routledge, 1995.

———. *Inscribing the Other*. Lincoln: U of Nebraska P, 1991.

———. *Jewish Self-Hatred: Anti-Semitism and the Hidden Language of the Jews*. Baltimore: Johns Hopkins UP, 1986.

———. *The Jew's Body*. New York: Routledge, 1991.

Ginsberg, Allen. *Collected Poems: 1947–1980*. New York: Harper, 1984.

———. *Howl: Original Draft Facsimile*. Ed. Barry Miles. New York: Harper, 1986.

Gleason, Philip. *Speaking of Diversity: Language and Ethnicity in Twentieth-Century America*. Baltimore: Johns Hopkins UP, 1992.

Goldstein, Sidney. "Jews in the United States: Perspectives from Demography." *American Jews: A Reader*. Ed. Marshall Sklare. New York: Behrman, 1983.

Gregory, Horace. "A Barrel of Poets." *The American Mercury* 33 (1934): 382–3.

———. "Correspondence." *Poetry* 38.1 (1931): 51–57.

Grumet, Elinor. "The Apprenticeship of Lionel Trilling." *Prooftexts* 4 (1984): 153–73.

———. "The Menorah Idea and the Apprenticeship of Lionel Trilling." Diss. U of Iowa, 1979.

Hallberg, Robert von. *Charles Olson: The Scholar's Art*. Cambridge: Harvard UP, 1978. 82–125.

Harap, Louis. "*The Menorah Journal*: A Literary Precursor." *Midstream* 30.8 (1984): 51–55.

Harshav, Benjamin. *Language in Time of Revolution*. Berkeley: U of California P, 1993.

———. *The Meaning of Yiddish*. Berkeley: U of California P, 1990.

———. "Texts and Subtexts in Chagall's Paintings: On Language, Culture, and Identity in Modern Art." *Modernism/Modernity* 1.2: 51–87.

Harshav, Benjamin, and Barbara Harshav, eds. *American Yiddish Poetry: A Bilingual Anthology*. Berkeley: U of California P, 1986.

Hatlen, Burton. "Objectivism in Context: Charles Reznikoff and Jewish-American Modernism." *Sagetrieb* 13.1–2 (1994): 147–68.

Hays, H. R. "A Poem of Protest." *Poetry* 46 (1935): 230–2.

Heller, Michael. *Conviction's Net of Branches: Essays on the Objectivist Poets and Poetry*. Carbondale: Southern Illinois UP, 1985.

Hindus, Milton. "Charles Reznikoff." Kessner 247–67.

———. *Charles Reznikoff: A Critical Essay*. Santa Barbara: Black Sparrow, 1978.

————, ed. *Charles Reznikoff: Man and Poet*. Orono: National Poetry Foundation., 1984.

Hohendahl, Peter Uwe, and Sander Gilman, eds. *Heinrich Heine and the Occident*. Lincoln: U of Nebraska P, 1991.

Homberger, Eric. *American Writers and Radical Politics, 1900–39: Equivocal Commitments*. New York: St. Martin's, 1986. 163–86.

Howe, M. A. DeWolfe. *Barrett Wendell and His Letters*. Boston: Atlantic Monthly P, 1924.

Hrushovski [Harshav], Benjamin. "Prosody, Hebrew." *Encyclopaedia Judaica* (1971–72): 13.1195–1240.

Henry Hurwitz Menorah Association Memorial Collection. American Jewish Archives, Cincinnati.

Hurwitz, Henry, and I. Leo Sharfman. *The Menorah Movement: History, Purposes, Activities*. Ann Arbor: Intercollegiate Menorah Assn., 1914.

Jenkins, Grant. "Totally Bound: Tracing a Levinasian Ethics from Objectivism to Language Poetry." Diss. U of Notre Dame, 1999.

Joselit, Jenna Weissman. *Our Gang: Jewish Crime and the New York Jewish Community, 1900–1940*. Bloomington: Indiana UP, 1983.

————. "Without Ghettoism: A History of the Intercollegiate Menorah Association, 1906–1930." *American Jewish Archives* 30.2 (November 1978): 133–54.

Kafka, Franz. *Letters to Friends, Family, and Editors*. Ed. Max Brod. Trans. Richard and Clara Winston. New York: Schocken, 1977.

Kallen, Horace. *Culture and Democracy: Studies in the Group Psychology of the American Peoples*. New York: Boni, 1924.

————. *Judaism at Bay: Essays toward the Adjustment of Judaism to Modernity*. New York: Bloch, 1932.

————. "Nationality and the Hyphenated American." *Menorah Journal* 1.2 (1915): 79–86.

————. "The Promise of the Menorah Idea." *Menorah Journal* 49 (1962): 9–16.

Kamenetz, Rodger. *The Jew in the Lotus: A Poet's Rediscovery of Jewish Identity in Buddhist India*. San Francisco: Harper, 1994.

Kenner, Hugh. *A Homemade World: The American Modernist Writers*. New York: Morrow, 1975.

Kessner, Carole S. "Marie Syrkin: An Exemplary Life." *The "Other" New York Jewish Intellectuals*. Ed. Carole S. Kessner. New York: New York UP, 1994. 51–70.

Klingenstein, Susanne. *Jews in the American Academy 1900–1940: The Dynamics of Intellectual Assimilation*. New Haven: Yale UP, 1991.

————. "'Not the Recovery of a Grave, but of a Cradle': The Zionist Life of Marvin Lowenthal." Kessner 206–27.

Konvitz, Milton, ed. *The Legacy of Horace M. Kallen*. New York: Herzl P, 1987.

Krupnick, Mark. *Lionel Trilling and the Fate of Cultural Criticism*. Evanston: Northwestern UP, 1986.

Lazarus, Emma, trans. *Poems and Ballads of Heinrich Heine.* New York: Worthington, 1881.

Lear, Elmer. "On the Unity of the Kallen Perspective." Konvitz 108–30.

Lowenthal, Marvin. "On a Jewish Humanism." Schwarz 64–76.

Marks, Elaine. *Marrano as Metaphor; The Jewish Presence in French Writing.* New York: Columbia UP, 1996.

Marsh, Alec. "Poetry and the Age: Pound, Zukofsky, and the Labor Theory of Value." Scroggins 94–111.

McAllister, Andrew. Introduction. *The Objectivists.* Ed. McAllister. Newcastle upon Tyne, Eng.: Bloodaxe, 1996. 9–15.

Michaels, Walter Benn. *Our America: Nativism, Modernism, and Pluralism.* Durham: Duke UP, 1995.

Miles, Barry. *Ginsberg: A Biography.* New York: Simon, 1989.

Miller, J. Hillis. *Poets of Reality.* Cambridge: Harvard UP, 1965.

Moore, Deborah Dash. *At Home in America: Second Generation New York Jews.* New York: Columbia UP, 1981.

Nadler, Allan. *The Faith of the Mithnagdim: Rabbinic Responses to Hasidic Rapture.* Baltimore: Johns Hopkins UP, 1997.

Nietzsche, Friedrich. *The Gay Science.* Trans. Walter Kaufmann. New York: Random House, 1974.

O'Hara, Daniel T. *Lionel Trilling: The Work of Liberation.* Madison: U of Wisconsin P, 1988.

Olson, Charles. *Charles Olson & Ezra Pound: An Encounter at St. Elizabeth's.* Ed. Catherine Seelye. New York: Grossman, 1975.

Omer-Sherman, Ranen. "The Stranger and the Metropolis: Partial Visibilities and Manifold Possibilities of Identity in the Poetry of Charles Reznikoff." *Shofar* 16.1 (Fall 1997): 43–73.

Oppen, George. *The Collected Poems of George Oppen.* New York: New Directions, 1975.

———. "On Charles Reznikoff." *Sagetrieb* 3.3 (1984): 7.

———. "On Reznikoff." *Sulfur* 13.1 (1993): 39–40.

———. *The Selected Letters of George Oppen.* Ed. Rachel Blau DuPlessis. Durham: Duke UP, 1990.

Oppen, George, and Mary Oppen. "An Interview with George and Mary Oppen." With Kevin Power. *Montemora* 4 (1978): 186–203.

———. "George and Mary Oppen: An Interview by Michael Englebert and Michael West." *American Poetry Review* 14.4 (1985): 11–14.

———. "Memorial Broadcast for Charles Reznikoff." *Sagetrieb* 3.3 (1984): 29–39.

Oppenheim, James. *The Nine-Tenths.* 1911. Upper Saddle River: Gregg, 1968.

———. *Songs for the New Age.* New York: Century, 1914.

Ouaknin, Marc-Alain. *The Burnt Book: Reading the Talmud.* 1986. Trans. Llewellyn Brown. Princeton: Princeton UP, 1995.

Palmer, Michael. "On Objectivism." *Sulfur* 10.1 (1990): 117–26.

Perelman, Bob. *The Trouble with Genius: Reading Pound, Joyce, Stein, and Zukofsky.* Berkeley: U of California P, 1994.

Perloff, Marjorie. "'Barbed-Wire Entanglements': The 'New American Poetry,' 1930–1932." *Modernism/Modernity* 2.1 (1995): 145–75.

———. *The Dance of the Intellect: Studies in the Poetry of the Pound Tradition.* New York: Cambridge UP, 1985.

Popkin, Richard H. "Epicureanism and Scepticism in the Early Seventeenth Century." *Philomathes: Studies and Essays in the Humanities in Memory of Philip Merlan.* Ed. Robert B. Palmer and Robert Hamerton-Kelly. The Hague: Martinus Nijhoff, 1971. 346–57.

———. "The Rise and Fall of the Jewish Indian Theory." *Menasseh Ben Israel and His World.* Ed. Yosef Kaplan, Henry Méchoulan, and Richard Popkin. Leiden: Brill, 1989. 63–82.

Pound, Ezra. *Literary Essays of Ezra Pound.* New York: New Directions, 1968.

———. "Preface to *Discrete Series.*" *Paideuma* 10.1 (1981): 13.

Quartermain, Peter. *Disjunctive Poetics: From Gertrude Stein and Louis Zukofsky to Susan Howe.* Cambridge, Eng.: Cambridge UP, 1992.

Ragussis, Michael. *Figures of Conversion: "The Jewish Question" and English National Identity.* Durham: Duke UP, 1995.

Ratner, Sidney. "Horace Kallen and Cultural Pluralism." Konvitz 48–63.

Reznikoff, Charles. *By the Waters of Manhattan.* 1930. New York: Wiener, 1986.

———. Charles Reznikoff Papers. MSS 9. Mandeville Special Collections Library, U of California, San Diego.

———. *Family Chronicle.* 1963. New York: Wiener, 1988.

———. "In Memoriam: 1933." *Menorah Journal* 22 (1934): 103–33.

———. *In Memoriam: 1933.* New York: Objectivist P, 1934.

———. *The Lionhearted: A Story About the Jews in Medieval England.* Philadelphia: Jewish Publication Soc., 1944.

———. *The Manner "Music".* Santa Barbara: Black Sparrow, 1977.

———. *Poems 1918–1975: The Complete Poems of Charles Reznikoff.* Ed. Seamus Cooney. 2 vols. Santa Barbara: Black Sparrow, 1976–77.

———. *Selected Letters of Charles Reznikoff 1917–1976.* Ed. Milton Hindus. Santa Rosa: Black Sparrow, 1997.

———. "A Talk with L. S. Dembo." *MP* 97–107.

———. *Testimony.* New York: Objectivist P, 1934.

Reznikoff, Charles, and Reinhold Schiffer. "The Poet in His Milieu." *MP* 109–26.

Reznikoff, Charles, with Uriah Engelman. *The Jews of Charleston: A History of an American Jewish Community.* Philadelphia: Jewish Publication Soc., 1950.

Roth, Henry. *Call It Sleep.* New York: Ballou, 1934.

Roth, Philip. *Operation Shylock: A Confession.* New York: Simon, 1993.

Rovner, Ruth. "Charles Reznikoff—A Profile." *Jewish Frontier* (April 1976): 14–18.

Rudolf, Anthony. "Is That Alter Brody?" *London Magazine* (April/May 1983): 108–13.

Sachar, Howard. *A History of the Jews in America.* New York: Knopf, 1992.

Schimmel, Harold. "Zuk. Yehoash David Rex." Terrell 235–45.

Schmidt, Sarah. "Horace M. Kallen and the Americanization of Zionism." Diss. U of Maryland, 1973.

———. "Horace M. Kallen: The Zionist Chapter." Konvitz 76–89.

Schwartz, Howard, and Anthony Rudolf, eds. *Voices within the Ark: The Modern Jewish Poets*. New York: Avon, 1980.

Schwarz, Leo, ed. *The Menorah Treasury: Harvest of Half a Century*. Philadelphia: Jewish Publication Soc., 1964.

Scroggins, Mark, ed. *Upper Limit Music: The Writing of Louis Zukofsky*. Tuscaloosa: U of Alabama P, 1997.

Seidman, Hugh. "Louis Zukofsky at the Polytechnic Institute of Brooklyn (1958–61)." Terrell 97–102.

Seidman, Naomi. *A Marriage Made in Heaven: The Sexual Politics of Hebrew and Yiddish*. Berkeley: U of California P, 1997.

Seltzer, Robert M. "Coming Home: The Personal Basis of Simon Dubnow's Ideology." *AJS Review* 1 (1976): 283–301.

Sharfman, I. Leo. "The Task of the Menorah." *Menorah Journal* 3 (1917): 47–50.

Sharp, Frederick Thomas. "'Objectivists' 1927–1934: A Critical History of the Work and Association of Louis Zukofsky, William Carlos Williams, Charles Reznikoff, Carl Rakosi, Ezra Pound, George Oppen." Diss. Stanford U, 1982.

———. "Reznikoff's *Nine Plays*." *MP* 267–73.

Shechner, Mark. *After the Revolution: Studies in the Contemporary Jewish-American Imagination*. Bloomington: Indiana UP, 1987.

———. *The Conversion of the Jews and Other Essays*. New York: St. Martin's, 1990.

Shevelow, Kathryn. "History and Objectification in Charles Reznikoff's Documentary Poems, *Testimony* and *Holocaust*." *Sagetrieb* 1.2 (1982): 290–306.

Silliman, Ron. "Third-Phase Objectivism." *Paideuma* 10.1 (1981): 85–9.

Sollors, Werner. "A Critique of Pure Pluralism." *Reconstructing American Literary History*. Ed. Sacvan Bercovitch. Cambridge: Harvard UP, 1986. 250–79.

Spiegelman, Art. *Maus, A Survivor's Tale, Part 1: My Father Bleeds History*. New York: Pantheon, 1986.

———. *Maus, A Survivor's Tale, Part 2: And Here My Troubles Began*. New York: Pantheon, 1991.

Spinoza, Benedict de. *A Spinoza Reader*. Ed. and trans. Edwin Curley. Princeton: Princeton UP, 1994.

Stern, David, ed. *Hellenism and Hebraism Reconsidered: The Poetics of Cultural Influence and Exchange*. *Poetics Today* 19.1–2 (1998).

Stone, Donald D. "Matthew Arnold and the Pragmatics of Hebraism and Hellenism." Stern 179–98.

Strauss, Lauren B. "Staying Afloat in the Melting Pot: Constructing an American Jewish Identity in the *Menorah Journal* of the 1920s." *American Jewish History* 84.4 (1996): 315–31.

Super, R. H., ed. *Culture and Anarchy.* Vol. 5 of *The Complete Prose Works of Matthew Arnold.* Ann Arbor: U of Michigan P, 1965.

——. *Lectures and Essays in Criticism.* Vol. 3 of *The Complete Prose Works of Matthew Arnold.* Ann Arbor: U of Michigan P, 1962.

Syrkin, Marie. "Charles: A Memoir." *MP* 37–67.

Syverson, M. A. "The Community of Memory: A Reznikoff Family Chronicle." *Sagetrieb* 11.1–2 (1992): 127–70.

Taggart, John. "Walk Out: Rereading George Oppen." *Chicago Review* 44.2 (1998): 29–93.

Terrell, Carroll, ed. *Louis Zukofsky: Man and Poet.* Orono: National Poetry Foundation, 1979.

Thoreau, Henry David. *Walden and Civil Disobedience.* Ed. Owen Thomas. Norton Critical Edition. New York: Norton, 1966.

Trilling, Diana. "Lionel Trilling: A Jew at Columbia." *Speaking of Literature and Society.* By Lionel Trilling. Ed. Diana Trilling. New York: Harcourt, 1980.

——. "The Other Night at Columbia: A Report from the Academy." 1959. Rpt. in *On the Poetry of Allen Ginsberg.* Ed. Lewis Hyde. Ann Arbor: U of Michigan P, 1984. 56–74.

Trilling, Lionel. "Genuine Writing." *Menorah Journal* 19.1 (1930): 88–92. Rpt. *MP* 371–76.

——. *Of This Time, of That Place and Other Stories.* New York: Harcourt, 1979.

——. *Sincerity and Authenticity.* Cambridge: Harvard UP, 1972. *r*

Untermeyer, Louis. *American Poetry since 1900.* New York: Holt, 1923.

——. *Heinrich Heine: Paradox and Poet.* 2 vols. New York: Harcourt, 1937.

——. "The Jewish Spirit in Modern American Poetry." *Menorah Journal* 7.3 (1921): 121–32.

——. *The New Era in American Poetry.* New York: Holt, 1919.

Van Doren, Mark. "Jewish Students I Have Known." *Menorah Journal* 13 (1927): 264–68.

Veblen, Thorstein. "The Intellectual Pre-Eminence of Jews in Modern Europe." *Political Science Quarterly* 34.1 (1919): 33–42.

Wagner, Richard. *Judaism in Music and Other Essays.* 1894. Lincoln: U of Nebraska P, 1995.

Wald, Alan. *The New York Intellectuals.* Chapel Hill: U of North Carolina P, 1987.

Weinberger, Eliot. "Another Memory of Reznikoff." *MP* 77–78.

Weinfield, Henry. "'Wringing, Wringing His Pierced Hands': Religion, Identity, and Genre in the Poetry of Charles Reznikoff." *Sagetrieb* 13.1–2 (1994): 225–32.

Weschler, Lawrence. *A Wanderer in the Perfect City: Selected Passion Pieces.* St. Paul: Hungry Mind P, 1998.

Williams, William Carlos. *The Autobiography of William Carlos Williams*. 1951. New York: New Directions, 1967.

Winokur, Mark. *American Laughter: Immigrants, Ethnicity, and 1930s Hollywood Film Comedy*. New York: St. Martin's, 1996.

Wirth-Nesher, Hana. "Between Mother Tongue and Native Language in *Call It Sleep*." *Prooftexts* 10 (1990): 297–312.

———. "Language as Homeland in Jewish-American Literature." Biale 212–30.

Wyman, David S. *The Abandonment of the Jews: America and the Holocaust, 1941–1945*. New York: Pantheon, 1984.

Yerushalmi, Yosef Hayim. *Zakhor: Jewish History and Jewish Memory*. 1982. New York: Schocken, 1989.

Yovel, Yirmiyahu. *Spinoza and Other Heretics*. Vol. 1: *The Marrano of Reason;* vol. 2: *The Adventures of Immanence*. Princeton: Princeton UP, 1989.

Zukofsky, Louis. *"A."* 1978. Baltimore: Johns Hopkins UP, 1993.

———. *Bottom: On Shakespeare*. 1963. Berkeley: U of California P, 1987.

———. "Charles Reznikoff: Sincerity and Objectification." MSS 400.0.1. Mandeville Special Collections Library, U of California, San Diego.

———. *Complete Short Poetry*. Baltimore: Johns Hopkins UP, 1991.

———. *Prepositions: The Collected Critical Essays of Louis Zukofsky*. Expanded ed. Berkeley: U of California P, 1981.

———. "Program: 'Objectivists' 1931." *Poetry* 37 (1931): 268–72.

———. "Sincerity and Objectification: With Special Reference to the Works of Charles Reznikoff." *Poetry* 37 (1931): 272–85.

———. *A Test of Poetry*. 1948. Hanover: Wesleyan UP, 2000.

———, ed. *An "Objectivists" Anthology*. Le Beausset, France: TO, Publishers, 1932.

———, ed. *Poetry: A Magazine of Verse* 37.5 (February 1931).

INDEX

Abrams, M. H., 64
Acosta, Uriel, 54–63, 64, 77, 78, 150
  Exemplar humanae vitae, 55, 61
Adorno, Theodor, 95
Aleichem, Scholem, 51
Allen, Woody, 133
Alter, Robert, 50, 51, 81–82, 92–93, 104–
  5, 169 n. 1, 170 n. 9
Altieri, Charles, 64
Antin, David, 3, 153
antinomianism, 54, 58–59, 78
anti-Semitism, 29, 78, 87, 89, 99, 113,
  128–30, 155
  See also Reznikoff, Charles, and anti-
  Semitism
Arendt, Hannah, 2
Arnold, Matthew, 8, 93–94, 96–97, 98,
  138, 139, 145, 154, 173 n. 8
Auden, W. H., 161
Auerbach, Erich, 140
Auster, Paul, 3, 14–15

Baron, Salo W., 12, 81, 87
Bellow, Saul, 158
Benét, William Rose, 120, 173 n. 5
Benjamin, Walter, 2, 170 n. 9
  "The Task of the Translator," 29–33,
  132–33
Bernstein, Charles, 136
  "Reznikoff's Nearness," viii, 11
betweenness, 27, 49–53, 55, 63, 68, 73, 77,
  79–80, 83, 94–96, 106, 113, 150–51
  See also identity, Jewish; Jewishness
Bhabha, Homi, 51–52
Blake, William, 10, 148–50, 160
Bloom, Harold, 9–11, 124, 147, 150
Boas, Franz, 98
Bodenheim, Maxwell, 117
Bourne, Randolph, 9, 105, 120
Boyarin, Daniel, 72–73, 170 n. 6
Boyarin, Jonathan, 72–73

Brody, Alter, 117, 121–24
Buber, Martin, 2
Bunting, Basil, vii, 167 n. 2
Burnshaw, Stanley, 172 n. 4
burnt book, 39–48, 78, 150, 171 n. 18

Carroll, Joseph, 94
Celan, Paul, 30, 31, 34–35
  Todesfuge, 34–35
Chagall, Marc, 51
cheder, 24–25, 107
Cohen, Elliott, 9, 125, 138, 143
Coleridge, Samuel Taylor, 63–64
Commentary, 9, 82
Communism, 49–50, 67–69, 74, 77, 78
Coolidge, Clark, 20
Cooney, Seamus, 45
Corman, Cid, 3
Corso, Gregory, 158
Creeley, Robert, 3, 136, 147
cultural pluralism, 8, 105, 106, 111–14,
  116, 150–51
  See also Kallen, Horace

Da Costa, Uriel. *See* Acosta, Uriel
Davidson, Michael, 68, 136, 171 n. 20
Dembo, L. S., 20, 167 n. 2
Deutsch, Babette, 117
Deutscher, Isaac, 67–68, 78
  "The non-Jewish Jew," 67–68, 78
Dewey, John, 9, 105, 108
Diaspora, 31, 41, 51, 72–80, 81, 85, 100
  See also exile
Dickinson, Emily, 116
Doolittle, Hilda (H.D.), 2, 5–6, 138–40,
  151
Dubnow, Simon, 84–87, 89, 91, 98, 105,
  110, 133, 173 n. 1
Duncan, Robert, 3, 136
DuPlessis, Rachel Blau, viii, 4–5
The Dybbuk (Anski), 54